AF708336

The Taiwan Independence Movement In and Out of Power

Dongtao Qi

East Asian Institute
National University of Singapore
Singapore

World Scientific

NEW JERSEY • LONDON • SINGAPORE • BEIJING • SHANGHAI • HONG KONG • TAIPEI • CHENNAI • TOKYO

Published by

World Scientific Publishing Co. Pte. Ltd.

5 Toh Tuck Link, Singapore 596224

USA office: 27 Warren Street, Suite 401-402, Hackensack, NJ 07601

UK office: 57 Shelton Street, Covent Garden, London WC2H 9HE

Library of Congress Cataloging-in-Publication Data
Names: Qi, Dongtao, author.
Title: The Taiwan independence movement in and out of power / Dongtao Qi
(East Asian Institute, National University of Singapore, Singapore).
Description: New Jersey : World Scientific, 2015. | Includes bibliographical references.
Identifiers: LCCN 2015017666 | ISBN 9789814689427 (alk. paper)
Subjects: LCSH: Min jin dang (China) | Nationalism--Political aspects--Tawain. |
Taiwan--Politics and government--2000– |
Taiwan--History--Autonomy and independence movements.
Classification: LCC JQ1539.A5747 Q25 2015 | DDC 324.251249/06090511--dc23
LC record available at http://lccn.loc.gov/2015017666

British Library Cataloguing-in-Publication Data
A catalogue record for this book is available from the British Library.

Copyright © 2016 by World Scientific Publishing Co. Pte. Ltd.

All rights reserved. This book, or parts thereof, may not be reproduced in any form or by any means, electronic or mechanical, including photocopying, recording or any information storage and retrieval system now known or to be invented, without written permission from the publisher.

For photocopying of material in this volume, please pay a copying fee through the Copyright Clearance Center, Inc., 222 Rosewood Drive, Danvers, MA 01923, USA. In this case permission to photocopy is not required from the publisher.

In-house Editors: Dong Lixi/Dr. Sree Meenakshi Sajani

Typeset by Stallion Press
Email: enquiries@stallionpress.com

Printed in Singapore

PREFACE AND ACKNOWLEDGMENTS

This book is a study of Democratic Progressive Party (DPP), Taiwan Independence Movement (TIM) and electoral politics in Taiwan during 2000–2012. It consists of two parts: the first part is my PhD dissertation aimed to understand fluctuating popular support for the DPP government during 2000–2008 when the DPP was in power, and the second part includes a series of studies on the DPP's quick but limited revival during 2008–2012 when it was out of power.

In the first part, I propose a movement government framework to explore the relations between the DPP's dual roles as both the movement leader and the government, which I believe is the key to understand the DPP's changing popular support during 2000–2008. A movement government is the new democratic government established through the popular democratic election by the opposition political party which has developed from the significant social and political movement. The 20th century has witnessed many movement governments in former authoritarian states such as Taiwan, South Korea and South Africa. It is also expected that movement government would emerge in more and more authoritarian countries through various democratic movements in the future. However, as an increasingly important political phenomenon, there have been neither theoretical frameworks nor systematic empirical studies of it. This study is the first attempt in the literature of state and movement to conceptually distinguish the movement government from the conventional democratic government, to provide an analytical framework of movement government, and finally, to study a case of movement government, the DPP government in Taiwan, with the proposed movement government framework.

Because of the movement government's origin in and long-term connection to the movement, it usually keeps its commitment to the movement's cause and continue its role as the movement leader even after it takes control of the government. Therefore, the movement government usually plays the dual roles of government and movement simultaneously, which often imposes significant strategic constraints on the government and damages its electoral performance because of the inherent tension between the role of government and that of movement in electoral politics. When the conflict between the two roles becomes apparent, the movement government faces a strategic dilemma in maintaining social support. The dilemma is that no matter which role it chooses to emphasize, it would have to downplay the other role and disaffect that role's support base. Because the movement government usually has a number of movement activists and supporters in its key administrative positions, it has a tendency to use a movement-oriented strategy to deal with the strategic constraints imposed by the role conflicts. In other words, it tends to emphasize movement principles and goals at the expense of government performance and mobilize the movement base to help secure power. However, when the movement-oriented strategy becomes too radical, it would consolidate movement fundamentalists' support, but on the other hand, alienate many moderates, which may finally lead to declined overall support for the movement government. During 2000–2008, the DPP government in Taiwan was a movement government with strong commitment and connection to the TIM. Therefore, the movement government framework may be applied to explain the wild fluctuation in the DPP's electoral fortunes during its two administrative terms. This study not only develops a general framework of movement governments but also reveals the symbiotic and interactive relations between government and movement. Therefore, it provides a corrective to the literature on state and movement which usually view the relations between two political forces as separate and antagonistic.

The second part of this book consists of five chapters on the DPP's quick revival since it lost power in 2008 (Chapter 6) as shown in the 2010 municipal elections (Chapter 7), and the limit of its revival revealed in the 2012 presidential election (Chapter 8) due to its China policy (Chapter 9), and finally, an explanation of the DPP's limited revival since 2008 with the perspective of political and economic nationalism in the context of increasing globalization and social justice concerns in Taiwan (Chapter 10). Since the DPP lost power in 2008, it was not a movement government anymore, but still a movement party because it has maintained its commitment and connection to the TIM. Nevertheless, the DPP has gradually adjusted its position on important independence issues and achieved a better balance between political and economic nationalism. As a result, the DPP has revived in local elections but still was defeated in the 2012 presidential election. The DPP's limited revival is mainly due to its China policy, which suggests that the DPP needs to further downplay its political nationalism to transfer its revival in local elections to the national presidential election. Chapters 6–9 have first appeared as Background Briefs of East Asian Institute, National University of Singapore.

For the first part of this book, I could not thank enough the following people. My PhD advisor, Professor Andrew Walder, had never failed to provide constant encouragement, insightful and critical comments, and a variety of generous support to me during my study at Stanford. Although I was a "black sheep" among his students because I chose a dissertation subject, Taiwan, which was not closely related to his long-term research subject, mainland China, he had never hesitated to encourage me to pursue my own research interest and support my every step during this process. Besides the research freedom and emotional support I received from him, his constructive and critical comments had been the strongest motor for me to pursue the right direction of research and also the most reliable source of ideas for me to revise the dissertation.

Professor Douglas McAdam, one of my dissertation reading committee members, was the key person in the development of my dissertation's theoretical framework. As early as in 2007, he had outlined this framework for me. Professor Gi-Wook Shin, another reading committee member, had inspired me with his excellent works on the nationalistic politics in the two Koreas; Taiwan and South Korea share many commonalities in their nationalistic politics. Therefore, some important components of my argument benefit greatly from reading his works on Koreas.

My special thanks to Professor Mau-Kuei Chang, Research Fellow in the Institute of Sociology at Academia Sinica and also my local sponsor during my 7 months fieldwork in Taiwan during 2006–2007. Before I went to Taiwan for fieldwork, I was completely an outsider of Taiwan. It was Professor Chang who kindly invited me to visit his prestigious institute and helped create many opportunities for me to gradually become a semi-insider of Taiwan. Without his support, the fieldwork would never be so fruitful and so much fun. My appreciations also go to all the other Taiwanese scholars, students, and friends in both Taiwan and the US who offered their time, advice and various other efforts to help me find right interviewees and also made me feel that Taiwan is my second hometown. They are Tai-Chun Kuo, Linda Gail Arrigo, members of Election Study Center at National Chengchi University including Lu-Huei Chen, Ching-Hsin Yu, Chi Huang, Su-Feng Cheng, members of Institute of Sociology at Academia Sinica including Fu-Chang Wang, Nai-Teh Wu, Yu-Yueh Tsai, Chih-Jou Chen, Ying-Hwa Chang, Su-Chuan Lee, Yuen-Ming Phoon, Chun-Kai Woo, Yu-Bin Chiu, Ming-Feng Liu, Wen-Pin Lin, James W.Y. Wang, Chung-Chi Chao, Wei-Hua Chen, Shu-Juo Chen, Chen-Yin Chiang, Ping Lin and so on. Especially, I thank those anonymous Taiwanese interviewees in the US and Taiwan for their time and cooperation.

My great appreciations also go to Larry Yung and the Freeman Spogli Institute for International Studies at Stanford University for the three-year Larry Yung Fellowship they offered to me. Without this generous financial support, my research and family life would be much more difficult at Stanford.

For the second part of this book, I am very grateful to Professor Yongnian Zheng and other colleagues at the East Asian Institute (EAI), National University of Singapore where I work as Research Fellow since I received my PhD in 2009. As Director of the EAI, Professor Zheng has provided unreserved encouragement to my research and useful comments on most works in this part of the book. My other colleagues, such as Dr. Litao Zhao and Dr. Wei Shan, also helped me shape some important research ideas through their insightful discussion with me. I need to especially thank Jessica Loon, Senior Research Officer (Editorial) at the EAI, who copyedited the Chapters 6–9 and greatly improved their readability.

In addition, a big thank you to my family: My wife Yanhua Liu and son Oliver Qi, my parents Maoshan Qi and Xianglian Zhang, my two sisters

Dongyun Qi and Dongmei Qi, for their unconditional love to me. I dedicate this book to them.

Finally, I wish to thank the World Scientific for its efforts in publishing the book, and especially Ms. Lixi Dong who was involved in the various stages of publication and Dr. Sree Meenakshi Sajani for her valuable copyediting work.

Dongtao Qi
Guangzhou

ABOUT THE AUTHOR

Dongtao Qi, PhD, is Research Fellow in the East Asian Institute, National University of Singapore, and was Professor and Executive Dean (January 2014–April 2015) in the Institute of Public Policy, South China University of Technology. He conducts research on state–society relations, nationalism, social movement, social policy and higher education in Taiwan and mainland China. His publications have appeared in *China Quarterly*, *Journal of Contemporary China, International Journal of China Studies, East Asian Policy* and so on. He co-edited two Chinese books: *State of Rural China*: *Peasants, Agriculture and Rural Society in the Reform Era* (Hong Kong: Tide Time Publishing) and *Social Development and Social Policies*: *International Experiences and China's Reform* (Beijing: Dongfang Publishing), and published some book chapters on Chinese working class and trade unions, Taiwan's politics, social movement and social welfare system, etc. He has consulted with governmental agencies and health care organizations on Taiwan's talent deficit crisis and healthcare system, and also played the leading role in organizing four international conferences in the US, the UK and China. His current research projects try to understand better the resource allocation mechanisms in the Chinese higher education system, the Chinese government's policy consulting processes, the role of think tanks in policy making, and development of the Taiwanese identity and nationalism.

TABLE OF CONTENTS

Preface and Acknowledgments v
About the Author xi
List of Figures and Tables xvii

PART I TAIWAN INDEPENDENCE MOVEMENT IN POWER: 2000–2008 **1**

Chapter 1: Fluctuation in the Social Support for the DPP and a Preliminary Framework of Movement Government **3**

Introduction 3
Movement Government Framework 9
Literature Review 16
Summary 26

Chapter 2: Differentiating The DPP's Two Support Bases **29**

Introduction 29
The Taiwan Independence Movement and the DPP from Movement to Political Party to Government 30
Differentiating the DPP Government's Two Support Bases at the Aggregate Level 48
The Correlations between Individuals' Dissatisfaction with the DPP Government's Performance and Their Support for the DPP and the TIM 59
The Changing Party Composition of the TIM's Support Base and the DPP's Weakened Monopoly on Taiwanese Nationalism 67

Summary 69

Chapter 3: Family Economic Fortune, Fondness of the President and Nationalistic Sentiment: Three Determining Factors in Taiwanese People's Party Support 71

Introduction 71

Evolution of the DPP Government's Strategies: From Concession to Confrontation, 2000–2004 74

Evolution of the DPP Government's Strategies: From Confrontation to Radicalization, 2004–2008 82

Data, Operationalization and Hypotheses 91

Method and Results 95

The Radical Strategy and Fondness of Chen 104

Summary 108

Chapter 4: The Movement Government's Radical Strategy: A Double-Edged Sword 111

Introduction 111

The Anatomy of the Radical Strategy 112

A Double-Edged Sword of the Radical Strategy 121

Summary 141

Chapter 5: Conclusion and Implications 143

Differences between Movement Governments and Conventional Democratic Governments 143

The Case of the DPP Government and the Limitations of the Movement Government Framework 146

Implications for the Literature on State-Movement Relations 152

Implications for the DPP's Future Development 154

PART II TAIWAN INDEPENDENCE MOVEMENT OUT OF POWER: 2008–2012 155

Chapter 6: Two Years in Opposition: Taiwan's Democratic Progressive Party Moves from Defeat to Revival? 157

The DPP's Quick Recovery from the 2008 Electoral Defeats 157
Tsai Ing-Wen and the Two Pro-Independence Factions in the DPP 158
Erasing Chen's Negative Legacy with Reforms in the DPP 162
Signs of Revival with Consecutive Electoral Victories 164
Proposing a New Agenda for Taiwan but More Challenges Ahead 165

Chapter 7: Taiwan's 2010 Municipal Elections 171

The Ma Administration's Mid-term "Exam" Concluded with Positive Implications 171
KMT's Lackluster Victory 173
DPP's Cheerful Defeat 178
Future Challenges to the Two Parties 181

Chapter 8: Taiwan's 2012 Presidential and Legislative Elections 183

Ma's Stability Card Defeats Tsai's Social Justice Card 183
Important Background to the 2012 Elections 185
Campaigns and Platforms 191
Post-Election Challenges for Ma and the DPP 196

Chapter 9: The China Policy of Taiwan's Democratic Progressive Party Since 2012: The Unfinished Last Mile 199

Three Lines of China Policy in the Democratic Progressive Party (DPP) 199
Loss of Core Supporters on China Policy Since 2012 202
The Three DPP Heavyweights and the Last Mile 209

Chapter 10: Globalization, Social Justice Issues, Political and Economic Nationalism in Taiwan: An Explanation of the DPP's Limited Revival During 2008–2012 213

Globalization, Social Justice Issues and the DPP's Efforts to Improve Taiwan's Social Welfare System 219
DPP's Support Base 227
Concerns of the Less Privileged Taiwanese and the DPP's Political and Economic Nationalism 232
DPP's Limited Resurgence, 2008–2012 238
Conclusion and Implications 244

REFERENCES **247**

Index 253

LIST OF FIGURES AND TABLES

Figure 1.1.	Vote Shares Received by the DPP in Presidential Elections in Taiwan: 1996–2008	5
Figure 1.2.	Dual Roles and Support Bases of the Movement Government	12
Figure 2.1.	DPP Membership: 1986–2008	39
Figure 2.2.	Legislative Election Results: 1986–2008, DPP	40
Figure 2.3.	County and County-Level-City Head Election Results: 1989–2005, DPP	40
Figure 2.4.	Trends of Taiwanese-Only Identity, DPP ID and Pro-Independence Attitude in Taiwan: 1992–2007	50
Figure 2.5.	The TIM's Development Stages after WWII	52
Figure 2.6.	Trend of Pro-Independence Attitude: 1994–2007 (Selected Years)	53
Figure 2.7.	Dual Roles and Support Bases of the DPP Government	54
Figure 3.1.	Trends of Taiwanese Identity and Pro-Independence Attitude in Taiwan, 1992–2007	76
Figure 3.2.	County and County-Level-City Head Election Results, 1989–2005, DPP	86
Figure 4.1.	Level of Nationalistic Sentiment in Different Social Groups: By Age, 1996–2008	128
Figure 4.2.	Level of Nationalistic Sentiment in Different Social Groups: By Education, 1996–2008	129
Figure 4.3.	Level of Nationalistic Sentiment in Different Social Groups: By Residence Region, 1996–2008	129
Figure 4.4.	Level of Nationalistic Sentiment in Different Social Groups: By Class, 1996–2008	130

Figure 7.1. KMT's and DPP's Vote Shares: 2008–2010 175
Figure 8.1. KMT's and DPP's Vote Shares: 2008–2010 188
Figure 9.1. Percentage of Nationalists in Two Social Groups: 1996–2012 203
Figure 9.2. Average Percentage of Social Welfare Budget in Taiwan's Central Government's Total Budget during Different Administrations, 1993–2012 204
Figure 9.3. Percentage of People in Different Social Groups Believing DPP/KMT Is Better/the Same on Cross-Strait Relations, 2012 207
Figure 9.4. Percentage of People in Different Social Groups Believing DPP/KMT Is Better/the Same on Economic Development, 2012 207
Figure 9.5. Percentage of People in Different Social Groups Believing DPP/KMT Is Better/the Same on Improving Taiwan's International Status, 2012 208
Figure 9.6. Percentage of People in Different Social Groups Believing DPP/KMT Is Better/the Same on Handling Social Inequality, 2012 208
Figure 9.7. Percentage of People in Different Social Groups Believing DPP/KMT Is Better/the Same on Improving Social Welfare, 2012 209
Figure 10.1. KMT's and DPP's Vote Shares in Local and Presidential Elections, 2008–2012 214
Figure 10.2. Development Trends of Investment, Unemployment and Inequality in Taiwan, 1995–2007 220
Figure 10.3. Percentage of People Who Believe that KMT/DPP Represents the Interests of the Rich and Powerful 224
Figure 10.4. Percentage of People Who Believe that KMT/DPP Represents the Interests of the Average People 224
Figure 10.5. Percentage of Social Welfare Budget in Central Government's Total Budget, 1993–2012 226
Figure 10.6. Ratio of Average Household Income of Highest 20% to that of Lowest 20% (Measure of Income Inequality): 1991–2011 226

Figure 10.7. Level/Percent of Nationalist Sentiment among the Less Privileged and the Privileged, 1996–2012 233

Table 1.1. Four Types of Government 11
Table 1.2. Dichotomous Characteristics of State and Movement 17
Table 2.1. Size of the DPP's Different Support Bases and Vote Share Received by the DPP in the Presidential Elections, 2000, 2004 and 2008 55
Table 2.2. Pearson Correlations between the Three Support Base Indicators: Before 2000 (Excluding 2000) 58
Table 2.3. Pearson Correlations between the Three Support Base Indicators: During 2000–2007 (Including 2000) 58
Table 2.4. Sample Means of the Variables Used in the Analysis, 2008 62
Table 2.5. Nested Multinomial Logistic Regressions of Party ID, 2008 64
Table 2.6. Nested Multinomial Logistic Regressions of National Identity, 2008 65
Table 2.7. Nested Multinomial Logistic Regressions of Attitude about Taiwan's Independence, 2008 66
Table 2.8. Party ID Composition in TIM's Support Base, 2000–2008 68
Table 3.1. Sample Means of the Variables Used in the Analysis of Party ID/Support and Fondness of Chen, 2004 and 2008 94
Table 3.2. Nested Multinomial Logistic Regressions of Party ID, 2004 96
Table 3.3. Nested Multinomial Logistic Regressions of Party ID, 2008 98
Table 3.4. Percent of People Having Worse off Family, DPP ID and Taiwanese Nationalistic Sentiment, and the Average Fondness Score of Chen in Different Social Groups, 2008 101

Table 3.5.	Percent of People Having Worse off Family, DPP ID and Taiwanese Nationalistic Sentiment in Different Social Groups, 2004	102
Table 3.6.	OLS Linear Regressions of Fondness of Chen, 2004 and 2008	106
Table 4.1.	Percent of People in Each Social Group Possibly Accepting the Open-Door Policy, 2008	125
Table 4.2.	Percent of People in Each Social Group Choosing Social Welfare as the Chen Government's Best Achievement in His Second Term, 2008	127
Table 4.3.	Percent of People in Each Social Group Agreeing or Disagreeing with the Statement: "If you love Taiwan, you must support local/Taiwanese regime." 2008	131
Table 4.4.	Percent of People in Each Social Group Choosing Ethnic Relations and Cross-Strait Relations as the Chen Government's Worst Performance, 2008	133
Table 4.5.	Binary Logistic Regression of Individual Voting Decision: Vote for the DPP vs. the KMT (ref.), 2008	138
Table 4.6.	Percent of People in Each Social Group Voting for the DPP or the KMT in the 2008 Presidential Election	140
Table 7.1.	KMT and DPP's Vote Share (%) in Five Municipal Governor Elections: 2005/2006 and 2010	175
Table 7.2.	Number of Mayoral Candidates' Facebook Fans	178
Table 8.1.	Comparison of Key Economic Indicators between Ma's and Chen's Presidency	186
Table 9.1.	Will You Be Better Off, Worse Off, Or the Same Under the Open-Door China Policy? (2008)	204
Table 9.2.	Average Rating of Tsai's and Ma's Capability of Protecting Taiwan Interests, 2012	206
Table 10.1.	Pearson Correlations between the Three Indicators of Investment, Unemployment and Inequality, 1995–2007	221
Table 10.2.	Binary Logistic Regression of Individuals' Votes for the DPP, 2008	227

Table 10.3. Percentage of Worse-Off Families and Votes for the DPP in Each Social Group, 2008 229
Table 10.4. Binary Logistic Regressions of Individuals' Votes for the DPP, 1996–2012 230
Table 10.5. Percentage of People in Each Social Group Choosing Social Welfare as the Chen Administration's Best Achievement in His Second Term, 2008 231
Table 10.6. Percentage of People in each Social Group Possibly Approving or Disapproving the Open-Door China Policy, 2008 234
Table 10.7. Comparison of Key Economic and Social Performance Indicators under the Ma and Chen Administrations 239
Table 10.8. Are You Satisifed or Dissatisfied with President Ma's Performance in Managing Cross-Strait Relations in the Past Three Years? 242
Table 10.9. Has Taiwan's Overall Economy Improved, Declined or Remained the Same because of ECFA? 242
Table 10.10. Should We Continue to Use "1992 Consensus" to Negotiate with Mainland China? 242

PART I

TAIWAN INDEPENDENCE MOVEMENT IN POWER: 2000–2008

CHAPTER 1: FLUCTUATION IN THE SOCIAL SUPPORT FOR THE DPP AND A PRELIMINARY FRAMEWORK OF MOVEMENT GOVERNMENT

Introduction

On 22 March 2008, Taiwan, a small island 100 miles off the coast of mainland China, received intensive global attention — not only for its extremely competitive and contentious presidential election that day, but also for the possible military attack from mainland China. It was thought that such an attack might be triggered by the pro-Taiwan's UN membership referendum the same day.[1] Since the largest pro-independence political party in Taiwan, the Democratic Progressive Party (hereafter, the DPP), won the presidential elections in 2000 and 2004, its support base had expanded greatly, emboldening the DPP to radicalize its pro-independence stance and to overtly confront military and diplomatic pressure from both the Chinese government and the international community.

However, the DPP failed dismally in both the presidential election and the referendum, which removed the possibility of an immediate

[1] http://tw.people.com.cn/GB/14812/14875/6059437.html, accessed on 18 June 2015; http://news.bbc.co.uk/chinese/trad/hi/newsid_7220000/newsid_7224300/7224319.stm, accessed on 18 June 2015.

military conflict between mainland China and Taiwan with the possible involvement of other world powers such as the United States (US) and Japan.[2] Because the DPP was also defeated badly by the old ruling party *Kuo Min Tang* (KMT)[3] in the legislative election two months prior to the presidential election, the KMT, which had governed Taiwan from 1945 through 2000, resumed its anti-independence regime as a majority government in 2008.

While the government leaders in the major countries involved in the so-called cross-strait relations, such as mainland China and the US, felt easy about the DPP's defeat in the elections and referendum, its defeat has received increasing attention from both Taiwanese and overseas scholars, because the dramatic decline in the social support for the DPP government may have significant and broad implications for Taiwan, mainland China and other countries undergoing similar political transformation.

The DPP, that had originated in the democracy and nationalism movements (i.e., the opposition movement and the Taiwan Independence Movement (TIM)) and developed into a strong opposition party in 1986, finally overthrew the 55-year one-party regime (i.e., the KMT authoritarian regime) in Taiwan via the popular presidential election in 2000 with 39.3% of the votes. For many Taiwanese, the DPP has shouldered their long-term expectation of a new democratic, clean and efficient government as opposed to the old authoritarian, corrupt and highly bureaucratic KMT government. For democracy scholars, Taiwan's peaceful regime change in 2000 represents one of the role models among the third-wave democracies that may be followed by other authoritarian countries, especially by the country on the other side of the Taiwan Strait — mainland China. Moreover, as Figure 1.1 shows, in the 2004 presidential election, the DPP successfully maintained its power with 50.1% of the votes, a 10.8% increase from the presidential election in 2000, which made the DPP even more promising as a pro-democracy and pro-independence government. Surprisingly, four years later, in 2008 the DPP received only

---

[2] See Taiwan Relations Act (US Congress, 1979) and The New US–Japan Defense Guidelines in 2005 for details, and also see http://www.reuters.com/article/worldNews/idUSN1934158120080319 for the news of two US carriers sent toward Taiwan before the election (accessed on 18 June 2015).

[3] i.e., The Chinese Nationalist Party or Kuo Min Tang in Chinese.

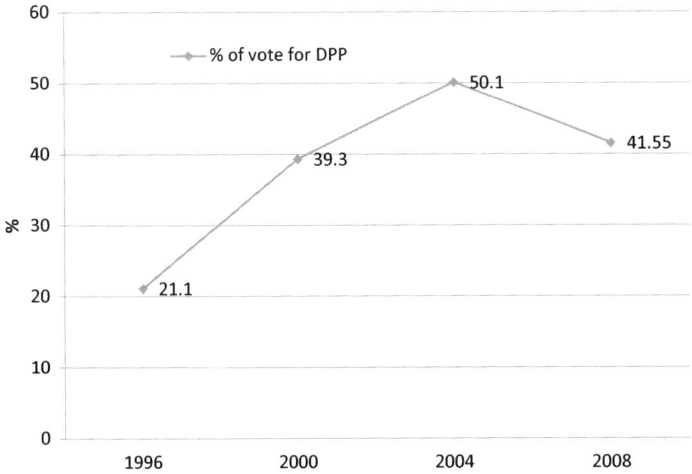

Figure 1.1 Vote Shares Received by the DPP in Presidential Elections in Taiwan: 1996–2008

Data source: Central Election Commission, http://www.cec.gov.tw/

41.6% of the votes, an 8.5% drop from the 2004 election. Why did the social support for this highly anticipated new democratic government fluctuate so radically from 2000 through 2008?

This question not only troubled the DPP's disappointed supporters in Taiwan and abroad, but also became a hot topic among many scholars and officials in mainland China and the US. During 2000–2008, the DPP government's dual images of pro-democracy and pro-independence exerted a significant impact on the stability of the triangular relations among Taiwan, mainland China and the US. For example, the DPP government's pro-democracy image was downplayed and even repressed by the Chinese government in mainland China. On the other hand, its pro-independence image was severely criticized by the Chinese government to mobilize nationalistic sentiment in domestic and overseas Chinese societies, which became a significant source of legitimacy for the Chinese government.

In contrast, the US government had always praised the DPP government's pro-democracy image and even urged mainland China to imitate it.[4]

[4] For example, see "Be more like Taiwan, Bush urges Beijing." http://www.guardian.co.uk/world/2005/nov/17/usa.china, accessed on 18 June 2015.

Meanwhile, the radicalized pro-independence image of the DPP government also troubled the US government which has long believed that maintaining the status quo between Taiwan and mainland China best serves its national interests. Therefore, the decline in the DPP's social support, indicated by its unprecedented electoral defeats in 2008, was surely welcomed by the Chinese government, but might have concerned the US government. Both governments were very interested in better understanding the changing support for the DPP and the TIM.

Exploring the changing social support for the DPP and the TIM is also important for other countries that have witnessed the new democratic governments springing from significant social and political movements against their respective old authoritarian rulers. These new democratic governments, referred to as *movement governments* in this study, had different fates after ousting the old authoritarian rulers and then taking power. Some of them managed to maintain state power for only one or two terms, such as the Solidarity government in Poland and the DPP government in Taiwan, whereas others have successfully stayed in power for longer periods of time without serious popular disapproval, such as the government of the African National Congress in South Africa. Therefore, a deeper understanding of the changes in the DPP and TIM's support base may provide an opportunity to develop a general framework to understand the diverse fates of these new democratic movement governments in other countries as well.

Popular accounts attribute the DPP's unprecedented defeat in this presidential election and referendum to two major reasons. On one hand, some scholars emphasized the DPP government's failure in mending Taiwan's economy and its serious corruption scandals as the major contributing factors to its electoral defeats.[5] On the other hand, the Chinese government proclaimed that the TIM led by the DPP had lost popular support in

[5] For example, see the interview with the Taiwan expert Shelly Rigger and the political critic Meng Xuan after the election: http://www.dwnews.com/gb/MainNews/SinoNews/Taiwan/2008_3_23_15_56_38_829.html, http://www.dwnews.com/gb/MainNews/Forums/BackStage/2008_3_23_11_52_51_452.html, accessed on 23 March 2008.

Taiwan, which caused the electoral defeats of the DPP in 2008.[6] However, as this study will show, these explanations are either inadequate or misleading. In fact, the DPP government's popularity had been negatively affected by its bad economic record and corruption scandals as early as in its first term of 2000–2004, but they still won the 2004 presidential election by largely increased votes. Therefore, the "poor government performance and corruption" argument is inadequate in explaining the fluctuation in the DPP's popular support. With regard to the declining support for the TIM, it is misleading to treat the DPP government and the TIM as the identical political force in Taiwan. It is true that the DPP has been the strongest leading force of the TIM since it was founded in 1986. However, during 2000–2008 the TIM has acquired a life of its own with the support base different from and even broader than the DPP government's support base; therefore, the withdrawal of support for the DPP government does not necessarily indicate that the TIM was losing popular support as well. On the contrary, this study contends that the TIM had developed into a new stage with much increased and stable popular support during 2000–2008.

To better explain the large fluctuation in the DPP's support base indicated by its unprecedented electoral victory in 2004 and defeats in 2008, and to shed some light on the different fates of similar movement governments in other countries, a framework of *movement government* is proposed in this study.[7] First of all, the framework identifies the DPP government as a unique type of government, the so-called movement government, which simultaneously plays two different but overlapping roles — the roles of the government and the nationalism movement leader, and as a result, its overall support base includes two different but overlapping supporters for each role. Therefore, to understand the changes in the movement government's overall support base, we should first distinguish

[6] For example, see the mainland Chinese government's statement after the election: http://tw.people.com.cn/GB/7033208.html, accessed on 18 June 2015.

[7] I thank Professor Doug McAdam for his help and encouragement in developing this framework. It was he who first called my attention to this framework in the case study of the DPP government.

between these two different groups of supporters and then study the changes in them separately. The framework proposes that the dynamics underlying the changes in the two support bases are different; therefore, the decline of one support base does not necessarily indicate the decline of the other. In the case of the DPP, although the DPP government's unsatisfactory performance, especially its corruption scandals, may reduce the social support for its government role (i.e., its government support base may decline), it does not necessarily exert the same negative impact on the social support for its movement role (i.e., its movement support base may not decline). Therefore, the argument that the lower social support for the DPP government indicated parallel declining support for the TIM may not be valid.

Regarding the factors leading to the changes in the movement government's overall support bases, the movement government framework emphasizes the movement government's strategies of dealing with the dynamic relations between its two roles. The movement government's role as the movement leader often contradicts its role as the government, which sets a strategic dilemma for the movement government in retaining both movement supporters and government supporters. The movement government may adopt different strategies to get rid of this dilemma, and these strategies have different impact on the movement government's two support bases.

In the case of the DPP government, during the first half of its first term from 2000–2002, it downplayed its radical role of movement leader and tried to establish the centrist role of government through conceding on important independence issues. As this government-oriented strategy failed to pacify the domestic and international oppositions, and at the same time, disappointed many of its movement supporters, the DPP government replaced the government-oriented strategy with the movement-oriented strategy to rely on its movement supporters for the 2004 presidential election. The movement-oriented strategy successfully mobilized greater Taiwanese sentiment and increased popular support for the DPP in the election, which also improved the DPP's confidence in the effectiveness of the movement-oriented strategy for expanding popular support. During the DPP government's second term, as President Chen Shuibian and his government were troubled by more serious scandals and unsatisfactory performance, they had to rely more heavily on the movement-oriented strategy to retain supporters. The movement-oriented strategy during this term became more radical — economically more conservative, ethnically more divisive, ideologically more fundamental and internationally more confrontational, which successfully consolidated the support of movement fundamentalists, but disaffected more moderates, and eventually led to the significant decline of the overall social support.

The above movement government framework is not only useful for a better understanding of the changes in the movement government's social support, but also may contribute to the literature on government-movement relations and the formation of political party's support base. The following sections further elaborate the movement government framework and then review the relevant literature to discuss the relationship and possible contribution of this framework to the related literature.

Movement Government Framework

The concept of movement government tries to reflect the concept of movement regime. The movement regime or its full term, the revolutionary mass-movement regime, was first defined by Tucker (1961) to refer to those dictatorship regimes established in the 20th century. It includes communist, fascist and nationalist single-party regimes, such as the Soviet Union under Lenin and Stalin, Germany under Hitler and Egypt under Nasser.

> Movement regimes are born in revolutions and rest upon and represent — or claim to — mass movements of a national or trans-national scope. In the typical case the mass movement is organized during the revolutionary struggle for power and as a means of waging this struggle. Once the regime is in being, the mass movement is enlarged and given new tasks of various kinds in the continuing revolution of national renewal. (Tucker, 1961: 284).

There are some similarities between the DPP government and movement regimes, but the DPP government is by no means a movement regime. In both cases of the DPP government and movement regimes, mass movements are important means by which the political party struggles for power, maintains power and pursues planned social changes. However, more substantial differences distinguish the DPP government from such movement regimes. First, the DPP government is not a single-party dictatorship or authoritarian, but is democratic; in contrast, movement regimes are always single-party totalitarian or authoritarian governments. Second, the TIM as a social movement is relatively independent of the DPP government and often criticizes it for its compromises on important independence issues, whereas mass movements under movement regimes are always controled by the regimes, and therefore, much less independent. Finally, the TIM's development and social impact are greatly constrained by the strong opposition and anti-independence forces in Taiwan (e.g., the KMT and other anti-independence political parties in Taiwan), but mass movements under movement regimes can penetrate almost every corner of the society due to the lack of significant opposition or constraints.

Although the DPP government is not a movement regime, the emphasis of the regimes' movement nature by the literature of movement regime inspires the author to conceptualize those new democratic governments that springs from significant social and political movements and maintains strong legacy and commitment to the movements, such as the DPP government in Taiwan, as a special type of government differing from both undemocratic movement regimes and conventional democratic governments without strong movement commitment. Based on whether a government is democratic and whether it has strong movement commitment, the governments in different countries may be classified into four categories as shown by Table 1.1.

We can see that the movement governments as defined by the above two criteria are those new democratic governments established through national popular elections in originally authoritarian or repressive regimes. It is not surprising that they are always closely affiliated with significant social movements in their own countries, because these movements, especially democratic and nationalistic movements, are usually opposition movements themselves from which the opposition parties draw popular support. Since it is expected that more and more non-democratic countries will eventually transform into democratic ones through a variety of

Table 1.1 Four Types of Government

	With Strong Movement Commitment	Without Strong Movement Commitment
Democratic	Movement governments, (e.g., DPP government in Taiwan, Solidarity government in Poland and African National Congress government in South Africa, etc.)	Non-movement democratic governments (mature and consolidated democratic countries, such as US, UK, etc.)
Undemocratic	Movement regimes (e.g., Soviet Union under Lenin and Stalin, Germany under Hitler and Egypt under Nasser, etc.)	Conventional undemocratic regimes (e.g., Saudi Arabia, Kuwait, United Arab Emirates, post-Mao China, etc.)

opposition movements, more and more movement governments will emerge in the world. Therefore, this case study of the DPP government in Taiwan with the movement government framework may have broader implications for these countries.

To describe and explain the changes in a movement government's support base, the movement government framework encompasses the following four elements:

1. The dual roles and support bases of the movement government. The most distinctive nature of the movement government is its distinguishable dual roles and support bases. Specifically, the movement government plays the role of the national government on one hand, and the role of the movement leader on the other. Its role as the movement leader is widely recognized and accepted by not only the domestic but also the international public opinion, and therefore, becomes one of its distinctive characteristics and powerful political resources which can differentiate it from other political forces domestically and internationally. In the case of the DPP government, the public opinion in Taiwan, mainland China, and among the government officials in the US recognize it as the leader of the TIM. Since the early 1990s, the DPP's role as the TIM leader has most conveniently distinguished it from other political forces in Taiwan, such as the old ruling party, the anti-independence KMT. Corresponding to the movement government's dual roles, two overlapping but still distinguishable support bases exist. For example, the DPP's overall support base includes the supporters of the DPP government and those of the TIM. The movement government's dual roles and support bases may be illustrated by Figure 1.2.

The figure illustrates the fact that the movement government's overall support base may be divided into three components represented by the letters A, B and C. A are those who only support the movement, C represents those who only support the government and B includes those supporting both the movement and the government, that is, the overlap between the two support bases. Therefore, A+B represents movement supporters and B+C are government supporters. Finally, the overall support base of the movement government is A+B+C. This refined categorization of the support base enables the movement government framework to argue that for a better understanding of the changes in the movement government's support base, it is necessary to study the changes in each type of support base and the factors leading to these separate changes.

2. The relations between the movement government's two roles. The framework proposes that the relations between the movement government's two roles are conditional, and therefore, dynamic — the two roles may contradict one another under some circumstances, but may be mutually-beneficial under others, which in turn may generate constraints or opportunities for the movement government to maintain its overall support base. The two roles' relations are usually determined by the different expectations of the two support bases, that is, the expectations of the

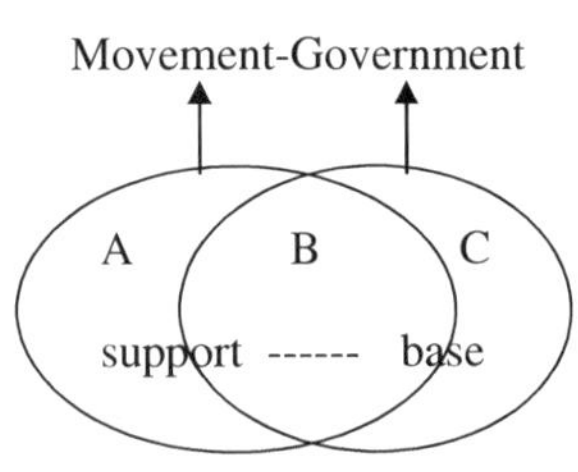

Figure 1.2 Dual Roles and Support Bases of the Movement Government

movement government's movement supporters and its government supporters. Conflicting expectations lead to role conflicts. If the expectations are harmonious, the two roles are in a harmonious relationship as well. In general, there is a persistent tension between the two roles, because as a government it is usually expected by its government supporters to perform as a centrist moderator in various social conflicts and deliver good economic and social performance; in contrast, as a movement leader it is usually expected by movement supporters to remain a contentious challenger on movement issues and deliver movement performance which often clashes with the government's economic and social goals. In other words, movement supporters are more radical than government supporters on important movement issues and are generally more ready to pursue the movement goals at the expense of the government performance.

For example, as a new government, the DPP was expected to rebuild Taiwan's economy as soon as possible. One of the most effective ways to mend the economy in the shortest time was to encourage more economic exchange between Taiwan and mainland China. Therefore, many Taiwanese, especially Taiwanese business persons expected the DPP government to build a more open and closer economic relationship with mainland China. However, the TIM's fundamentalist supporters within and outside of the DPP government worried that the closer economic relationship with mainland China might improve the Chinese government's influence in Taiwan and consequently hindered Taiwan from pursuing full independence of mainland China. Therefore, they strongly opposed improving the economic relationship with mainland China. These conflicting expectations from different supporters led to the role conflict of the DPP government — it is just impossible for this movement government to fulfill one role without sacrificing the other in this case. Such role conflicts had been the major challenge to the DPP government during 2000–2008 because it was caught in a strategic dilemma caused by conflicting expectations from the two support bases — no matter which side it turned to for support, it would lose the support of the other side. In contrast, a harmonious relationship between the two roles, although rare, may enable the movement government to maintain the support of both sides.

3. Strategies for dealing with the tension between the two roles and their impact on different support bases. To deal with role conflicts, the movement government may have three options. It may adopt the *government-oriented strategy* which emphasizes its role as the government and moderator and reduce its movement nature by conceding on controversial movement issues. This strategy may discourage movement development, and as a result, alienate some, especially fundamentalist, movement supporters, but may retain and expand government supporters.

In contrast to this strategy, the movement government may adopt *the movement-oriented strategy* which emphasizes its role as the movement leader and challenger and try to maintain support through various movement activities. This strategy may further develop the movement, radicalize the movement government on movement issues and retain and expand movement supporters, but alienate some of the government supporters.

The final strategy may be referred to as *the shifting strategy* because the movement government tries to balance the two conflicting roles and cater for both types of supporters and even non-supporters by shifting its position on controversial movement issues. This option is reasonable in theory, but in reality it may be extremely difficult for the movement government to please its supporters on different sides of the issue. The most probable outcome under this option is that the movement government switches its position on movement issues back and forth, trying to escape the criticism of both sides, but eventually losing each side's trust and support.

The three strategies discussed above are only idealizations. The actual political conditions faced by the movement government may be very complex, and therefore, may force it to adopt diverse or even mixed strategies in different periods of time. For example, within this framework, the DPP government's two terms in 2000–2008 may be generally divided into three stages according to the strategies it adopted. In the early period of its first term from 2000–2002, the DPP government strategically conceded on important pro-independence issues and adopted the government-oriented strategy, trying to expand its support base by pacifying the opposition forces. In the later period of its first term from 2002–2004, it abandoned this strategy, returned to the movement-oriented strategy and became confrontational to the domestic and international oppositions. After the DPP won the 2004 presidential election, the DPP government relied more greatly on the movement-oriented strategy and became more radical on controversial pro-independence issues.

The impacts of these strategies on the two support bases are contingent on other factors. For example, the DPP government's movement-oriented strategy usually alienated many of its government supporters, but when the Chinese government reacted against the strategy too aggressively, such as launching military exercises to threaten the DPP government, those government supporters who initially opposed the movement-oriented strategy might turn to support the DPP, because external threats to the nation would justify the government's role as the nationalism movement leader on one hand, and on the other hand, improve nationalistic sentiment among the government supporters. This framework calls for attention to these strategies and their impact on the different types of supporters in understanding the changes in the movement government's support base over time. A major part of this study is devoted to exploring these strategies and their impacts on the different support bases of the DPP government from 2000 through 2008.

4. The factors influencing the adoption of different strategies. The movement government framework further suggests that the adoption of different strategies is constrained by domestic and international factors, such as the movement government's performance in managing economy and social affairs, the strength of the government, the strength of the movement and its independence of the government control, the level of international support, and so on. Specifically, if the movement government is a weak or minority government with poor administrative performance, if the movement is strong and more independent of the government control, and if the international support is weak, the movement government will be forced to rely on the movement-oriented strategy to maintain social support. In contrast, if these factors are favorable, that is, if the movement government performs well in managing the economy and social affairs, is a strong or majority government, faces a movement that is easy to control, and finally, receives strong international support. It is more likely to choose the government-oriented strategy to expand social support.

The most distinctive aspect of the above framework is its argument for the dynamic relationship between the movement government's two roles, which form the basis for subsequent strategy adoption followed then by changes in the two support bases. To more completely understand the relationship between the movement government's two roles, we must review the literature on state/government-movement relations theoretically and the DPP government's movement nature empirically. With a more detailed discussion of the DPP and the DPP government's movement nature, I argue that the popular framework of the separate and antagonistic relationship between state and movement is not applicable to the case of movement governments. Movement governments usually have a symbiotic relationship with movements, but this symbiotic relationship may result in role conflicts and hinder the movement government from fulfilling its government role.

Literature Review

Literature on government-movement relations

In general, states/governments and movements are viewed as two different political forces with distinct natures. This distinction originates in the most popular dichotomy in social science: the dichotomy between state and society (e.g., Skocpol, 1979; Tarrow, 1998; Tilly, 1978). Social movements, especially violent revolutions, are usually viewed as one of the most significant challenging forces from the society against the state. Therefore, by virtue of the dichotomous definition of state and society, there should be a clear boundary between state and movement as well, just as the distinction between state and society. Table 1.2 summarizes these basic and dichotomous characteristics of state and movement based primarily on Tilly (1978), Tarrow (1998), McAdam (1999) and Goldstone (2003).

To put it simply, popular perspectives in this field suggest that the most basic distinction between state and movement is the difference between

Table 1.2 Dichotomous Characteristics of State and Movement

Characteristics	State	Movement
Level of Institutionalization or Routinization	Highly routinized and institutionalized politics	Non-routine, non-institutional politics
Main Actors	Power holders/elites/ bureaucrats/dominant groups in the society / rulers/political insiders	Citizen/ordinary people/ powerless/ruled/political outsiders
Relationship	Target/challenged/shaped	Challengers/shapers
Role in Confrontation	Source of stimulus/ opportunities/constraints	responders
Role in Mediation	Moderator	Competing and disputing agencies
Objectives/Functions	Maintaining power and status quo	Social and political changes

institutional and non-institutional politics, and the most common relationship between them is "separate and antagonistic" (Goldstone, 2003: 2) that is, the challenging movement vs. the challenged state. Within this general framework, it is not surprising to observe that two generally separate literatures, although equally rich, exist with each centering on its own subject — either state or movement. Especially in the social movement literature, most studies focus on identifying the mechanisms and factors internal to the movement (McAdam, 1999).

On the other hand, the complex relationships between the two subjects are relatively less studied (Goldstone, 2003). When the relationships become the focus of research, normally they are explored with reference to a separate and antagonistic framework. For example, studies of state roles in the emergence, development and decline of movements typically emphasize the opportunities and constraints inherent in state building, state mobilization, state crisis, state co-optation or repression (or to use a more popular term, the changes in political opportunity structures) (McAdam, 1999; Tarrow, 1998). On the other side, studies of movement roles in state politics often focus on how the state is forced to change its policies, programs, norms, members and even entire institutions under the movement's pressure (Tarrow, 1998).

Many findings and insights from the above literature are useful for the study of the DPP government and TIM in Taiwan. They will be referred to when relevant issues are discussed. Nevertheless, the case of movement government generally and that of the DPP government specifically do not fit into this *separate and antagonistic* framework, simply because the relationships between the movement government and the movement from whom it draw support are not separate and antagonistic, but rather symbiotic. The following case of the DPP government illustrates this point.

The symbiotic relationship between the DPP and the TIM and the DPP's movement nature

The DPP was founded as a pro-democracy and pro-independence party by the coalition of various opposition forces in Taiwan in 1986 under the KMT's authoritarian regime. Due to the martial law imposed by the KMT government from 1949 through 1987, Taiwan's opposition movement had survived and developed not as official political parties but as various movement organizations. Therefore, the relationship between the KMT government and the opposition movement was indeed separate and antagonistic as suggested by the above literature. However, in terms of the relationship between the DPP and these movements, especially the TIM, it is obviously neither separate nor antagonistic, but symbiotic. Since 1991 when the DPP officially proclaimed its pro-independence goal in the party platform, it has been recognized and accepted domestically and internationally as the largest leading force of the TIM. Although there have been many pro-independence movement organizations outside of the DPP, in the mid-1990s, the overall pro-independence forces had converged under the DPP's leadership.

According to the above dichotomous definitions of state and social movement, once it became a legal political party and joined routine and institutional politics of the state, the DPP ceased to be a movement organization. Based on the same definition, the institutional and political activities such as elections cannot be treated as non-institutional social movement activities either. Only its allied pro-independence organizations outside of institutional politics are social movement organizations engaging in social movement activities. If we still place the TIM in the social movement category, it should be confined to these affiliated organizations and their activities, rather than the DPP and its major political activities such as elections.

It seems reasonable to draw such a boundary between the DPP as the formal and institutionalized political party and the TIM as the non-institutional social movement organization. The history of the DPP also justifies such differentiation to some extent. For example, for a long time there was a serious debate between supporters of two different strategic lines within the DPP. One was the "congress line," which believed that completely joining institutional politics such as participating in electoral politics and running according to institutional requirements and norms would be the best way for the DPP to achieve the objective of Taiwan's complete independence. The other line was the "street/movement line," which viewed institutional politics as dangerous traps imposed by the KMT government to co-opt pro-independence and pro-democracy activists. They more respected the DPP's movement legacy and believed that the real power for the DPP emerged from the masses and other kinds of social movement organizations, especially those TIM organizations, which had been fighting with the DPP as its most sincere allies. Therefore, supporters of the "street/movement line" urged the DPP to stop pursuing official positions in the government through the institutional politics, such as elections, and to return to the street to mobilize the masses and develop social movement organizations to enhance pressure on the KMT government for additional political and social changes. Eventually, the "congress line" won the debate due to the fact that the KMT government released more and more important government positions to be filled via popular elections. When the presidential election was finally opened up to the public in 1996, the DPP was determined to take this most powerful position in the institutional politics for their pro-independence and pro-democracy purpose.

However, the victory of the "congress line" within the DPP and the institutionalization of the DPP within Taiwan's politics do not necessarily translate into its isolation and purification from "street" and movement.

On the contrary, the DPP has maintained a significant level of its *movement* nature and built up a symbiotic relationship with many, especially pro-independence, movement organizations. It is true that the DPP, as in the case of a political party in a democratic society, has been highly institutionalized to be an election-driven party; but as long as its *movement nature* and the support from movement sectors can help it achieve electoral victories, there is no reason for the DPP to abandon them.

It is easy to describe and understand the symbiotic relationship between the DPP and other TIM organizations, but more difficult to identify its movement nature. A symbiotic relationship means that since the DPP became the strongest pro-independence political force in Taiwan, all of the TIM organizations and supporters need to rely on it to realize their independence dream, and for this purpose, provide their support for the DPP. On the other hand, the DPP also needs these organizations' help to recruit activists, maintain the support base, and mobilize participants for all kinds of political activities, and so on. The relationship between the DPP and the TIM organizations is symbiotic, but does not represent an absolute "leader–follower" style. These pro-independence organizations share some basic goals, strategies, and principles with the DPP, but do not necessarily support the DPP's specific stance under some circumstances. For example, when the DPP strategically compromised on independence issues for electoral victories or other political benefits, radical pro-independence organizations have not hesitated to harshly criticize the DPP's betrayal of the independence movement.

Regarding the DPP's movement nature, it is better to discuss it by comparing the DPP to the KMT, the once dominate and ruling party in Taiwan before 2000. This comparison should begin with the fact that while the DPP was allowed to join the arena of institutional politics as an official political party since the late 1980s, the economic, political and cultural resources under its control were far less than those controlled by the KMT. With such poor resources, the DPP was unable to follow the conventional electoral norms cultivated by the KMT in the past three decades, which included vote buying through money and gifts, vote mobilization through local elites, the mafia, state-controlled media and state-sponsored organizations, such as workers' unions and farmers' unions, election manipulation through election officers, and so on. The only advantage of the DPP was its movement legacies — its direct connection to the mass, allied social movement organizations, its creativity and skills in framing issues and organizing protests, and having a large group of social movement entrepreneurs as its key leaders. Therefore, the DPP's disadvantaged position within institutional politics left its leaders no choice but to continue its movement strategies and activities for better electoral performance.

It is not uncommon that "[l]eaders of new political parties are likely to act like social movement entrepreneurs seeking to mobilize potential supporters in light of varying opportunities, resources, and ways of framing their claims" (Glenn, 2003: 165).[8] In addition, as Tilly (2003: 250) points out, together with other elements, the "sustained challenge" and the "direction of that challenge to power holder" "set off social movements from other forms of politics." To the public and the KMT, the DPP was no more than an always challenging and contentious movement organization with the name of a political party. The DPP's principal weapons were all sorts of protests. They even brought protests into the Congress and established the Congress norm of fistfights. Not surprisingly, the DPP leaders were constantly hated by their opponents as "trouble makers," "norm breakers," and "instability creators." As Tarrow (1998: 208) indicates, social movements participating in institutional politics "can become imbued with their [institutional politics'] logic and values," it is true that the DPP has been institutionalized since it joined institutional politics, but it is also the case that the DPP has brought "movement" into institutional politics by breaking old political norms and establishing new ones with its movement actions.

In general, both the symbiotic relationship between the DPP and pro-independence organizations and the DPP's movement nature were maintained after the DPP assumed power in 2000. As an inexperienced and weak government, the DPP strategically conceded on important independence issues and concealed its challenging nature at

[8]The author cites the finding from McAdam, D, JD McCarthy and MN Zald (1996). *Comparative Perspectives on Social Movements: Political Opportunities, Mobilizing Structures, and Cultural Framings.* Cambridge [England]; New York: Cambridge University Press.

the beginning of its first term to establish a better relationship with strong domestic and international opposition forces. This strategy disappointed some radical pro-independence organizations and individuals for a while. However, the DPP never stopped promoting its pro-independence agenda in both institutional and non-institutional (i.e., movement) ways. For example, pro-independence activists were assigned to important government positions, such as the ministers for foreign affairs and education, to promote Taiwan's full independence in the international community and add pro-independence educational materials to Taiwan's education system. On the other hand, all kinds of pro-independence organizations, protests and mass gatherings were sponsored by the DPP and the government to develop pro-independence sentiment in Taiwan. Especially after it realized that the concession strategy was not helping to improve its relationship with the opposition forces, and on the other side, it needed to rely on the expanding pro-independence support base to maintain power, it quickly reverted to the more confrontational stance on independence issues and resumed its challenging nature. The study will present more details about the DPP government's movement-oriented strategies in the later chapters. For now, it is sufficient to conclude that the relationship between the DPP government and the TIM does not fit within the *popular* framework of the separate and antagonistic relationship. According to Goldstone (2003: 12), "[u]nderstanding how social movements give rise to parties, shape political alignments and interact with normal political institutions has become essential to comprehending political dynamics," it is hoped that this case study of such a symbiotic relationship between the government and the movement may make some contribution to investigating this topic.

In the case of the DPP government, the above discussion has shown that generally the popular separate and antagonistic framework is not applicable to the cases of movement government where the government usually maintains a symbiotic relationship with movements. Instead, the movement government framework is proposed to analyze such cases and then elaborated in terms of the movement government's differences and similarities to other types of governments, its dual roles and support bases and role conflicts, the three general strategies dealing with the role conflicts and their different impact on the two support bases, and finally, the domestic and international factors influencing the movement government's strategy adoption. I do not think that the movement government framework alone can fully explain changes and continuities in the movement government's support base. Rather, this framework complements the *popular* accounts of support base formation. As shown by the following literature review, the popular perspectives of support base formation have a strong structuralistic tendency and may be inadequate to explain the significant fluctuation in support base. In contrast, although some relevant structural factors are omitted in the movement government framework, it is a more interactive and dynamic perspective for understanding the support base changes of a special type of government — the movement government.

Literature on support base formation

Studies of the support base of political parties, movements, ideologies and so on, have a long tradition in political sociology. Scholars in this field tend to focus their studies on various social structures influencing peoples' political orientations, which consequently divide individuals into different political camps (i.e., different support bases). To list some examples, these social structures include class, organization, mode of production, and social network.

The most classic and influential works on class analysis were written by Marx (e.g., 1964), who proposed that an individual's position in a class structure, i.e., which class he or she belongs to, is the most significant factor determining his or her political orientation. The class is defined as a group of individuals who share the same relation to the property in the production. There are two basic types of relations to the property — possessing and non-possessing; therefore, the two fundamentally different classes are the exploiting class who possess the property and the exploited class who do not. These two classes have distinctly opposite interests; consequently, they also have opposite political orientations in a conflict. One of the historical cases used to examine the above class theory is the Parisian insurrection in June 1848. As Marx argued based on the above class theory, the insurrection is a class struggle between proletariat and bourgeois who used lumpenprolitarians as the repressing weapon. Therefore, different classes naturally form different support bases with different interests and political orientations.

However, Traugott's study (1980) negates Marx's class struggle argument in the above case of Parisian insurrection and provides an organization-based argument on the same case. His study shows that the insurrection did not develop along a clear class boundary. First, there was no well-developed proletariat in 1848 Paris due to industrial underdevelopment. Second, the class bases for the two antagonistic sides were almost identical. What really distinguished one group from the other were age and organizational experience. It is the difference of work experience, economic vulnerability and marital status primarily associated with the age disparity, and the difference of loyalty and solidarity principally determined by different organizational experience, that account for these two groups' opposite political orientations. Therefore, different organizational experience may group individuals into different political camps.

The mode of production is another social structure suggested by Marx to differentiate individuals into different political camps. Recent scholars such as Brustein (1988, 1991), in his study of the rise of Fascism in Italy and Belgium, follows Marx's argument concerning the importance of mode of production in forming "the economic base of society" and shaping "its social characteristics" (Brustein, 1988: 70). He demonstrates that voting preference for Fascist Party "was directly attributable to the different constellations of interests surrounding distinctive modes of production" (Brustein, 1991: 652).

Social networks are probably the most significant social structure identified by movement scholars to account for differential recruitment questions, the core of which is explaining why one individual becomes involved in movements, whereas another remains inactive (McAdam and Paulsen, 1993). The question of differential recruitment actually is an individual level question of being or not being a member of certain movements' active support base. By logical extension, it may be applied to the question of individual participation in the active support base of many other political entities such as political parties.

According to the social network literature in the study of social movements, a type of personal ties, that is, the connection between potential recruits and movement activists, is most commonly found to predict an individual's participation in social movements (Snow, Zurcher and Olson, 1980). Organizational ties, which are created among members of the same organization, can profoundly influence their decision to participate as well (Traugott, 1980). The importance of organizational ties in movement recruitment explains why pre-existing organizations often become the most important vehicles for movement mobilization (McAdam and Paulsen, 1993). Furthermore, the interaction between informal personal ties (e.g., neighborhood ties) and formal organizational ties (e.g., membership ties in a movement organization) can even determine the movement participants' commitment level to the movement and the degree of their resistance to repression (Gould, 1991, 1995).

The above literature on the relationship between social structures and individuals' political orientations may help explain some aspects of my study. For example, it has been shown that ethnicity is a very important structural factor associated with individuals' political orientation in Taiwan. Specifically, mainlanders (i.e., those mainland Chinese who migrated to Taiwan from mainland China with the KMT during 1945–1949 and their descendents in Taiwan) are more likely than the other ethnic groups (i.e., Hoklo and Hakka who are the local Taiwanese) to oppose the DPP and the TIM. Therefore, the ethnic structure in Taiwan is a convenient tool to differentiate support bases of pro and anti-independence parties. Nevertheless, the above literature has a strong tendency towards structural determinism which implies that as long as the individual's structural position remains unchanged, he or she will remain in the old support base. In reality, however, it is not uncommon to see that people change their political orientation without changing their social structure position, which, in turn, leads to the fluctuation in the political party's support base. For example, in the DPP's case, a preliminary finding reveals that individuals with higher education (i.e., college or above) have dramatically changed their support for the DPP. Their support for the DPP was not significantly different from others in and prior to 2000. But during the period of the DPP regime from 2000 to 2008, they have become increasingly less likely than others to vote for the DPP. If better educated people's position in the educational structure did not change, why did their political attitudes change? To address the research question of support base fluctuation, we need to bring factors other than social structures into the analytic framework.

One of such factors is the "owner" of the support base such as the movement organization, the political party and the government that the support base supports. As suggested by the movement government framework, the support base owner's strategies of maintaining support are constrained by the support base's expectations on one hand, and have significant impacts on the support base on the other. Therefore, the support base fluctuation may be better understood within an interactive and dynamic framework involving both the support base and the owner of that support base. In the proposed movement government framework, four major political forces including the government, the movement, and their two support bases are woven into an interactive framework. Therefore, it may be able to complement the above structuralistic accounts of support base formation.

Summary

As a highly anticipated new democratic government in Taiwan since 2000, the DPP successfully maintained power by significantly increased votes in the 2004 presidential election. However, in early 2008, the DPP failed dismally in the legislative and presidential elections. Why did the social support for the DPP government fluctuate so radically from 2000 through 2008? This chapter first indicates the importance and broader implications of this research question for the studies of so-called movement government, and then, discusses the inadequacy of the popular answers to this question which either emphasize the DPP government's poor economic record and corruption scandals or the declining support for the TIM. As an alternative account, this chapter proposes a movement government framework to clarify and explain the fluctuation in the DPP's support base. According to this framework, the DPP government is a typical case of movement government which plays the dual roles of government and movement and has two overlapping but different support bases supporting the two roles. This chapter also theoretically elaborates the movement government framework to introduce the key characteristics of movement government including their dual roles and support bases, the inherent tension between the two roles, the three strategies dealing with role conflicts and their different impact on the two support bases, and finally, the factors influencing the adoption of different strategies. To illustrate how this framework may connect and contribute to the literature on government-movement relations and support base formation, this chapter reviews these two groups of literature and suggests that (1) the popular framework of the separate and antagonistic government-movement relations is not applicable to the case of movement government, and (2) structuralistic perspectives on support base formation may be inadequate to explain the fluctuation in the movement government's support base. Therefore, the proposed movement government framework may complement the existing perspectives.

The next chapter begins to analyze the case of the DPP, the TIM and the changes in their support bases within the movement government framework. The principal purpose of Chapter 2 is to differentiate between the DPP government's two support bases in terms of their sizes, developing trends at the aggregate level and their different correlations to individuals' dissatisfaction with the DPP government's performance. Moreover, this two-level analysis will also facilitate examining the argument that the DPP's electoral defeats in 2008 indicate the decreased popular support for the TIM in Taiwan.

CHAPTER 2: DIFFERENTIATING THE DPP'S TWO SUPPORT BASES

Introduction

The previous introduction and theory chapter raises the general research question of this study: Why did the social support for the government of the Democratic Progressive Party (DPP) fluctuate so much during its two administrative terms in 2000–2008? That chapter also discusses the empirical, theoretical and broader significance of this research question with the case study of the DPP government in Taiwan; the inadequacy and weakness of the popular answers to this question are briefly presented. Moreover, the movement government framework is proposed and elaborated as an alternative account for the fluctuation in the DPP's support base. Finally, relevant literatures on government-movement relations and support base formation are reviewed; the connection and possible contribution of the movement government framework to the literature are discussed as well in the previous chapter. The current chapter begins the analysis of Taiwan's case within the proposed movement government framework.

Specifically, this chapter first reviews the history of the Taiwan Independence Movement (TIM), the DPP, Taiwan's independence issues and party politics to provide the context for this case study. Then, based on the movement government framework and previous studies, it proposes three attitudinal indicators — the DPP ID (i.e., identification with DPP), the Taiwanese identity and the pro-independence attitude, to identify which one of the two support bases each DPP's potential supporter belongs to, and the gap and overlap between the two support bases.

Finally, to examine the argument that the lower social support for the DPP indicates parallel declining support for the TIM, this chapter presents the two support bases' divergent development trends during 2000–2008 and then uses nested multinomial logistic models to show how individuals' dissatisfaction with the DPP's government performance is differently correlated with their support for the DPP government and for the TIM in 2008.

The Taiwan Independence Movement and the DPP from Movement to Political Party to Government

Origin of the TIM

A popular justification for pursuing Taiwan's independence of mainland China is Taiwan's unique colonial history and resulting long separation from mainland China (Shi, 2001; Wang, 1993). Although the causality between the long history of separation and the necessity of Taiwan's independence is still a highly debated issue (Nan, 1980; Lin, 1993; Chen, 1994; Zhang, 2002), it is not wrong to say that Taiwan's long colonial experience prepared a rich soil for the emergence and the development of the TIM. This was especially the case for the half a century occupation by Japan.

From 1895 through 1945, Taiwan was a colony of Japan under the Treaty of Shimonoseki with the Chinese Qing dynasty. As a rising economic and military power in the late 19th century, the Japanese government's objective in Taiwan was to build a foreign base of raw production materials for Japanese domestic economy and a model colony to gain respect from its western competitors (Roy, 2003; Gold, 1986:33). Therefore, the Japanese government invested a great amount of money, technology and human resources in Taiwan to give it a new image. By the year of 1945 when the Nationalist Party government (i.e., *Kuo Min Tang* in Chinese; or, the KMT) from mainland China reclaimed Taiwan from the defeated Japanese government after World War II (WWII), Taiwan had undergone profound social and economic changes which made it distinct in many aspects from war tortured mainland China.

The standard of living and the education level of typical Taiwanese, and the general infrastructure conditions in Taiwan were much higher and better than those in mainland China (Roy, 2003; Wang, 1993). On the other hand, Taiwan's organized and armed resistance against the Japanese occupation ceased as early as 1902 (Roy, 2003: xi; Brown, 2004: 8). Nevertheless, a non-violent "self-government" movement led by the local business elite and political activists persisted through the entire colonial period. Partly due to the pressure of this movement, Taiwan saw a gradual transition in governance from an authoritarian system to a limited democratic system. A group of local business elites had the opportunity to join the government and became the political elites as well (Roy, 2003; Wang, 1993, 2002; Zhang *et al.*, 2000).

In the 1930s, the Japanese government in Taiwan began a new policy of assimilation called "imperial-subjectization" (i.e., "kominka" in Japanese or "Huangminhua" in Chinese) (Roy, 2003:41). The impact of this decade-long assimilation campaign on Taiwan society was double sided: on one hand, many local/Chinese cultural practices were overtly discriminated against or even destroyed; on the other hand, more educational and political resources under Japanese control were opened up to local Taiwanese. To the extent that some local elites and their children, through working or studying with Japanese in the same government agencies, enterprises or schools, became familiar with the Japanese language, the Japanese lifestyle and the Japanese political culture and system, the effect of this assimilation policy was not totally in vain (Wang, 1993, 2002; Zhang *et al.*, 2000).

The TIM might never have emerged despite all the above changes in Taiwan, had the newly-arrived KMT government and troops not systematically discriminated against the Taiwanese and greedily transferred all kinds of public resources in Taiwan to mainland China. Actually, after the defeat of Japan in 1945, most Taiwanese including the local elites who had been getting along with Japanese government were extremely excited about Taiwan's return to motherland China. They also had a very high expectation for the troops and administrative staff sent by the KMT government from mainland China. However, their excitement and expectations were crushed within a couple of months by the punitive treatment they received from their "mainland brethren." The KMT government believed that the Taiwanese had been Japanized and were not trustworthy. In most cases, the more prestigious a Taiwanese was, the more connections he or she had with the Japanese colonial government, and therefore the more discrimination he or she would face from the KMT government. The KMT government also discretionarily transferred public resources in Taiwan such as machines, products, raw materials and even entire plants to mainland China to support its civil war effort against the Chinese Communist Party (hereafter, the CCP) (Roy, 2003; Lin, 1993; Wang, 1993, 2002; Zhang *et al.*, 2000; Brown, 2004: 9).

Not surprisingly, Taiwanese society experienced deteriorating living standards, an unsecured environment for life and property and a highly authoritarian government soon after Taiwan's return to the KMT government. Local Taiwanese also saw a variety of overt corruptions in both the KMT troops and the government, which they believed to be much worse than they experienced under the Japanese regime. As a result of all these frustrations, deep disillusion with their "mainland brethren" was widespread among Taiwanese. The once higher standard living and educational level, the long-existing tradition of a "self-government" movement and the impact of the Japanization policy during the Japanese occupation all made these frustrations more obvious and unbearable (Roy, 2003; Wang, 1993, 2002; Lin, 1993). On 28 February 1947, after one Taiwanese was shot by a KMT officer during a skirmish on the previous day, protests erupted in Taiwan's capital city, Taipei, and then quickly developed into armed rebellion, spreading across the entire island in a few days.

Nevertheless, an island-wide rebellion did not directly lead to the emergence of the independence movement. Ironically, it was the KMT government's aggressive attempt to repress this rebellion through massacre, persecution and martial law that finally gave birth to the TIM. To escape from severe persecution, a small group of Taiwanese activists fled first to Hong Kong and then to Japan (Zhang *et al.*, 2000; Zhang, 2002). They began the TIM by establishing formal movement organizations.

It is impossible to draw a comprehensive picture of the TIM in this short review, not only because of its long history, but also because of the complexity inherent in almost every facet of its development. To give only a few such examples, its central locus changed from Japan to the US and finally back to Taiwan; its organizations have undergone splits, mergers and severe internal conflicts; different factions of the TIM held different, sometimes opposite ideologies, strategies and plans for Taiwan's independence; many activists of the TIM were ideologically driven and devoted themselves to the movement. However, others actively promoted the movement for their own political gains, and in a few cases, some movement leaders surrendered to the KMT government. Furthermore, the TIM had a long and complicated interaction with other social movements in Taiwan, such as the opposition movement (i.e., democracy or Dangwai movement in Chinese); moreover, the KMT government's reaction towards the TIM varied greatly at different periods of time. After the DPP won the presidential elections in 2000 and 2004, the role of the TIM in both Taiwan's electoral politics and its international relations became more and more salient and critical. In the following review, I do not intend to cover all of the above aspects of the movement, but only to sketch the TIM's development from movement to political party and finally to government to present the general historical context of the study. Other relevant history will be discussed in other chapters of the study when needed.

The Overseas TIM

Under Taiwan's 38-year martial law from 1949–1987, three types of opposition activists including those pro-independence, pro-democracy and pro-mainland China (i.e., communists) were identified by the KMT government as the most dangerous enemies to its regime and were persecuted relentlessly. Therefore, the TIM activists had to develop the movement overseas in Japan and the US and did not return to Taiwan until the late 1980s, when martial law was finally lifted and the domestic TIM — disguised within the democracy movement in Taiwan — started going public.

(a) Japan: 1947 — the 1960s. During this period, Japan seemed predetermined to become the first center for the TIM. First of all, Japan had far more Taiwanese immigrants than any other country at that time. Second, due to various connections between Japanese and Taiwanese established during the Japanese occupation, Japan became Taiwanese students' first choice for overseas higher education. Especially for dissident students in Taiwan, Japan was an accessible haven for a less repressive environment. Therefore, Japan provided a relatively rich support base (e.g., dissident Taiwanese students), resources (e.g., donations from Taiwanese immigrants) and an open political environment for the TIM's first stage of development (Chen, 1998, 2006; Zhang *et al.*, 2000; Wang, 2002).

There were several factions within the TIM in Japan during this period. The faction leaders were almost all from well-known local Taiwanese elite families (Zhang *et al.*, 2000). The frustration of their family fortune and personal careers as a result of discrimination and persecution by the KMT government might have been one underlying reason for their rebellious activism. In addition to this frustration, scholars in mainland China believe that these activists were actually a group of highly Japanized Taiwanese, who represented a very small percent of Taiwanese (Zhang, 2002; Lin, 1993). Although it is hard to definitely conclude the causality between Japanization and some Taiwanese's support for the TIM, it is fair to say that these activists were, indeed, well connected to Japan in one way or another: they received higher education in Japan; they spoke fluent Japanese; they once had positions in Japanese colonial government; their families had good business connections with the Japanese; finally, they received support from some high-level Japanese politicians for their pro-independence activities (Song, 1996; Zhang *et al.*, 2000; Wang, 2002).

The dominant faction of the TIM in Japan during this period was led by Liao Wenyi, who established the "Provisional Government of Taiwan Republic" in 1956 and was the self-appointed "President" of this "independent state." The strategy they chose to achieve an independent Taiwan was to put Taiwan under the trusteeship of the United Nations first and then legitimize Taiwan's independence through a referendum in Taiwan. Most members of this faction were those Taiwanese exiled after the 28 February Incident, their family members and close friends in Taiwan. However, in 1965, the "President" Liao first and then some of his followers returned to Taiwan and surrendered to the KMT government, which hit the entire TIM badly (Chen, 1998, 2006; Zhang *et al.*, 2000).

On the other hand, under the KMT government's pressure, the Japanese government tightened the political environment for the TIM: some pro-independence activists were forcefully repatriated to Taiwan. Additionally, more and more Taiwanese students shifted their country preference of overseas study from Japan to the US. Therefore, by the end of the 1960s, the US became the new central locus for the TIM (Chen, 1998, 2006).

(b) The US: the 1970s — the late 1980s. Besides an increasing pool of potential participants, two other factors attracted the TIM activists to shift the movement's center to the US. One was the American government's ability to influence the KMT government in Taiwan and the other was the proximity to the UN headquarter in New York City (Chen1998, 2006). It was a successful move. The organizations, memberships and activities of the TIM thrived in the US during this period and further spread to other countries such as Canada and many European countries.

The major objective chosen by the largest and the most influential TIM organization, the World United Formosans for Independence (hereafter, the WUFI), in the US was to overthrow the KMT regime by any means possible. In practice, some of its local groups were even labeled "terrorist organizations" by the California government due to their members' violent activities (e.g., bombing and assassination) against individuals and companies of the KMT government in the US and Taiwan (Chen, 1998, 2006). On the other hand, the TIM activists often lobbied bills on Taiwan through the US Congress to gain better political treatment in the US and to put pressure on the KMT government. Another major activity of the TIM was supporting the opposition (i.e., pro-democracy) movement in Taiwan. Although these two movements did not share completely same agenda for Taiwan, both of them had the same "enemy" — the authoritarian KMT government. In the open political environment of the US and with the help of some Congressmen, the TIM organizations mobilized numerous resources to support the opposition movement in Taiwan (Chen, 1998, 2006; Shi, 2001). The contribution of the TIM to Taiwan's democratization facilitated its subsequent merger with the opposition movement in Taiwan.

DPP: From Movement to Political Party to Government

The political history of Taiwan since it reverted to the KMT government in 1945 was a long and painful struggling process between Taiwan's opposition forces and the KMT authoritarian government. As a result of this process, Taiwan gradually transformed from an authoritarian to a democratic regime. Generally, the history of this political transformation may be divided into five stages with a different president in each stage: (1) the "hard authoritarian regime" or the period of "white terror" dictated by Chiang Kai-shek, the leader of the KMT, in 1945–1975 (Zhang and Qiu, 2005); (2) the "soft authoritarian regime" or the period of localization governed by Chiang's son, Chiang Ching-kuo, in 1976–1988; (3) the period of further localization and democratization under President Lee Teng-hui, the first Taiwanese leader of the KMT and also the first president elected by the popular election, in 1989–2000; (4) the democratic and pro-independence regime under President Chen Shui-bian, the leader of the main opposition party DPP, in 2000–2008; finally, (5) the democratic but anti-independence regime under President Ma Ying-jeou , the leader of the KMT, since May, 2008.

Due to the highly repressive political environment, the TIM had not existed as a significant mass movement in Taiwan until the 1980s, except some sporadic pro-independence activities either spontaneous or influenced by the overseas TIM. In contrast, because the KMT government opened its local elections in 1950 (Chu and Lin, 2001), the opposition movement has been able to develop through various electoral and social movement activities. In the late 1970s, all kinds of opposition forces including those pro-democracy, pro-independence, pro-socialism (i.e., leftists), pro-unification, and various social movement activists started coalescing to fight against their common enemy, the authoritarian KMT government. However, the pro-independence sentiment and agenda had been disguised under the popular and democratic appeal for self-determination and improving human rights within the opposition movement until 1979, when Kaohsiung Incident occurred.

In December, 1979, a large protest in Kaohsiung organized by the opposition movement was crushed down by the KMT government. Almost all of the important opposition activists in Taiwan were arrested soon afterward. However, the subsequent trials became a unique opportunity for these activist defendants to intensively propagandize their pro-democracy and pro-independence ideas all over the island, because somehow the KMT government allowed Taiwan's and international media to freely report the trials (Chen, 2006).[1]

After the trials, although most old opposition activists were put in jail, the new activists who were the spouses and the lawyers of those arrested activists carried on the opposition movement. Since then, the pro-independence ideology and agenda gradually became explicit, and therefore, the domestic TIM which was different from the overseas one started emerging within the opposition movement. When the opposition coalition finally established its own political party, the DPP, in 1986, the majority of the party leaders and key members were also pro-independence activists (Chen, 2006).

It should be noted that martial law was not lifted until 1987 and the legal persecution of non-violent pro-independence activities did not stop until 1992 when the relevant law[2] was amended. Nevertheless, the pro-independence ideology and agenda gradually became the same important pillar as pro-democracy for this illegally founded political party. In 1991, the DPP added explicit pro-independence goals into its official party platform, claiming its identity as a pro-independence party to the public. Around this time, the overseas TIM started returning to Taiwan to join the DPP's pro-democracy and pro-independence movement. After 1992, the largest overseas TIM organization, WUFI, officially returned to Taiwan.[3] The two TIMs finally converged in Taiwan under the leadership of the DPP, starting a new era for the TIM.

The DPP had a very practical reason for promoting the TIM — the TIM was a most effective mobilizing instrument for expanding its support base. This is because the KMT government's policies of "internal colonialism" (Hechter, 1999; Olzak, 2004) justified the TIM and made it appealing to many local Taiwanese. When the KMT was defeated by the CCP in the

[1] Some of my mainlander interviewees in Taiwan told me that soon after these trials, they started feeling local Taiwanese's rising anti-China and anti-mainlanders sentiment, which had been the first time for local Taiwanese publically expressing such sentiment since mainlanders arrived in Taiwan.

[2] The Article 100 of the Criminal Law on the Crime of Insurrection.

[3] See the WUFI's official website: http://www.wufi.org.tw/, accessed on 18 June 2015.

Chinese civil war and fled to Taiwan in 1949, it brought one to two million mainland Chinese soldiers and ordinary immigrants to this small island (Brown, 2004: 9). To secure the authoritarian regime, the KMT government made most of those important and rewarding positions in the public systems, such as the systems of military, government, education and state enterprises, available only to mainlanders. Consequently, a "cultural division of labor" (Hechter, 2000; Olzak, 2004) emerged in Taiwan soon after 1949, discriminating and disadvantaging local Taiwanese mainly including Hoklo and Hakka. In her book *Is Taiwan Chinese*, Brown (2004: 10) summarizes other scholars' findings on this issue: "'Taiwanese,' for example, were largely (but not entirely) excluded from political power and national corporations in Taiwan during the period of martial law, and 'Mainlanders,' in turn, were largely (but not entirely) excluded from small and medium-sized businesses owned and operated by Taiwanese." From many local Taiwanese's point of view, the KMT governed Taiwan in the same way as the former Japanese colonizer, or even in a worse way. Therefore, the independence movement was justified for overthrowing this new colonizer and liberating local Taiwanese from the authoritarian regime. (Xiao, 1999; Li, 2003)

Chiang Ching-kuo's "soft" authoritarian regime was handed over to Lee Teng-hui after he died in 1988, which began a new era for Taiwan's localization, democratization and the independence movement. Lee, the first local Taiwanese President and the leader of the KMT, was a skillful and sophisticated politician with conflicting faces, and influenced Taiwan's transformation profoundly. He was called "Mr. Democracy" by many of his supporters for his gradual reforms of localization and democratization in Taiwan.[4] Meanwhile, he was hated by many mainlanders in Taiwan and called "a KMT traitor" for his implicit support for the DPP and the TIM when he served as the President. He was also blamed by opposition forces for the KMT government's involvement in "black-gold" corruptions (i.e., corruptions involving mafia, money and politicians) under his leadership. Not surprisingly, Chinese government also labeled him "the nation's traitor" and "troublemaker" and believed he tried to mobilize another TIM within the KMT government when he defined

---

[4] http://news.bbc.co.uk/hi/chinese/news/newsid_695000/6957441.stm, accessed on 18 June 2015.

Taiwan and mainland China as the "state-to-state" relation in 1999 (Brown, 2004: 4).[5]

For the DPP and the TIM, Lee was both a friend and an enemy. In general, many of Lee's reforms met or sometimes were even beyond the DPP's demands on democratization and pro-independence. On the other hand, the DPP's political resources associated with these two appeals had also been skimmed away by the KMT government's reforming progress under Lee's leadership. In other words, since the Lee's government had become more and more democratic and pro-independence, there seemed to be less and less space for the DPP to exploit in Taiwan's politics. However, in 2000 presidential election, the severe split of the KMT by two presidential candidates led to an unexpected victory of the DPP with only 39.3% of vote. After 55 years of one-party regime, Taiwan finally achieved peaceful regime change with a new President from the DPP, Chen Shui-bian.

The DPP's historical victory in the 2000 presidential election did not completely rely on good luck, because before 2000 its political influence in Taiwan had grown steadily since it was founded in 1986. We can see its increasing political influence in the following Figures 2.1–2.3 which

Figure 2.1 DPP Membership: 1986–2008

Data source: The DPP's official website, http://www.dpp.org.tw/ accessed on 10 June 2015

[5]Also see http://www.gwytb.gov.cn/hxlt/hxlt0.asp?offset=400&hxlt_m_id=218, accessed on 13 February 2008.

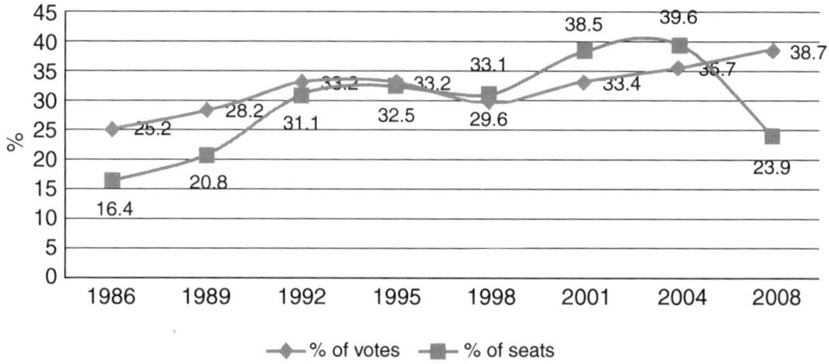

Figure 2.2 Legislative Election Results: 1986–2008, DPP

Data source: The DPP's official website, http://www.dpp.org.tw/; Central Election Commission, http://www.cec.gov.tw/ accessed on 10 June 2015

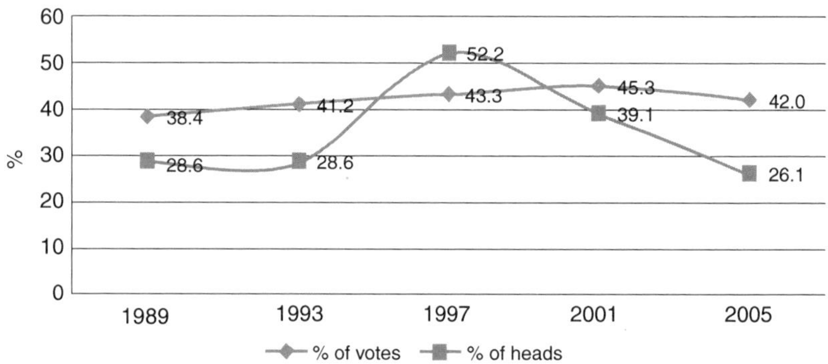

Figure 2.3 County and County-Level-City Head Election Results: 1989–2005, DPP

Data source: The DPP's official website, http://www.dpp.org.tw/; Central Election Commission, http://www.cec.gov.tw/

show the DPP's annual membership, its electoral performance in national legislative (i.e., parliamentary) elections and local county/county-level-city head elections.

As these above figures show, the DPP's membership had increased from a little over 1,000 in 1986 to over 200,000 in 1999, an increase by over 180 times in 13 years. In 1997, it controlled more than half of the counties and county-level cities in Taiwan which covers about 71.6% of Taiwan's population.[6] In 1998, it has controlled about one-third of parliamentary seats. Therefore, although the DPP's victory in the 2000 presidential election might be unexpected to many Taiwanese, nobody could deny its great development during the past 15 years.

The DPP Government: Controversial Government Performance but Successful Movement Development

The new DPP government was a typical minority government — its president was a "minority president" with less than 40% of popular support and the DPP was the minority party in the parliament. The international community, especially mainland China and the US, together with the new opposition party KMT, worried about the DPP government's quick move towards Taiwan's complete independence and imposed heavy pressure on the new government. Therefore, it was not surprising to see the new President Chen Shui-bian adopt a series of compromising strategies trying to pacify and co-opt various oppositions at the beginning of his presidency (Lin, 2006). For example, he promised "four noes and one without"[7] in his inauguration and appointed the former defense minister of the KMT government as his premier.

However, all these efforts did not stop constant conflicts between the government and the opposition party — now it was the KMT's turn to be the opposition. The DPP government and the KMT fought each other in almost every policy arena. In addition, as an inexperienced government, the DPP's incapability in rebuilding Taiwan's economy received severe public criticism. Social movement activists also started criticizing the DPP government for its quickly reversed position favoring richer and

---

[6] http://www.huaxia.com/zt/rdzz/06-018/2006/00464662.html, accessed on 18 June 2015.

[7] Chen declared that "as long as the CCP regime has no intention to use military force against Taiwan, I pledge that during my term in office, I will not declare independence, I will not change the national title, I will not push forth the inclusion of the so-called 'state-to-state' description in the Constitution, and I will not promote a referendum to change the status quo in regards to the question of independence or unification. Furthermore, the abolition of the National Reunification Council or the National Reunification Guidelines will not be an issue." http://info.gio.gov.tw/ct.asp?xItem=12725&ctNode=3763, accessed on 24 March 2009.

privileged groups. Even worse, the media exposed more and more corruption scandals involving some high-level DPP government officials. In the eyes of the public, this young and highly anticipated government seemed to be quickly KMTized — it became more and more like its enemy, the former ruler KMT, in many respects.

On the other hand, the TIM, which became a state-sponsored nationalism movement since 2000, developed substantially. The most obvious indication of this development was that a large group of pro-independence activists were assigned to key positions in public systems, such as military, government, education, state enterprise systems, and so on. Consequently, the TIM was able to control a huge amount of military, political, economic, educational and cultural resources which might be utilized for their pro-independence purpose. Furthermore, as Figure 2.1 shows, the DPP's membership increased hugely from a little over 200,000 in 1999 to over 370,000 in 2000, an increase by over 170,000 people, which is an undeniable signal of the TIM's significant development. Additionally, an increasing number of pro-independence organizations were established and received generous financial support from the DPP government. Most importantly, the public started showing stronger pro-independence sentiment since 2000. Gradually, "pro-China" activities became politically incorrect and none of the politicians would like to receive such condemnation from their political rivals. According to Tarrow (1998), all these changes signal a successful development of the movement. In 2002, seeing the failure of his concession strategy and the rising trend of pro-independence sentiment in Taiwan, President Chen Shui-bian and the DPP changed their mild stance on pro-independence issues to be much more radical and confrontational (Lin, 2006). In 2004, Chen Shui-bian won the presidential election again with 50.1% of vote, a much higher popular support than four years ago.

The DPP government at the beginning of its second term was much stronger with improved popular support and increased number of seats in parliament. However, its performance in managing economy and anti-corruption was not improved as expected. The fatal hit to the government came from its own President Chen's family — his wife, son-in-law and even the President himself were accused of corruptions in 2006, which triggered large scale anti-President protests all over the island. For this troubled government, it seemed the TIM was its last hope to prevent its support base from drifting away. Relying on its dominant position in the TIM, the DPP government pushed the radical strategy to be more divisive, contentious and conflict-creating to fight against opposition forces and consolidate its core support base. However, these strategies seemed to be much less effective than they had been before 2004. In the legislative and presidential elections in 2008, the DPP encountered the worst electoral defeats in its history — the percent of seats they took in the legislative election was only about 24%, a 16% drop from the last term's 40%, and the vote share they received in the presidential election was 41.55%, a 8.5% drop from 50.1% of four years ago (Taiwan Central Election Commission[8]). As a result, the eight-year pro-independence regime ended in May 2008, and the KMT returned to power and resumed the anti-independence regime.

Taiwan's Independence Issues and the Two Political Camps

Although the TIM originated in a tragic event in Taiwan, the 28 February Incident in 1947, international factors, especially the changing relationship between mainland China and the US, have always had significant impact on Taiwan's independence issues. After the CCP defeated the KMT in the Chinese civil war and established the People's Republic of China (PRC) in 1949, the two Chinas which are the CCP's PRC in mainland China and the KMT's Republic of China (ROC) in Taiwan fought with each other for the national representation in the international community. Before 1971, although many countries had switched their official diplomatic relations from the ROC to the PRC, it was the ROC, not the PRC, which was the official member of the United Nations (UN). The UN membership had been extremely important for the KMT regime to maintain its legitimacy in both Taiwan and the international community. In the context of the Cold War, the main reason that the ROC could maintain its UN membership was the support of the US. However, since the PRC finally replaced the ROC as the official member of the UN, and meanwhile, the ROC quit the UN in 1971, an increasing number of countries severed their official diplomatic relations with the ROC and accepted the

[8] http://www.cec.gov.tw/, accessed on 18 June 2015.

PRC's "one-China" policy which states that there is only one China in the world, the government of the PRC is the sole legal government of all of China, and Taiwan is an inalienable part of the territory of the PRC. The last straw to the ROC's endangered international position came in 1978 when the US, the ROC's most important supporter and protector, abandoned the ROC and embraced the PRC. Nowadays among nearly 200 countries in the world, there are only 23 countries maintaining official diplomatic relations with the ROC (Ministry of Foreign Affairs, Republic of China (Taiwan)).[9]

The almost complete defeat in the battle of national representation has shaken the ROC's legitimacy in Taiwan, and on the other hand, created opportunities for pro-independence challenges (Jacobs, 2005). The legitimacy of the ROC is primarily based on the old Constitution established in 1947 when the KMT still held state power in mainland China. After the KMT fled to Taiwan in 1949, to maintain the ROC's legitimacy, it was necessary for the KMT to keep this Constitution intact. Therefore, although the ROC's actual governance has been constrained within Taiwan and some small nearby islands since 1949, the Constitution still stipulates that the territory of the ROC includes both mainland China and Taiwan. During the period of Chiang Kai-shek and Chiang Ching-kuo, the KMT had taken great effort to educate people in Taiwan to believe that the ROC still existed as the only legitimate representative of China in the international community and Taiwan was not part of the PRC. Moreover, according to the KMT, Taiwan was KMT's "base for revival". According to the KMT's propaganda, the CCP would finally be defeated by the KMT and mainland China would be reunited with Taiwan. However, when most countries in the world accepted the PRC as the only China and the ROC lost its UN membership, the above propaganda about the ROC's international legitimacy became ungrounded. Then the question is, if Taiwan is not part of the PRC as the KMT government insisted and the ROC is not recognized by the international community, what should Taiwan be? For many Taiwanese, the easy and reasonable answer is that Taiwan should be a country independent of both the PRC and the ROC.

---

[9] http://www.mofa.gov.tw/AlliesIndex.aspx?n=0757912EB2F1C601&sms=26470E539B6FA395, accessed on 11 June 2015 .

Therefore, pro-independence activists have tried to justify their pursuing of Taiwan's independence at both the domestic and the international level: domestically, the KMT is an outside colonizer imposing an authoritarian regime on local Taiwanese; internationally, the ROC exists in name only and its Constitution is way too outdated and inconsistent with Taiwan's political reality. Along this line of argument, in the DPP's Party Member Representatives Meeting in September, 2007, Normal Nation Resolution was passed and specified the major tasks for the DPP in the future: "actively pursue name-rectification and promulgate a new Constitution, accede to the United Nations as an equal member, and implement transitional justice and policies aimed at nurturing a Taiwan-centric consciousness." (Normal Nation Resolution, English version, page 4)[10] This Normal Nation Resolution was called "the new pro-independence platform" and severely criticized by the Chinese government,[11] which however suggests that both the mainland Chinese government and the DPP have recognized that political actions such as name-rectification (change the ROC to Taiwan Republic or whatever else), constitution renewal (to exclude mainland China from the stipulated territory of the future independent Taiwan state), and joining the UN would equal Taiwan's independence.

In general, the two antagonistic political camps in Taiwan, the so-called pan-green and pan-blue,[12] can be distinguished by their different positions on the above three issues. But before we try to understand the difference between the two camps, we need to briefly review the origins of the major parties in each camp. The major party in the pan-green camp in addition to the DPP is the Taiwan Solidarity Union (TSU) which was founded in August 2001, a year after the DPP took power, with the former President Lee Teng-hui as their "spiritual leader." Its members and supporters mainly include two types of people — pro-independence fundamentalists and previous KMT members who supported Lee Teng-hui and therefore

[10] http://www.dpp.org.tw/upload/policy/20071029100043_link.pdf, accessed on 18 June 2015.

[11] http://news.xinhuanet.com/newscenter/2007-10/01/content_6821206.htm, accessed on 18 June 2015.

[12] The two camps are named by the background colors of the DPP and KMT party flags. The DPP party flag's background color is green and the KMT's is blue.

opposed the anti-Lee Teng-hui campaign in the KMT right after the KMT lost the presidential election in 2000. Many believed that the TSU originally had tried to position itself in the middle ground of the independence-unification spectrum with a moderate pro-independence agenda. However, as the DPP quickly moved to the same moderate position on pro-independence issues after 2000, this position seemed to be unavailable for the TSU. Therefore, the TSU strategically decided to occupy the radical pro-independence position to prevent pro-independence fundamentalists from being alienated by the DPP's concession strategy. Since then, the TSU has been the DPP's most sincere ally and viewed by the public as the most radical pro-independence party in Taiwan.

In the pan-blue camp, there are two other major parties in addition to the KMT, the New Party (NP) and the People First Party (PFP), both of which were founded by previous KMT leaders. The NP was founded in 1993 by a small group of young mainlander KMT cadres to fight against prevalent corruptions and the President Lee Teng-hui's pro-independence policies in the KMT (Wang, 2005: 79). Since its foundation, it has been the most explicit anti-independence and pro-unification party in Taiwan. Its members and supporters mainly are mainlanders, therefore, it is often called a "mainlanders' party" by pro-independence people. The PFP was founded by an important former KMT leader James Soong right after he lost the presidential election as an independent candidate in March 2000.[13] Its members and supporters mainly come from the KMT and the NP. Therefore, it has very close connections with both parties.

We can see that the pan-blue camp is basically composed of previous or current KMT members and supporters excluding Lee Teng-hui's pro-independence faction in the KMT, and the pan-green camp mainly includes the DPP and the new supporters brought by Lee. The major difference between the two camps is their positions on Taiwan's independence issues such as name-rectification, constitution renewal, pursuing

---

[13] James Soong received 36.8% of vote which is higher than the KMT candidate's votes (23.1%) but lower than the DPP candidate's (39.3%). In 2004 presidential election, he ran as the Vice President candidate together with the KMT chairman as the President candidate. They received 49.9% of vote and the DPP candidates received 50.1%.

the UN membership, and economic and social policies related to these issues. In general, the pan-green camp supports all these pro-independence agendas, and the TSU usually appears more radical than the DPP in pursuing them. In contrast, the pan-blue camp opposes the first two agendas — they have insisted on keeping the name and the Constitution of the ROC intact, but do not oppose Taiwan joining the UN. From the two camps' similar attitudes about Taiwan's UN membership, we can find the common ground between them despite their significant conflicts on other issues — both camps believe Taiwan is a *de facto* independent country and deserves the official UN membership. However, the pan-green camp argues that Taiwan is independent of the PRC, but not as the ROC with an outdated Constitution; the pan-blue camp insists that it is the ROC that is independent of the PRC and one of the most important objectives of the pan-blue parties is to pursue the eventual reunification between mainland China and Taiwan.

Another important policy difference between the two camps is about the economic and social relations between Taiwan and mainland China. In general, the pan-blue camp promotes closer, wider and more open economic and social relations with mainland China and emphasizes the opportunities brought by the better relations to Taiwan. A better relationship may help rebuild Taiwan's economy; on the other hand, it may establish mutual understanding between the two sides and especially may reduce hostilities of mainland China towards Taiwan. However, the pan-green camp sees more threats from such an improved relationship. They argue that such a relationship with mainland China will definitely encourage more capital to move from Taiwan to mainland China and therefore "empty" Taiwan's own economic resources and increase unemployment in Taiwan. Moreover, Taiwan's pro-independence course may be compromised by such an open relationship with mainland China, because this will provide the Chinese government with more opportunities to integrate Taiwan with mainland China economically and culturally. Specifically, during 2000–2008 the debate was mainly on two issues: whether or not to increase or even remove the 40% capital investment cap of Taiwanese business in mainland China, and whether or not to implement the "three direct links" (i.e., direct trade, transport and mail services) between

Taiwan and mainland China. While the pan-blue camp supported the increase of the capital investment cap and the three direct links, the pan-green camp opposed both during 2000–2008.

Since the 2001 legislative election, the term "green" and "blue" are not only used to distinguish between the two camps of political parties, but also popular labels differentiating supporters of each camp — organizations and individuals in Taiwan are usually labeled "green" or "blue" as well to indicate which camp they support. In addition, the support base of each camp is further divided into two components — deep-greens/blues and light-greens/blues. The deep-greens/blues are those most likely to vote for the pan-green/blue parties and light-greens/blues those relatively less likely to vote for the pan-green/blue parties in elections. Although many organizations and individuals in Taiwan refuse to be labeled in such a partisan way and claim to be neutral voters, as long as they come to vote in elections, they have to vote for one camp or the other, and therefore, will fall into this "green vs. blue" categorization. Since the turnout rates in Taiwan's major elections, such as the presidential election, are usually over 75%,[14] the majority of eligible voters in Taiwan may actually be classified this way.

Differentiating the DPP Government's Two Support Bases at the Aggregate Level

The movement government framework suggests that the DPP government is a typical movement government. Therefore, it should have two overlapping but still different support bases. The question is: what are the indicators to differentiate the two support bases? Without a doubt, the most convincing support base indicator is the individuals' voting decision — people who vote for the DPP are members of its support base. However, an individual's voting decision can only indicate whether he or she belongs to the DPP's overall support base, and we cannot tell from their voting decisions which one of the two support bases, the government's or the movement's support base, they are in. Therefore, we need to identify

[14] The turn-out rates in the 1996, 2000, 2004 and 2008 Presidential elections are 76%, 83%, 80% and 76% respectively (Taiwan Central Election Commission).

some other indicators which are not only highly correlated with individuals' voting decisions, but also can indicate which specific support base the individual belongs to.

Fortunately, previous studies on this topic have identified such support base indicators, which are three attitudinal indicators — the party ID, the national identity and the attitude about Taiwan's independence. They have been collected through the following three questions in a variety of surveys in Taiwan since the early 1990s:

1. The question about the party ID: which political party do you feel identified with — the DPP, the KMT…? Please note this is not asking about party membership — the number of party ID is usually much higher than that of party membership.
2. The question about the national identity: do you consider yourself to be Taiwanese only, Chinese only, or both?
3. The question about the attitude on Taiwan's independence: what is your opinion about Taiwan's future relation with mainland China: pro-independence, pro-unification or pro-status quo?

Previous studies have found that the above three attitudinal indicators, especially individuals' party ID, are highly correlated with their voting choices. In other words, people who identify with the DPP (including other pro-independence/pan-green parties), or have the Taiwanese-only identity or the pro-independence attitude are significantly more likely than those not having such attitudes to vote for the DPP in national elections (e.g., Xu, 2002; Chen, 2000; Sheng, 2002; Wang, 1998; Hsieh and Niou, 2005). Therefore, people with the DPP ID, or the Taiwanese-only identity, or the pro-independence attitude may generally be viewed as the members of the DPP's support base. The following Figure 2.4 shows the trend of each indicator from the early 1990s to 2007.[15]

---

[15] Original data for Figure 2.4 are semi-annually collected by different national surveys through the Election Study Center at National Cheng-chi University (Taiwan). To make the trends more apparent, averaged annual data are used for Figure 2.4. The study does not use the same kinds of data collected by different media in Taiwan because those data are generally biased with much lower quality.

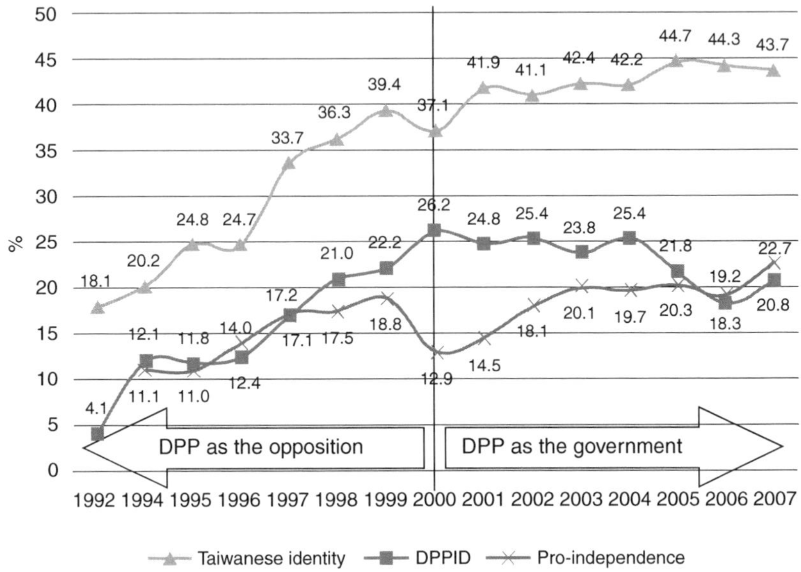

Figure 2.4 Trends of Taiwanese-Only Identity, DPP ID and Pro-Independence Attitude in Taiwan: 1992–2007

Data source: Election Study Center, N.C.C.U., important political attitude trend distribution.

It is not difficult to see that the percent of DPP ID indicates the level of popular support for the DPP no matter what the DPP's major role is. That is, it indicates the popular support for the DPP as the opposition party before 2000 and as the government after 2000. Regarding the other two support base indicators of the Taiwanese identity and the pro-independence attitude, it is reasonable to relate them to the social support for the TIM.

The pro-independence attitude seems to most apparently indicate the popular support for the TIM, although this indicator is also believed to be an "repressed opinion", which means many Taiwanese do not express their pro-independence attitude publicly only because they realize the huge cost or impossibility for Taiwan's complete independence of mainland China — mainland China definitely will attack and defeat Taiwan if Taiwan claims *de jure* independence of mainland China. If asking Taiwanese people by hypothetical questions trying to remove the effect of mainland China's threat on people's opinions, such as "do you agree that if after Taiwan announced its independence, it could maintain peaceful relations with the Chinese communist government, then Taiwan should become an independent country?" 51.5% of the respondents answer "yes" in 2003 (Taiwan's Election and Democratization Survey 2003, i.e., TEDS 2003), which is much higher than the highest percent of the pro-independence attitude detected by the traditional question used for the trend in Figure 2.4: "what's your attitude about Taiwan's future relations with mainland China: pro-independence, pro-unification or pro-status-quo?" Therefore, the percents of the pro-independence attitude in Figure 2.4 may be viewed as the conservative or minimum estimation of popular support for the TIM.

However, this conservative indicator might be the most accurate one showing the stage of the TIM's development. One piece of evidence is from the comparison between the following two trends. Figure 2.5 shows the TIM's development stages from 1949 to 2006 (Chen, 2006: 533), and Figure 2.6 is an excerpt trend of the pro-independence attitude originally shown in Figure 2.4. We can see that the two trends are almost identical with the same significant rise or decline in the same year, especially before 2004.

The author of Figure 2.5 argues that the TIM's development since 1949 is a long struggling process from Taiwan's *de facto* independence towards its *de jure* independence of mainland China. Before accomplishing the *de jure* independence, the TIM will need to lead Taiwan to go through three different levels of independence status, which are the substantial independence, the popularly supported independence and the institutionalized independence. Since 2000, the DPP government's major policy changes on important independence issues are viewed as the key indication of the TIM's development stage — either achieving a higher stage or retreating to a lower one. For example, right after the DPP took power in May 2000, it announced a series of concession policies on important independence issues. Some scholars and politicians (Chen, 2006; Lin, 2006) believed that these policies impair the TIM significantly and made Taiwan retrogress from a higher independence status to a lower one. In contrast, as the DPP stopped conceding and resumed its radical pro-independence stance in 2002–2003, Taiwan was able to progress towards the higher status of independence which was the institutionalized independence (Chen, 2006).

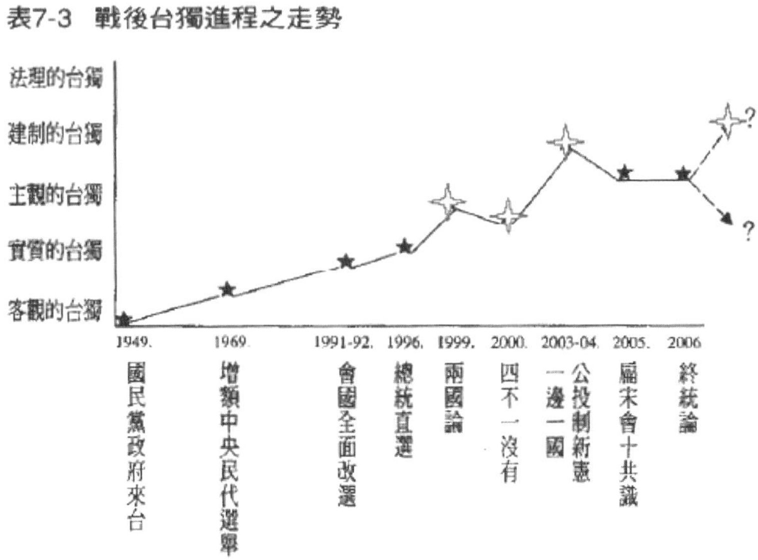

Figure 2.5 The TIM's Development Stages after WWII

Source: (Chen 2006: 533).

Translation notes:

The vertical axis from bottom to top represents the five stages of the TIM development: *de facto* independence, substantial independence, popularly supported independence, institutionalized independence, and *de jure* independence.

The horizontal axis from left to right represents the specific years of major political changes leading to the TIM's progress or decline:

1949: the KMT government came to Taiwan;
1969: election for extra Central People's Representatives;
1991–1992: complete parliamentary re-election;
1996: the first popular presidential election;
1999: President Lee Tenghui raised the "state-to-state" theory;
2000: President Chen Shuibian promised "four noes and one without;"
2003–2004: President Chen Shuibian raised the theory of "two countries in each side (of the Taiwan Strait)" and the proposal of revising the Constitution through referendum;
2005: the ten agreements between President Chen Shuibian and the head of PFP, James Soong;
2006: President Chen Shuibian proposed to terminate the government's pro-unification institute and outline.

The above argument about the relation between the DPP government's pro-independence policy and the level of the TIM's development may also be applied to explain the changing pro-independence attitude. For example, in Figure 2.6, we see a surprisingly large drop of the pro-independence attitude in 2000 from the peak of a constantly rising trend

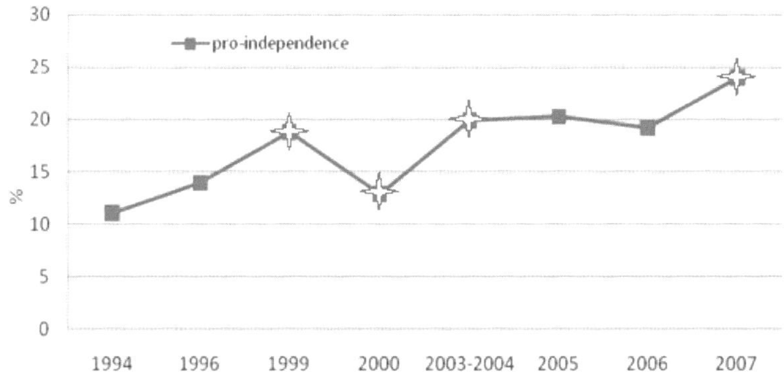

Figure 2.6 Trend of Pro-Independence Attitude: 1994–2007 (Selected Years)

Data source: Election Study Center, N.C.C.U., important political attitude trend distribution.

(i.e., from 18.8% in 1999 to 12.9% in 2000 which is even below the percent in 1996, 14%). This significant decline of the pro-independence attitude may be caused by the DPP government's concession policies as well. After 2000, the pro-independence attitude resumed the rising trend steadily with especially large boost around 2003 and 2004. This rising trend generally corresponds to the TIM's development stage in Figure 2.5, and therefore, may be related to the DPP government's more aggressive pro-independence policies as well.

In general, the trend of Taiwanese identity shown in Figure 2.4 is similar to the above two trends in Figures 2.5 and 2.6. Specifically, Taiwanese identity also encountered an unexpected large drop in 2000 from a steadily rising trend, and then slowly resumed its rising trend, although with more fluctuations. It implies that the percents of the Taiwanese identity may be correlated to the TIM's development level, and therefore, may indicate the popular support for the TIM as well. Indeed, the increase of the Taiwanese identity has long been chosen as one of the TIM's most important goals by famous TIM leaders. For example, in December 2007, the previous President Lee Teng-hui, now the "spiritual leader" of the most radical TIM party, the Taiwan Solidarity Union, expressed his deep disappointment that the goal of over 75% of Taiwanese holding Taiwanese identity would be unable to achieve in 2008.[16]

[16] http://www5.chinesenewsnet.com/MainNews/SinoNews/Taiwan/cna_2007_12_30_09_00_16_549.html, accessed on 13 February 2008.

As previous studies have shown, people who have the DPP ID, the pro-independence attitude and the Taiwanese identity are more likely to vote for the DPP and may be viewed as the support base of the DPP; meanwhile, as the above discussion shows, the DPP ID may indicate the social support for the DPP's government role, and the other two indicators, the pro-independence attitude and the Taiwanese identity may indicate the social support for the TIM, we may apply Figure 1.2 in Chapter 1, which illustrates the dual roles and support bases of movement governments, to the case of the DPP government. Figure 2.7 illustrates the dual support bases of the DPP government indicated by the three attitudinal indicators, as suggested by the movement government framework and the above discussion of these three indicators.

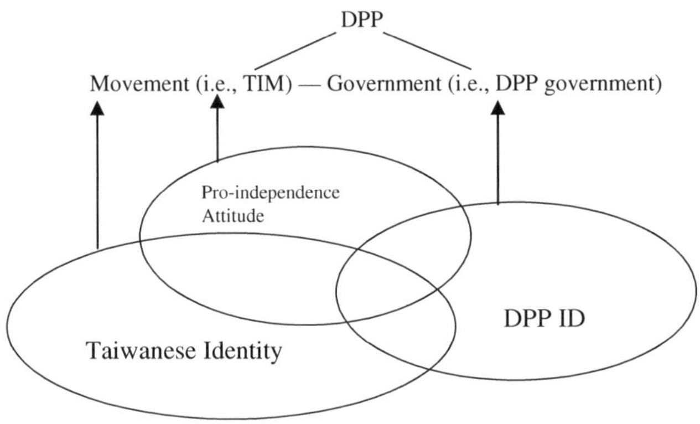

Figure 2.7 Dual Roles and Support Bases of the DPP Government

Source: Illustrated by author.

The figure indicates the fact that the DPP government played two roles as the government and the TIM leader at the same time, and, correspondingly, the two roles have different but overlapping support bases. Specifically, the support base of its movement role includes those having the pro-independence attitude or the Taiwanese identity, and that of its government role includes those having the DPP ID.

To what extent is this method of defining the support base effective in finding the real size of the DPP's support base? To what extent are the two support bases different and overlapping in terms of size? The answers to these two questions are very important, because they will not only examine the effectiveness of the movement government framework, but also pave the way for the further study of the relationships between the two support bases. The following Table 2.1 provides necessary data to answer these two questions.

In Table 2.1, as defined in Figure 2.7, the first row is the DPP's support base for its government role indicated by the percent of people with the DPP ID; the second row is its movement's support base indicated by the percent of people with either the Taiwanese identity or the pro-independence attitude. The third row is the overlap between the two

Table 2.1 Size of the DPP's Different Support Bases and Vote Share Received by the DPP in the Presidential Elections, 2000, 2004 and 2008*

(Unit: the rows 1–5 in the table are percents of the surveyed sample)

	2000	2004	2008	Average
1. Government's support base	26.6	28.7	20.8	25.37
2. Movement's support base	44.4	51.7	48.5	48.20
3. Support base overlap	19.5	22.4	17.5	19.80
4. Gap between the two support bases	17.8	23	27.7	22.83
5. Overall support base (excluding people with pan-blue party ID)	44.5	50.8	41.7	45.67
6. Vote share received in the presidential election†	39.3	50.1	41.6	43.67
7. Difference between overall support base and vote share in election	5.2	0.7	0.1	2.00

* Original data from the following three datasets are recoded and calculated for this table:

1. An Interdisciplinary Study of Voting Behavior in the Presidential Election in 2000 (NSC 89-2414-H-004-021-SSS). Principal Investigator: Professor Yih-yan Chen, Executive Institution: the Election Study Center, National Cheng-Chi University.
2. Taiwan's Election and Democratization Studies, 2004: The Presidential Election, (TEDS2004P) (NSC92-2420-H-031-004). Principal Investigator: Professor Shiow-duan Hawang, Executive Institution: Department of Political Science, Soochow University; Survey Research Center, National Chung-Cheng University; Department of Political Science, National Taiwan University.
3. Taiwan's Election and Democratization Studies, 2008: Telephone Interview of the 2008 Legislative Elections (TEDS2008L-T) (NSC 96-2420-H-002-025). Principal Investigator: Professor Yun-han Chu, Executive Institution: Department of Political Science, National Taiwan University; Election Study Center, National Chengchi University.

The author appreciates the assistance in providing data by the institutes and individuals aforementioned. The author is alone responsible for views expressed herein.

† From Central Election Commission (Taiwan).

support bases indicated by the percent of people with the DPP ID on one hand, AND the Taiwanese-only identity or the pro-independence attitude on the other. The fourth row is the gap between the two support bases which is the result of the movement's support base minus the government's. The fifth row is the overall support base of the DPP government indicated by the percent of people holding either the DPP ID or the Taiwanese-only identity or the pro-independence attitude excluding those with the pan-blue party ID. People with the pan-blue party ID are excluded from the DPP's overall support base because they are less likely to vote for the DPP. The table also provides the percent of the votes for the DPP in each presidential election (i.e., the sixth row) to compare with the size of its overall support base in that election year (i.e., the seventh row which is the result of the overall support base minus the vote share in each election year). We can have the following findings from this table to answer the previous two questions:

1. To what extent is this method of defining the support base effective in finding the real size of the DPP's support base? Because the vote share received by the DPP in the presidential election is usually believed to most accurately indicate the size of its support base, we can examine the effectiveness of the proposed support base definition by comparing the proposed overall support base (i.e., the fifth row) to the vote share in each election year (i.e., the sixth row) to see how different the two measurements are (i.e., the seventh row). The smaller the difference, the more effective the proposed definition of support base. As the seventh row of the table shows, the differences between the vote shares for the DPP and the sizes of its overall support base defined by the movement government framework are very small — the average difference is only 2%. Furthermore, the difference has become smaller and smaller since 2000 when the DPP took power the first time — it became less than 1% (i.e., 0.7%) in 2004 and only 0.1% in 2008. It seems that the longer the DPP holds the two roles of government and movement, the more accurate the proposed definition of its support base is. In conclusion, the finding shows that the movement government framework provides an effective way of revealing the size of the DPP's support base.

2. To what extent are the two support bases different in terms of the size? The fourth row of the table shows that the size of the movement's support base was always much larger than that of the government's. From 2000 through 2008, on average, the movement's support base is approximately twice as large as the government's. Moreover, since 2000, the gap between the two support bases has become larger and larger. In short, we see a large difference between the two support bases in terms of size. Obviously, the two support bases are not identical political forces.

3. To what extent are the two support bases overlapping in terms of the size? The third row of the table indicates that the overlap between the two support bases, on average, is about 20% (i.e., 19.8%). This overlap has different meanings for the two support bases. On average, for the government's support base, 20% of the support base overlap means that the majority of it (i.e., 78%) also belongs to the movement's support base; in contrast, for the movement's support base, it means only the minority of it (i.e., 41%) is also in the government's support base. In other words, while most supporters of the DPP's government role support its movement role as well, most supporters of the DPP's movement role (i.e., about 59%) do not support its government role. Therefore, this finding makes the commonality and difference between the two support bases much clearer to us.

While the above discussion shows the difference and commonality between the two support bases in terms of their size, their relationship may be further understood through studying their development trends. Let us look back at Figure 2.4, which shows the trends of the DPP ID, the Taiwanese identity and the pro-independence attitude before and after the DPP took power in 2000. In general, a common rising trend shared by every support base indicator ends in 1999 and then becomes divergent since 2000.

Specifically, from the early 1990s through 1999, the percents of people with the DPP ID, the Taiwanese identity and the pro-independence attitude increased by 18.1%, 21.3% and 7.7% respectively. However, since 2000, although the rising trend has been maintained by two indicators, which are the Taiwanese identity and the pro-independence attitude, the DPP ID's trend stagnated in the DPP government's first

Table 2.2 Pearson Correlations between the Three Support Base Indicators: Before 2000 (Excluding 2000)

	Taiwanese Identity (%)	Pro-Independence Attitude (%)
DPP ID (%)	0.95** (n = 12)	0.90** (n = 10)
Taiwanese identity (%)	1	0.92** (n = 10)

Note: ** Correlation is significant at the 0.01 level (2-tailed); original semi-annual percents are used in calculating the above correlations.
Data source: Election Study Center, N.C.C.U., Important Political Attitude Trend Distribution.

Table 2.3 Pearson Correlations between the Three Support Base Indicators: During 2000–2007 (Including 2000)

	Taiwanese Identity (%)	Pro-Independence Attitude (%)
DPP ID (%)	–0.66** (n = 16)	–0.49 (n = 16)
Taiwanese identity (%)	1	0.70** (n = 16)

Note: ** Correlation is significant at the 0.01 level (2-tailed); original semi-annual percents are used in calculating the above correlations.
Data source: Election Study Center, N.C.C.U., Important Political Attitude Trend Distribution.

term in 2000–2003 and then declined during its second term in 2004–2007. Therefore, the trend of DPP ID was divergent from those of the other two support base indicators during 2000–2008. The correlations among the percents of people with the DPP ID, the Taiwanese identity, and the pro-independence attitude in each half-year before and after 2000 further confirm these divergent trends during 2000–2007 (Tables 2.2 and 2.3).[17]

Table 2.2 indicates that the correlations among the three support base indicators are significant, positive and extremely large before 2000; however, as shown by Table 2.3, during 2000–2007 the correlation between the percents of DPP ID and the Taiwanese identity is still significant and large but the direction becomes NEGATIVE, whereas that between the percents of Taiwanese identity and the pro-independence attitude is still significant, positive and large. Therefore, the finding about the divergent

[17] Original semi-annual data are used in calculating these correlations.

trends in the development of the two support bases during 2000–2007 is supported by the above dramatically changed correlations.

This dramatic change of the correlation between the percents of people with the DPP ID and the other two support base indicators may be understood through the movement government framework. According to the framework, after the DPP took the government role and became the movement government in 2000, its overall support base might be divided into two overlapping but different groups, supporting its government and movement roles separately. While the DPP did not achieve satisfactory government performance since 2000 and became especially unsatisfactory since 2004, which resulted in decreased popular support for its government role, its movement's support base might not be negatively impacted so much by the disappointing government performance. Therefore, at the aggregate level and in terms of the development trend, the above finding does not support the argument that the decreased social support for the DPP government indicates parallel declining support for the TIM. In the following section, with individual level data, I further examine whether individuals' dissatisfaction with the DPP's government performance has the same negative effect on their support for the DPP's government role and for the movement role.

The Correlations between Individuals' Dissatisfaction with the DPP Government's Performance and Their Support for the DPP and the TIM

Based on the above finding about the divergent development trends of the two support bases and the account proposed by the movement government framework, I propose the following individual level hypothesis:

> **H2.1: While people dissatisfied with the DPP's government performance are less likely to hold the DPP ID, they are not less likely to hold the Taiwanese identity or the pro-independence attitude. In other words, while people's dissatisfaction with the DPP's government performance has negative effect on their support for the DPP's government role, it has no net effect on their support for the DPP's movement role.**

The dataset used to examine this hypothesis was collected through TEDS2008L-T (i.e., Taiwan's Election and Democratization Studies, 2008: Telephone Interview of the 2008 Legislative Elections)[18] which was conducted by the Election Study Center at National Cheng-Chi University from December 2007 through January 2008. It is a random sample based on the most complete phone book in Taiwan. The survey collected data on each respondent's basic social demographic background, political participation, knowledge about the 2008 legislative election, positions on various issues and party ID.

In the following regressions, the dependent variables are the three support base indicators — party ID, national identity, and attitude about Taiwan's independence, all of which are recoded polytomous variables with three categories for each variable.

The three categories in the party ID variable are: the pro-independence/pan-green party ID including the DPP ID and the TSU ID (i.e., the Taiwan Solidarity Union which is the most radical pro-independence party and the DPP's ally), the neutral ID (i.e., no party preference), and the anti-independence/pan-blue party ID including the KMT ID, the PFP ID and the NP ID. The following analysis does not treat the TSU ID as a different party ID from the DPP ID, because (1) the percent of the TSU ID is only 1.8% and that of the DPP ID is 19%, therefore, the combination of the two party IDs will not change the attributes of the DPP ID holders substantially; (2) the nature of the two IDs are very close, because the TSU ID holders usually vote for the DPP's candidate in the presidential elections where the TSU, without its own candidates, supports the DPP completely. In the following models, the interested category of party ID is the DPP ID (including the TSU ID). The other two categories, the neutral ID and the anti-independence/pan-blue party ID, are chosen to be the reference categories.

---

[18] Data analyzed in this section were from "Taiwan's Election and Democratization Studies, 2008: Telephone Interview of the 2008 Legislative Elections (TEDS2008L-T) (NSC 96-2420-H-002-025)." The coordinator of multi-year project TEDS is Professor Chi Huang (National Chengchi University). TEDS2008L-T is a project on the legislative election in 2008. The principal investigator is Prof. Yun-han Chu. More information is on TEDS website (http://www.tedsnet.org, accessed on 10 June 2015). The author appreciates the assistance in providing data by the institute and individuals aforementioned. The author is alone responsible for views expressed herein.

The national identity variable includes three categories of identity: the Taiwanese identity, the dual identity (i.e., self identified as both Chinese and Taiwanese), and the Chinese identity. The Taiwanese identity is the interested category; the other two categories which are the dual identity and the Chinese identity are chosen to be the reference categories. The recoded variable of the attitude about Taiwan's independence includes three categories of attitude: pro-independence, pro-status quo and pro-unification. Similarly, the attitudes of pro-status quo and pro-unification are the reference categories to be compared to the pro-independence attitude.

The independent variable of interest is recoded as a dichotomous opinion about the DPP's government performance — satisfied or dissatisfied. We want to examine whether individuals' opinion about the DPP's government performance is significantly correlated with their party ID, national identity and attitude about Taiwan's independence. "Satisfied" is chosen as the reference category. Hereafter, we call it the "dissatisfaction" variable.

The control variables in the models include social demographic variables such as ethnicity, gender, cohort and education. Additionally, since previous studies have shown significant correlations among the three support base variables, when one of them is selected to be the dependent variable, the other two are also included in the same model as the control variables to make the model more rigorous. The following Table 2.4 provides the sample means of all these variables.

Because the dependent variables are polytomous outcome variables, a group of multinomial logistic models are used in the analysis. These models can show us, after controlling for all the control variables, whether individuals' dissatisfaction has a significant and independent effect on their party ID, national identity and attitude about Taiwan's independence. For example, the multinomial logistic model of party ID can show us, after controlling for ethnicity, gender, cohort, education, individuals' national identity and their attitude about Taiwan's independence, whether those dissatisfied with the DPP administration are less likely than those satisfied to have the DPP party ID.

To clarify the potential confounding effect between the "dissatisfaction" variable and the other two support base variables which are also

Table 2.4 Sample Means of the Variables Used in the Analysis, 2008

Variables	Mean
Dependent Variables	
Party ID: "which political party do you feel identified with?"	
1. Pan-green parties: DPP and TSU	0.21
2. Neutral	0.33
3. Pan-blue parties: KMT, PFP, and NP	0.43
National identity: "do you consider yourself to be Taiwanese, Chinese or both?"	
1. Taiwanese	0.41
2. Chinese	0.06
3. Both	0.46
Attitude about Taiwan's independence: "what's your opinion about Taiwan's future relation with mainland China?"	
1. Pro-independence	0.18
2. Pro-status quo	0.57
3. Pro-unification	0.13
Independent Variables	
Opinion about DPP admin's performance	
1. Dissatisfied	0.71
2. Satisfied (ref.)	0.14
Ethnicity	
1. Mainlander	0.13
2. Hakka	0.13
3. Hoklo (ref.)	0.70
Gender	
1. Male	0.48
2. Female(ref.)	0.52
Cohort	
1. Older (born in or before1942)	0.08
2. Middle (born during 1943~1960)	0.27
3. Younger (born in or after 1961) (ref.)	0.65
Education	
1. Higher (college or above)	0.47
2. Middle (senior high or vocational)	0.30
3. Lower (junior high or below) (ref.)	0.21

Data source: TEDS2008L-T, $N = 1514$.

attitudinal and believed to be significantly correlated with the dependent variable, I use two-level nested multinomial logistic models in the analysis. The starting model (i.e., the constrained model) includes the "dissatisfaction" variable and all of the social demographic control variables — ethnicity, gender, cohort and education. The full model adds the other two support base variables, both of which are attitudinal variables and different in nature from the social demographic control variables. I assess the impact of adding these two attitudinal variables on the significance level of the "dissatisfaction" variable. Tables 2.5–2.7 show each independent and control variable's coefficients and significance levels in these models.

As the constrained model A1 and B1 in Table 2.5 show, people who are dissatisfied with the DPP's government performance are indeed less likely to have the DPP party ID, that is, less likely to support the DPP. The full model A2 and B2 in Table 2.5 show that adding the other two attitudinal variables, national identity and attitude about Taiwan's independence, into the models does not reduce the significant level of the correlation between individuals' opinion about the DPP's government performance and their party ID. In other words, dissatisfied people are still less likely to hold the DPP ID, and instead, more likely to hold the neutral or the anti-independence party ID. This finding supports the previously proposed argument that the percent of the DPP ID may indicate the level of popular support (i.e., satisfaction) for the DPP's government role. Therefore, the declined percent of the DPP ID indicates the declined popular support (satisfaction) for the DPP's government role.

Does individuals' dissatisfaction with the DPP administration also reduce their support for the TIM? Tables 2.6 and 2.7 give the negative answer. As shown by the two tables, although the "dissatisfaction" variable is significant in the constrained models, it is not significant at all in the full models after including the other two attitudinal variables. This means people's satisfaction or dissatisfaction with the DPP's government performance has no net effect on their national identity and attitude about Taiwan's independence, because its seeming effect completely disappears after controlling for the other two attitudinal variables. Therefore, people who are dissatisfied with the government performance are the same likely (i.e., neither less likely nor more likely) as those satisfied to hold the

Table 2.5 Nested Multinomial Logistic Regressions of Party ID, 2008

	(A) DPP ID vs. Neutral ID		(B) DPP ID vs. Pan-Blue Party ID	
	Model A1	**Model A2**	**Model B1**	**Model B2**
Independent Variables	**Co-ef.**	**Co-ef.**	**Co-ef.**	**Co-ef.**
Ethnicity	—	—	—	—
Mainlander	1.039*	–0.828†	–2.045***	–1.700***
Hakka	–0.533†	–0.563	–1.260***	–1.176***
Hoklo (ref.)				
Gender				
Male	0.270	0.325	0.269	0.317
Female (ref.)	—	—	—	—
Cohort				
Older (born in or before1942)	0.233	0.427	–0.370	–0.375
Middle (born during 1943~1960)	0.550*	0.447†	0.045	–0.017
Younger (born in or after 1961) (ref.)	—	—	—	—
Education				
Higher (college or above)	0.491†	0.269	0.087	0.400
Middle (senior high or vocational)	0.262	–0.006	0.076	0.278
Lower (junior high or below) (ref.)	—	—	—	—
Opinion about DPP admin's performance				
Dissatisfied	**–1.838*** **	**–1.710*** **	**–3.164*** **	**–2.706*** **
Satisfied (ref.)	—	—	—	—
Attitude about Taiwan's independence	—	—	—	—
Pro-unification	—	–0.738†	—	–2.301***
Pro-status quo	—	–1.035***	—	–1.899***
Pro-independence (ref.)	—	—	—	—
National identity	—	—	—	—
Chinese	—	–1.469*	—	–2.252***
Both Taiwanese & Chinese	—	–0.809***	—	–1.906***
Taiwanese (ref.)	—	—	—	—
Intercept	–1.219***	0.099	–1.198***	1.170**
–2LL	378.335***	702.671***	378.335***	702.671***
N	1190	1066	1190	1066

Note: TEDS2008L-T

† p ≤ 0.1, * p ≤ 0.05, ** p ≤ 0.01, *** p ≤ 0.001.

Table 2.6 Nested Multinomial Logistic Regressions of National Identity, 2008

	(A) Taiwanese vs. Dual Identity		(B) Taiwanese vs. Chinese	
	Model A1	**Model A2**	**Model B1**	**Model B2**
Independent Variables	**Co-ef.**	**Co-ef.**	**Co-ef.**	**Co-ef.**
Ethnicity	—	—	—	—
Mainlander	–0.677***	–0.074	–1.536***	–0.893**
Hakka	–0.508**	–0.096	–0.321	0.375
Hoklo (ref.)	—	—	—	—
Gender	—	—	—	—
Male	–0.007	–0.246	–0.332	–0.421
Female (ref.)	—	—	—	—
Cohort	—	—	—	—
Older (born in or before1942)	–0.090	–0.262	–1.228**	–1.511**
Middle (born during 1943~1960)	0.223	0.218	–0.630*	–0.695*
Younger (born in or after 1961) (ref.)	—	—	—	—
Education	—	—	—	—
Higher (college or above)	–0.674***	–0.637*	–0.113	–0.016
Middle (senior high or vocational)	–0.638**	–0.672**	–0.139	–0.215
Lower (junior high or below) (ref.)	—	—	—	—
Opinion about DPP admin's performance	—	—	—	—
Dissatisfied	**–1.373*** **	**–0.425†**	**–2.616*** **	**–1.273**
Satisfied (ref.)	—	—	—	—
Attitude about Taiwan's independence	—	—	—	—
Pro-unification	—	–1.850***	—	–2.478***
Pro-status quo	—	–1.602***	—	–1.282*
Pro-independence (ref.)	—	—	—	—
Party ID	—	—	—	—
DPP ID	—	–1.901***	—	–2.329***
Neutral ID	—	–0.796***	—	–1.576*
Pan-blue party ID (ref.)	—	—	—	—
Intercept	0.262	2.804***	2.480***	5.396***
–2LL	392.809***	694.361***	392.809***	694.361***
N	1160	1066	1160	1066

Note: TEDS2008L-T

† $p \leq 0.1$, * $p \leq 0.05$, ** $p \leq 0.01$, *** $p \leq 0.001$.

Table 2.7 Nested Multinomial Logistic Regressions of Attitude about Taiwan's Independence, 2008

	(A) Pro-independence vs. Pro-status quo		(B) Pro-independence vs. Pro-unification	
	Model A1	**Model A2**	**Model B1**	**Model B2**
Independent Variables	**Co-ef.**	**Co-ef.**	**Co-ef.**	**Co-ef.**
Ethnicity	—	—	—	—
Mainlander	–0.863**	–0.277	–1.590***	–0.736†
Hakka	–0.418	0.080	–0.948**	–0.423
Hoklo (ref.)	—	—	—	—
Gender	—	—	—	—
Male	0.060	0.126	0.099	0.228
Female (ref.)	—	—	—	—
Cohort	—	—	—	—
Older (born in or before1942)	0.297	0.406	0.752	1.063†
Middle (born during 1943~1960)	0.130	0.049	0.300	0.284
Younger (born in or after 1961) (ref.)	—	—	—	—
Education	—	—	—	—
Higher (college or above)	–0.382	–0.330	–0.392	–0.425
Middle (senior high or vocational)	–0.303	–0.211	–0.314	–0.308
Lower (junior high or below) (ref.)	—	—	—	—
Opinion about DPP admin's performance	—	—	—	—
Dissatisfied	**–1.480*** **	**–0.303**	**–0.319*** **	**–0.192**
Satisfied (ref.)	—	—	—	—
National identity	—	—	—	—
Chinese	—	–1.349*	—	–2.499***
Both Taiwanese & Chinese	—	–1.595***	—	–1.846***
Taiwanese (ref.)	—	—	—	—
Party ID	—	—	—	—
DPP ID	—	–1.947***	—	–2.352***

(Continued)

Table 2.7 (*Continued*)

	(A) Pro-independence vs. Pro-status quo		(B) Pro-independence vs. Pro-unification	
	Model A1	**Model A2**	**Model B1**	**Model B2**
Independent Variables	**Co-ef.**	**Co-ef.**	**Co-ef.**	**Co-ef.**
Neutral ID	—	−1.038***	—	−.745
Pan-blue party ID (ref.)	—	—	—	—
Intercept	−1.122	0.584	0.459	2.620***
−2LL	385.614***	720.036***	385.614***	720.036***
N	1128	1066	1128	1066

Note: TEDS2008L-T
† $p \leq 0.1$, * $p \leq 0.05$, ** $p \leq 0.01$, *** $p \leq 0.001$.

Taiwanese identity and the pro-independence attitude. In other words, the popular support for the TIM is not negatively influenced by people's dissatisfaction with the DPP's government performance, while the support for the government is. In summary, the results from the above models support the previous hypothesis H2.1 but do not support the argument that the lower support for the DPP government indicates parallel decreasing support for the TIM.

The Changing Party Composition of the TIM's Support Base and the DPP's Weakened Monopoly on Taiwanese Nationalism[19]

How to interpret the divergent popular support for the DPP and the TIM during the DPP's two administrative terms of 2000–2008? The direct but superficial interpretation is that popular support for the TIM did not transform to popular support for the DPP. In other words, more and more

[19] This section is excepted from the author's paper published in 2012: Divergent Popular Support for the DPP and the Taiwan Independence Movement in Taiwan, 2000–2012, *Journal of Contemporary China*, 21(78), 973–991.

Taiwanese people started to view the TIM and the DPP as two different political forces, and therefore, showed different levels of support for them. A further speculation is that the DPP's monopoly of the TIM has been weakened as the KMT started to show its stronger identification with Taiwanese nationalism since 2000. Analysis of the party ID composition in the TIM's support base since 2000 provides evidence for this speculation.

Following the previous discussion, we define the TIM's support base as the people who either have a pro-independence attitude or have a Taiwanese identity. Table 2.8 shows the party ID composition in the TIM's support base in 2000, 2004 and 2008.

Table 2.8 Party ID Composition in TIM's Support Base, 2000–2008

	TIM Support Base
2000	
DPP/pan-green Party ID	45% (20%)
Neutral	40% (18%)
KMT/pan-blue Party ID	15% (7%)
Total	100% (45%)
2004	
DPP/pan-green Party ID	51% (27%)
Neutral	34% (18%)
KMT/pan-blue Party ID	15% (8%)
Total	100% (52%)
2008	
DPP/pan-green Party ID	40% (20%)
Neutral	38% (19%)
KMT/pan-blue Party ID	22% (11%)
Total	100% (51%)

Note: Percentages in parentheses are cell percentages.

Source: An Interdisciplinary Study of Voting Behavior in the Presidential Election in 2000, TEDS2004P, TEDS2008L. See the data source information of Table 2.1 for details.

First of all, Table 2.8 shows that the TIM's overall support base increased from 45% of the population in 2000 to 52% in 2004 and then remained stable at 51% in 2008. In general, this is consistent with the two development trends in pro-independence attitude and Taiwanese identity during the same time period shown in Figure 2.4. Secondly, we can see that from 2000 to 2004, the proportion of DPP supporters in the TIM's support base increased from 45% to 51%, that is, more than half of the TIM's support base supported the DPP as well in 2004. However, from 2004 to 2008, the proportion of DPP supporters decreased to 40%, which is even lower than that in 2000. In other words, a large proportion of the TIM's support base (i.e., about 11%) withdrew their support for the DPP in 2008. In contrast, those neutral people or supporters of the KMT/pan-blue parties in the TIM's support base showed a different development pattern. From 2000 to 2004, the proportion of the neutral people in the TIM's support base decreased from 40% to 34%, and that of supporters of the KMT/ pan-blue parties did not change. However, from 2004 to 2008, the proportions of these two groups of people increased significantly in the TIM's support base. In particular, the share of the KMT/ pan-blue parties' supporters, who were supposedly anti-independence or pro-status-quo, increased by 7% in the TIM's support base from 2004 to 2008. Therefore, the pan-blue camp actually provided an increasing number of Taiwanese nationalists in 2008, stabilizing the popular support for the TIM. This also implies that the KMT has weakened the DPP's monopoly on Taiwanese nationalism. As a result, right before the 2008 presidential election, the majority of the TIM's support base (i.e., about 60%) did not support the DPP.

Summary

The principal purpose of this chapter is to differentiate the DPP's two support bases, that is, the supporters of its government role and those of its movement role. Based on the movement government framework and previous studies, this chapter uses three attitudinal indicators which are the DPP ID, the Taiwanese identity, and the pro-independence attitude to make this distinction. Specifically, the percent of the DPP ID indicates the level of popular support for the DPP's government role; on the other hand, the percents of the Taiwanese identity and the pro-independence attitude indicate the level of support for the TIM and the DPP's movement role.

With this method of defining the DPP's two support bases, this chapter provides accurate estimation on the sizes of the two support bases and the gap and overlap between them. The data show that, during 2000–2008, (1) this method of defining the DPP's support base is very effective because the size of the DPP's overall support base defined by this method is very close to the vote share it received in the presidential election; (2) the movement's support base has been almost twice as large as the government's; (3) while the majority of the government supporters support the TIM, only the minority of the TIM supporters support the DPP's government role. Additionally, the correlation analysis among the development trends of the three support base indicators at the aggregate level shows that during 2000–2007 while the trend of the DPP ID was stagnated and then declining, the Taiwanese identity and the pro-independence attitude resumed and then maintained their rising trends. At the individual level, this chapter shows that although individuals' dissatisfaction with the DPP's government performance has negative effect on their support for the DPP's government role, it has no net effect on their support for the TIM and the DPP's movement role. The further analysis of the party identification composition of the TIM's support base indicates that the pan-blue camp supporters actually contributed to the stablization of the TIM, and as a result, reduced the DPP's monopoly on the Taiwanese nationalism. In conclusion, the findings at both the aggregate and the individual levels do not support the argument that the lower support for the DPP government indicates parallel declining support for the TIM.

CHAPTER 3: FAMILY ECONOMIC FORTUNE, FONDNESS OF THE PRESIDENT AND NATIONALISTIC SENTIMENT: THREE DETERMINING FACTORS IN TAIWANESE PEOPLE'S PARTY SUPPORT

Introduction

In Chapter 1, I have introduced the two factors that are popularly believed to contribute to the declined social support for the Democratic Progressive Party (DPP) during its second administrative term of 2004–2008, which are the DPP government's dissatisfactory economic performance and President Chen and his family members' corruption scandals. I have also shown the popular interpretation in mainland China about the lower support for the DPP, that is, the lower support for the DPP indicates parallel declining support for the Taiwan Independence Movement (TIM). In Chapter 2, based on the movement government framework proposed in Chapter 1, I have defined the two overlapping but different support bases of the DPP's government role and its movement role, and demonstrated that during the DPP's second administrative term and at the aggregate level, while the popular support for the DPP decreased, the support for the TIM did not; on the other hand, at the individual level, while individuals' dissatisfaction with the DPP government made them less likely to support the

DPP, it had no net effect on their support for the TIM. In this chapter, at the individual level, I critically examine the effect of the DPP government's economic performance and President Chen's family corruption scandals on individuals' support for the DPP. In Chapter 2, we find that individuals' general dissatisfaction with the DPP government could reduce their support for the DPP. In addition, it was widely believed that it was the two factors, i.e., the DPP government's poor economic performance and President Chen's family corruption scandals that led to Taiwanese people's dissatisfaction with the DPP government. Therefore, this chapter examines the two major possible causes of Taiwanese people's dissatisfaction with the DPP government. I want to examine whether these two factors, as popularly believed, reduced individuals' support for the DPP.

In addition to the above two factors, I also try to generally examine the effect of Chen's radical movement strategy on individuals' support for the DPP. According to the movement government framework, I propose that when a movement government fails on one role, it tends to radicalize its effort to succeed on the other role and tries to use the success of this role to retain social support. In the case of the DPP government, as President Chen and his government were severely troubled by the government's poor economic performance and his family's corruption scandals during his second term, he radicalized the movement strategy to promote popular Taiwanese nationalism and tried to retain social support through enhancing Taiwanese people's nationalistic sentiment. Previous studies have found a long term positive correlation between Taiwanese people's nationalistic sentiment and their support for the DPP. Specifically, people who have Taiwanese identity and pro-independence attitude were more likely than others to have the DPP ID and vote for the DPP in national elections (e.g., Xu, 2002; Chen, 2000; Sheng, 2002; Wang, 1998; Hsieh and Niou, 2005). If Chen's radical strategy successfully enhanced popular nationalistic sentiment, as expected by Chen and the DPP, this enhanced nationalistic sentiment would help people overcome their concern about Chen government's poor economic performance and his family's corruption scandals, which in turn would help retain popular support for the DPP. Therefore, in the following examination, the individuals who had pro-independence attitude or Taiwanese identity are defined as people having Taiwanese nationalistic sentiment, which also indicates the radical movement strategy's effect on individuals. Through adding this third factor of nationalistic sentiment to the examination, I hope to reveal that to what extent the radical movement strategy reduced the negative effects of the government's poor economic performance and corruption scandals on people's support for the DPP.

The last important purpose of the examination in this chapter is to pave the way for a more delicate argument based on the movement government framework to explain the declining support for the DPP. In Chapter 1, I have briefly argued that the popular explanation of the lower support for the DPP, which focused on the two factors of the DPP government's poor economic performance and the Chen family's corruption scandals, was inadequate, because as early as in Chen's first term of 2000–2004, his government was troubled by the similar two factors (although they were not so severe as in the second term), but Chen won the re-election with significantly increased popular support. Now the question is, if the popular explanation is inadequate, which is to be shown in the following examination, and if the movement government framework proposes that Chen's radical movement strategy might successfully reduce the negative impact of his government's poor performance and his family's corruption scandals on popular support for the DPP, then how can the movement government framework explain the lower popular support for the DPP at the end of Chen's second term? This chapter provides initial clues for a more delicate argument about the double-edged sword effect of the radical movement strategy on people's support for the DPP, which is also based on the movement government framework, arguing that although the radical movement strategy may consolidate support of movement fundamentalists, at the same time, it may disaffect moderates and eventually lead to the decline of the overall social support for the DPP. The elaboration and examination of this argument will be the task of the next chapter. Before examining the above three factors, it is necessary to review the evolution of the DPP government's strategies from concession to confrontation and finally to radicalization during 2000–2008 to provide the historical context for the subsequent examination and discussion. The materials for the following review are mainly from the online versions of the major Taiwanese newspapers such as *The Liberty Times, China Times, United Daily News*, and a Hong Kong online newspaper *ifeng.com*.[1]

Evolution of the DPP Government's Strategies: From Concession to Confrontation, 2000–2004

When the DPP's candidate Chen Shuibian won the 2000 presidential election with 39.3% of vote, it not only shocked the *Kuo Min Tang* (KMT), the party in power since 1945 in Taiwan, but also surprised the DPP itself and its supporters. Almost nobody had expected this great victory to come to this young opposition party so early, especially when it only enjoyed minority support in the presidential election. The DPP, lacking able personnel, political resources and administrative experience, did not seem ready to lead Taiwan out of its deepening economic downturn, widely spreading political corruptions and escalating ethnic conflicts. On the other hand, the domestic and international oppositions against this new minority government were extremely strong. The defeated KMT and its allies held about 65% of the Congress seats and could block almost any legislative and administrative initiatives proposed by the DPP administration. The political, economic and cultural legacies of the old KMT regime remained strong and antagonistic in the new administrative bureaucracy, national enterprises, military and education systems. On the other side of the Taiwan Strait, the mainland Chinese government determined to defeat the new government's substantial steps toward Taiwan's independence, and tried harder to further isolate Taiwan in the international community. The US government, which has long been viewed as Taiwan's most important and reliable supporter and protector by all the major parties and the general public in Taiwan, hailed Taiwan's peaceful regime change and consolidated democracy, but did not change its support for the Chinese government's one-China policy and did not want the DPP government to deviate from the old KMT government's policy of maintaining the status quo relation with mainland China. In short, soon after enjoying

[1]For example, http://forums.chinatimes.com/report/960927/main.htm, http://news.ifeng.com/special/chenshuibian/, accessed on 18 June 2015.

their unexpected victory, the new DPP government found itself in a very difficult situation where the great opportunity offered by holding power may turn to be an overwhelming challenge.

Therefore, it is quite understandable when the new President Chen decided to appease the domestic and international oppositions and minimize challenges through downplaying the DPP government's role as the TIM leader and building its centrist image as a neutral government. In his inauguration speech in May 2000, Chen promised "four noes and one without" which stated "as long as the CCP regime has no intention to use military force against Taiwan, I pledge that during my term in office, I will not declare independence, I will not change the national title, I will not push forth the inclusion of the so-called 'state-to-state' description in the Constitution, and I will not promote a referendum to change the status quo in regards to the question of independence or unification. Furthermore, the abolition of the National Reunification Council or the National Reunification Guidelines will not be an issue."[2] Clearly, he promised the domestic and international oppositions a moderate position on the important independence issues. In addition to this promise, the novice government also initiated a series of reforms to liberalize Taiwanese investment in mainland China and lifted some restrictions on the economic and cultural exchange between the two sides of the Taiwan Strait. The most important reform during this period was the abolition of "no haste and be patient" investment policy which had restricted significant Taiwanese investment in mainland China since 1996. In 2001, the DPP government replaced this highly restrictive policy with a more liberal one called "pro-active liberalization and effective management" to free Taiwanese investment to mainland China to a much greater extent. To further pacify the KMT and especially its military force, Chen also appointed the KMT's former Defense Minister as his first premier to form a coalition government.

Following the DPP government's efforts to build up a centrist government, a strategic dilemma soon emerged for this movement government. On the one hand, the oppositions did not seem to be pacified by these conciliatory efforts. The KMT, frustrated and enraged by their electoral defeat, had determined to fight against the new government on all fronts.

---

[2] http://info.gio.gov.tw/ct.asp?xItem=12725&ctNode=3763, accessed on 24 March 2009.

Within five months, the premier from the KMT resigned and the new coalition government collapsed due to a severe conflict between the KMT and the DPP on the construction of a nuclear plant. On the other hand, the TIM supporters, including most fundamentalists and some moderates, believed that the new government conceded too much on the independence issues and were disappointed with Chen. One of the founding members of the DPP and a senior legislator, Lin (2006), who was also known as the TIM's master theorist and a moderate, believed that the new DPP government tried to clean out the pro-independence elements through the aforementioned concessions and criticized Chen for ignoring and even impeding the development of Taiwanese nationalism after 2000. As mentioned in Chapter 2, the following Figure 3.1 may support Lin's argument about the negative impact of the new government's concessions on the TIM. We can see that in 2000, both the percent of people supporting Taiwan's independence and that of people having Taiwanese identity declined unexpectedly and significantly from a constantly rising trend. From the perspective of the movement government framework, this strategic dilemma caused by the inherent tension between the movement government's dual roles, its government and movement roles, is almost unavoidable. From the above review, we have seen that facing this

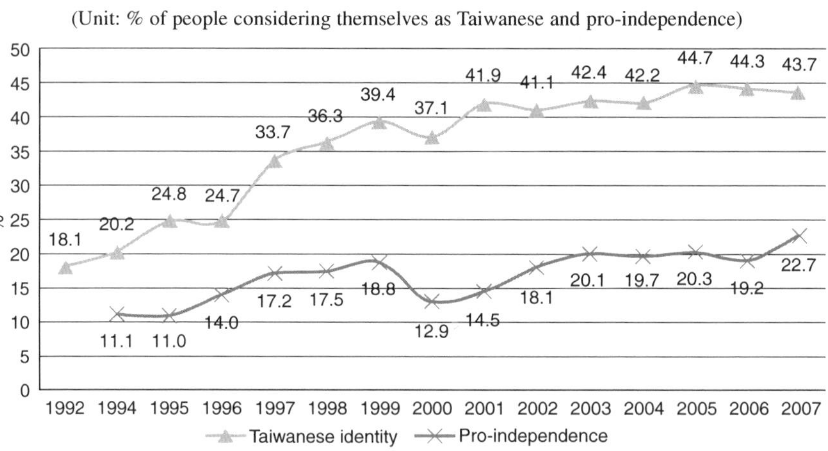

Figure 3.1 Trends of Taiwanese Identity and Pro-Independence Attitude in Taiwan, 1992–2007

Data source: Election Study Center, N.C.C.U., important political attitude trend distribution.

dilemma, Chen's government initially adopted a government-oriented strategy through compromising its movement role, which disappointed movement supporters.

When it was time for Chen and the DPP to start preparing for the 2004 re-election, Chen and the DPP government had been trapped in the above dilemma for about a year and a half. With the government-oriented and concession strategy, they did not see much benefit but more and more challenges from both sides. Partly as a result of this dilemma, the DPP government also failed to accomplish satisfactory performance in mending the economy. It seemed necessary for Chen to consider a new strategy to ensure his re-election. On the other hand, in the legislative election in December 2001, the DPP won more seats in the Congress. Together with its ally, the Taiwan Solidarity Party, they controlled about 45% of the Congress seats. In January 2002, to prepare for his re-election campaign, Chen thoroughly reshuffled the government. Now the government with stronger congress support seemed to be ready to try a new strategy. However, nobody had anticipated that the debut of the confrontation strategy was triggered by a humiliating diplomatic frustration of the DPP government.

In July 2002, as one more effort to ensure his re-election, Chen started leading the DPP officially as its chairman. To show his moderate position again to the KMT and the mainland Chinese government, he assigned a senior DPP member, who was known to be friendly to mainland China and supported a more liberal economic relation with mainland China, as the director of the DPP's China Affair Office. However, this "gift" that was supposed to mollify the Chinese government received unanticipated response. On the exact day of his inauguration as the chairman, Nauru, one of the 21 countries maintaining official diplomatic relations with Taiwan, terminated its official diplomatic relations with Taiwan and embraced mainland China instead. It was clearly prearrangement by the mainland Chinese government to humiliate and further isolate the DPP government in the international community. Facing such a humiliating diplomatic frustration, if Chen still maintained his moderate position, he would lose his authority within the DPP (Lin, 2006). About 10 days later, in a speech at a teleconference organized by an important pro-independence organization, World Taiwanese Association,

Chen characterized the relation between Taiwan and mainland China as "one country on each side (of the Taiwan Strait)" and declared that Taiwan needed a referendum to determine its future,[3] which immediately received all the 500 meeting participants' stand-up applause. This speech marked the turning point for the DPP government. To those TIM supporters, especially those movement fundamentalists, it showed Chen and the DPP had decided to return to the movement course and continue their commitment as the movement leader. To the domestic and international oppositions, it showed the DPP government's strategy changed from concession to confrontation on the independence issues.

However, the speech did not get Chen and his government out of the dilemma. As they won back the hearty support of the pro-independence people, the pressure from Taiwan's economic sectors and the domestic and international oppositions grew stronger immediately and significantly. Worrying about the cross-strait relations to be exacerbated by the speech, Taiwan's stock market plunged disastrously on the first business day after the speech. Taiwanese business people who invested or worked in mainland China complained that the speech would ruin their bright future in mainland China. The KMT and its allies blamed Chen for breaking the presidential inauguration promise and losing trust domestically and internationally. On the other side of the strait, it was not surprising to see that the mainland Chinese government, enraged by the speech, launched not only official denunciation through its Taiwan office and national media, but also military exercises including a large scale aerial defense exercise in Shanghai where more than half a million Taiwanese business people and their families lived. The US government was troubled by the speech, too, and reiterated that they did not support Taiwan's independence and remained supportive to the Chinese government's one-China policy.[4]

Foreseeing the storm, on the first work day after the speech, the DPP government clarified to the public that the government would still keep President Chen's inauguration promise and would not pursue Taiwan's independence. In the same day's afternoon, Chen met with the

---

[3] http://issue.udn.com/FOCUSNEWS/TWOSIDES/index.htm, accessed on 26 March 26 2009.

[4] ibid.

director of American Institute in Taiwan to assure the US government that he would not break his inauguration promise. Soon after that, the Minister of Mainland Affairs Council came to Washington to clarify the DPP government's position on the independence issues to the US government. Gradually, the storm faded away. Chen and his government successfully managed to survive the storm, which might have improved their confidence to continue the new confrontation strategy. According to the movement government framework, we can see from the above review that Chen stopped using the government-oriented strategy and started emphasizing the government's movement role with the movement-oriented confrontation strategy. However, as suggested by the movement government framework and shown by the above review, although the movement-oriented strategy retained the movement support for the DPP government, it disappointed other social groups such as business people whose interests might be hurt by the movement-oriented strategy. Therefore, the new strategy did not make Chen's government get out of the strategic dilemma.

As the 2004 presidential election was approaching, it became clearer to Chen that he needed to shift the public's attention from his government's poor performance to something favorable to his re-election. As we have seen from the above discussion, the old concession strategy did not work well, and in contrast, the new confrontation strategy could maintain the fundamentalists' support at least. Therefore, he needed to create some confrontational topics which he could easily take advantage of and could maintain the fundamentalists' support and even attract moderates' sympathy. During the world severe acute respiratory syndrome (SARS) crisis in early 2003, the mainland Chinese government presented such an opportunity to Chen again.

In March 2003, a highly infectious and fatal disease, SARS, broke out in mainland China and then quickly spread to the rest of the world. The world media blamed the Chinese government for their covering up the initial cases of SARS as early as in November 2002, which led to the worldwide SARS crisis. The Chinese government also disappointed the world by its slow cooperation with the World Health Organization (WHO) in investigating and reporting the SARS cases in mainland China. Therefore, when Taiwanese found that they were among the most severely infected population due to Taiwanese business people's frequent trips between Taiwan and mainland China, they felt victimized by the mainland Chinese government's misconducts. To make the public resentment even stronger, the DPP government told the public that the mainland Chinese government had also tried to prevent the WHO's investigators from coming to Taiwan, which delayed their arrival and therefore exacerbated the SARS crisis in Taiwan. The SARS crisis also provided a better opportunity for the DPP government to seek the WHO membership, which the Taiwanese government had tried since 1997 but always failed due to the Chinese government's objection in the WHO. In the midst of the SARS crisis, when the DPP government's application for the WHO membership was rejected again in May due to the same reason, Chen declared that it was necessary to make a referendum law and then hold a referendum in the 2004 presidential election to show the world Taiwanese people's determination of joining the WHO.

Referendum is a highly challenging political activity to the mainland Chinese government because since the DPP's founding date, it has promoted the referendum as the most democratic and therefore legitimate means for achieving Taiwan's *de jure* independence of mainland China. Although the three referendum topics proposed later by Chen, which were about seeking the WHO membership, constructing a nuclear plant and congress reforms, did not seem directly related to Taiwan's independence, the mainland Chinese government believed that the legalized referendum practice on public affairs was paving the way for future referendum on Taiwan's independence. Therefore, it launched a new wave of denunciation campaigns in mainland China and the international community to criticize and warn Chen and his government. Under China's diplomatic pressure and worried about possible military conflict between mainland China and Taiwan, the US and the Japanese governments also raised their objection to Chen's referendum proposal. As usual, the opposition parties in Taiwan including the KMT and its allies, the People First Party (PFP) and the New Party (NP), blamed Chen for breaking the inauguration promise again.

Nevertheless, Chen and his government determined to stick to their confrontation strategy, mainly because this might be the best strategy to ensure Chen's re-election in 2004. By then, they have realized that the popular Taiwanese nationalism was the most reliable sentiment that they could effectively exploit to ensure Chen's re-election. Their decade-long conflict experience with the Chinese government taught them that the latter's denunciation, warning and especially military exercises against Taiwan had always aroused Taiwanese people's nationalistic sentiment, which then turned into higher popular support for the DPP in elections. The confrontation strategy was effective in stimulating the Chinese government to react vigorously and aggressively. On the other hand, although the referendum was highly confrontational to the Chinese government and in the international community, its legitimacy was supported by Taiwan's Constitution and generally accepted by most Taiwanese. Therefore, it did not take long for the opposition parties in Taiwan to realize that an absolute objection to the referendum proposal would reduce the popular support for them. They stopped opposing the legislation of the referendum law, and instead, proposed a different version of the law in the congress. The final result seemed to satisfy the opposition — their version of the referendum law defeated the DPP's and was passed in the congress; but the DPP did not lose completely. Even according to the opposition's version of the referendum law, President Chen had the right to hold a "defensive referendum" under the condition of serious foreign threat which might be defined at his own disposal. Certainly Chen would not waste his right — he declared that because of the sustained military threat from mainland China, a "defensive referendum," which asked the public whether the DPP government should reinforce Taiwan's defense capability and hold equal-status negotiations with the Chinese government, was to be held in the 2004 presidential election.

The referendum issue, which lasted for almost one year, contributed greatly to Chen's successful re-election campaign. While the KMT's presidential election campaign focused on exposing and criticizing Chen and his government's incompetence in mending the economy, the DPP's resorted to popular Taiwanese nationalism through confrontational and sensitive nationalistic issues such as the referendum and making a new Constitution. The KMT camp was in an obviously leading position at first, but later the competition became extremely tight until the day right before the election, when Chen and his running mate were shot and slightly injured in a campaign activity. The unverified news that the Chinese government's killer tried to assassinate Chen quickly spread all over the island. The failed assassination brought Chen many sympathetic voters which finally helped him win the election by 50.1% of vote.[5]

The movement government framework can provide a straightforward interpretation about the evolution of Chen's government strategy in its first term. As a minority government, to pacify the strong domestic and international oppositions and expand its support base, Chen's government first conceded on important movement issues, downplayed its movement role and adopted government-oriented strategies, trying to establish a neutral and moderate image of government. While this strategy failed to mollify the oppositions and was criticized by the government's movement base, Chen had to replace the government-oriented and concession strategy with the movement-oriented and confrontation strategy, which instead downplayed the government role but relied on the movement role to retain and expand social support. The confrontation strategy successfully shifted popular attention from the government's poor economic performance to the confrontational issues such as the referendum. The mainland Chinese government's aggressive reaction to the confrontational issues motivated Taiwanese people's nationalistic sentiment which then turned to stronger popular support for Chen and the DPP.

Evolution of the DPP Government's Strategies: From Confrontation to Radicalization, 2004–2008

The re-election of Chen with significantly increased votes enhanced the DPP's confidence of maintaining power — some even believed that the DPP would stay in power for at least the next 12 years, that is, three consecutive presidential terms until 2016. However, four years later in 2008, the DPP lost the presidential election miserably with 41.6% of vote, which not only disappointed the DPP's supporters, but also surprised the KMT;

[5] Political pundits and scholars have acknowledged the artificial inflation of the popular support for the DPP caused by this assassination attempt, although there was no consensus how much inflation the DPP enjoyed. Generally, it was widely believed that the popular support for the DPP has significantly increased during 2000–2004, even if without taking into account the assassination effect.

they had expected the DPP to lose, but never expected it to lose so badly. The popular explanation of the DPP's electoral defeat emphasizes Chen and his family members' corruption scandals and his government's continuous failure in developing the economy. However, according to the movement government framework, I argue that during 2004–2008, the radicalization of Chen's movement-oriented strategy in economic, political, and social fields, which was intended to shift popular attention from the scandals and economic failure to nationalistic fronts, actually alienated many moderate supporters, although the radicalization successfully consolidated the movement fundamentalists' support for the DPP. Therefore, it was not only the corruptions and economic failure per se, but also the strategy that Chen and his government used to deal with these problems, which reduced the popular support for the DPP. Now I discuss Chen and his government's radicalization in more detail.

Before the detailed description of the DPP government's radical strategy, it is better to first clarify the major differences between the confrontation strategy used in 2002–2004 and the radical strategy used in 2005–2008 by Chen and his government. With the confrontation strategy, the major "enemy" that was chosen by Chen and his government to challenge was usually the Chinese government, that is, an outsider enemy. They tried to first stimulate the Chinese government with confrontational issues such as the statement of "one state on each side" and the referendum proposal, and then took advantage of the Chinese government's aggressive reactions to mobilize popular Taiwanese nationalistic sentiment. In contrast, the radical strategy expanded the scope of enemies to include not only the Chinese government but also those Taiwanese who had presupposed "connections" with mainland China such as the KMT and mainlanders in Taiwan, and major world powers who did not support Taiwan's independence course such as the US government. Among these three enemies, the domestic one, not the Chinese government, became the major target for the radical strategy. The radical strategy was also different from the confrontation strategy in the scope of battlefields. While the confrontation strategy was mainly applied in the political arena, the radical strategy permeated many fields of Taiwan's political, economic and social life, which was called by some Taiwanese scholars Taiwan's "Cultural Revolution." (e.g., Nan, 2008) The third difference was that the radical strategy demonstrated more illiberal and undemocratic nature during its implementation than the confrontation strategy. The final difference was that the radical strategy caused more conflicts, especially violent conflicts, among different social groups in Taiwan than the confrontation strategy. These differences are discussed in more detail in the following sections.

The 2004 Presidential election had a significant and lasting impact on both the DPP and the opposition and also was an important reason for Chen and his government to become radical. For the DPP, Chen's re-election with much increased popular support seemed to suggest that the right strategy could significantly improve people's nationalistic sentiment, and then the improved nationalistic sentiment could help people overcome their concern about the government's poor performance. Therefore, it is important to emphasize the government's role as the TIM leader to maintain the movement's support, especially when the government's performance is not satisfactory. For the KMT, Chen's re-election was unacceptable due to the election fraud — they believed that the failed assassination was a plot directed by the DPP itself and the voting process in many places was also manipulated by the DPP. Therefore, the opposition started week-long protests, filed the election fraud case in court and proposed to investigate the assassination by a special committee. Because of the constant and severe confrontations between Chen's government and the opposition, the whole year of 2004 seemed to be the extended and highly confrontational election campaigns of the two camps until the Supreme Court declined the opposition's accusation of election fraud at the end of the year. The enduring confrontations created a political atmosphere that favored the radicalization of the DPP government.

The remaining three years from 2005 through 2008 were full of challenges against the corruptions of Chen's high officials, his own family members and himself. The criticism came not only from the KMT and other opposition parties but also from those moderate, liberal and democratic TIM advocates. The radicalization of Chen's movement-oriented strategy was mainly the outcome of these confrontational interactions. Put simply, facing the confrontations from broader forces including his previous supporters, Chen seemed to believe that he had to become more radical to secure his last hope, the movement fundamentalists' support.

However, the more radical he became, the less support he received from moderate, liberal and democratic supporters. He then faced a strategic dilemma similar to the one in his first term, but with much broader oppositions. The radical strategy might not be good for the DPP to maintain popular support as a whole, but could help Chen consolidate fundamentalists' personal loyalty to him, which then would help him resist legal accusations after he finished the second presidency.

In August 2005, Chen and his government's corruption nightmares were first exposed through a violent riot by a group of Thai contract workers in a subway construction site in Taiwan's second largest city, Kaohsiung. The investigation of the riot showed that these workers had been treated inhumanly for about two years, and a high level officer from Chen's office, who had close association with Chen, was involved in the corruption of this construction project. The government's reputation was nearly shattered by these scandals because, although Chen's government failed to compete with the previous KMT government in developing the economy, the government had tried to persuade the public that the major distinction between them and the KMT government was that they were "a human right defender" and "a clean government," while the previous KMT government was "a human right offender" and "a corrupt government." Now it turned out that Chen's government was as bad as the KMT's on human rights and corruptions, or even worse, because the KMT government at least developed Taiwan's economy well. These scandals also contributed to the DPP's unprecedented defeat in the local election in December 2005 — the DPP only won six out of the 23 local head positions, which, as the following Figure 3.2 shows, was the lowest in terms of share in the DPP's local election history.

After these events, the dissatisfaction and criticism against Chen and his government mounted up not only in the opposition camp but also within the DPP and its supporters. To change the unfavorable situation, Chen resorted to the popular Taiwanese nationalism again, but in a more radical way this time. In his 2006 New Year Talk, he declared that the liberal policy for Taiwanese investment in mainland China called "pro-active liberation and effective management," which he promoted in his first presidency, needed to be replaced by a more conservative one called "pro-active management and effective liberation." Taiwanese business persons were certainly

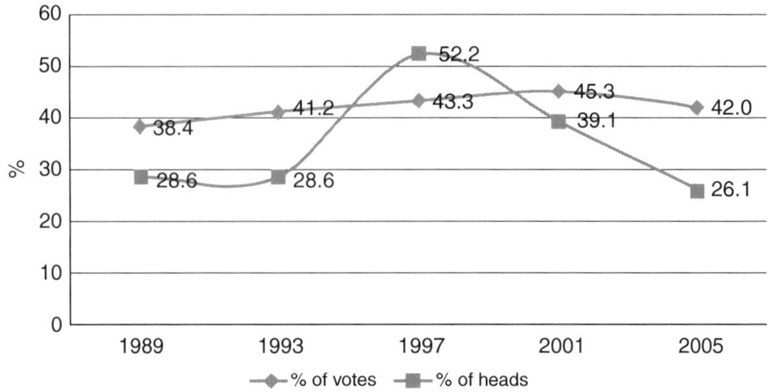

Figure 3.2 County and County-Level-City Head Election Results, 1989–2005, DPP

Data source: the DPP's official website, http://www.dpp.org.tw/; Central Election Commission, http://www.cec.gov.tw/.

frustrated by the policy change, but the TIM fundamentalists applauded for it because they had long argued that a liberal investment policy would endanger Taiwan both economically and politically. Economically, they argued, freer investment in mainland China would empty Taiwan's economic resources and significantly increase unemployment in Taiwan; politically, the more Taiwan invested in mainland China, the more dependent Taiwan became on mainland China, which in turn would prevent Taiwan from pursuing its complete independence of mainland China. It was widely believed that Chen tried to use this close-door policy to secure fundamentalists' support at the expense of Taiwan's economy.

About one month later, in a talk during the Chinese New Year, Chen declared that the National Reunification Council and the National Reunification Guidelines needed to be abolished since they had not functioned since 2000. Established in the early 1990s by the KMT government based on the one-China principle, the Council and the Guidelines were seen by the Chinese government as Taiwanese government's symbolic commitment to the future reunification with mainland China. Understandably, the abolition of them would imply Taiwan was going closer to the independence of mainland China. Therefore, in his inauguration speech in 2000, to show his moderate position on Taiwan's independence, Chen had promised that he would not abolish the Council and the Guidelines. As discussed previously, Chen's concessions on the independence issues in his first presidency disappointed many fundamentalists and even some moderates. Although in 2002 right after the Chinese government's diplomatic humiliation, he declared "one state on each side" to challenge the Chinese government's one-China policy and tried to retain the fundamentalists' support, the fundamentalists still complained that since then Chen had done almost nothing concrete to make Taiwan more independent of mainland China. The abolition of the National Reunification Council and the National Reunification Guidelines could be seen as a concrete step toward Taiwan's further independence, and therefore, might consolidate the fundamentalists' support for Chen.

The immediate domestic and international criticism against this speech was nothing unusual to Chen and the DPP's supporters, but it was disappointing to many of them when the subsequent confrontation between the DPP and the US governments on the "abolition issue" significantly deteriorate Taiwan–US relations. The US government did not want either side of the Taiwan Strait to initiate anything that could lead to the change of status quo between mainland China and Taiwan, and therefore, warned Chen not to abolish the National Reunification Council and Guidelines. Chen "compromised" to the warning through a word game — in the official order of abolishment a month later, the word "abolish" was replaced by "cease to function/apply," but then a government official told the public that there was no substantial difference between "cease to function/apply" and "abolish." Obviously, the US government was annoyed by Chen's trick and asked for his clarification. In April 2006, the US government did not allow Chen to stop in the US during his diplomatic trip, which was a clear signal of the US government's dissatisfaction with him. Nevertheless, Chen determined to continue the radical strategy no matter what the US government's response would be because, to him, retaining the fundamentalists' support was much more urgent and useful than maintaining a good relationship with the US government.

Shortly after the abolition issue quieted down, more corruption scandals involving Chen's son-in-law, his wife, his friends and even himself were exposed one by one in May through November 2006, which then was ranked the world's number five scandal on the 2006 *Time*'s Top 10

Scandals List.[6] Now Chen and his government faced stronger challenges not only from the opposition but also from the DPP's previous leaders and ordinary Taiwanese. The opposition parties proposed the recall of the President twice in Congress but failed due to the DPP and its allied party's objection. As Chen did not feel really threatened by the institutional challenge from the opposition, the non-institutional challenges, especially those from the DPP's previous leaders and supporters, were overwhelming. In July 2006, a group of pro-democracy and pro-independence activists, mainly including famous professors, researchers, lawyers and social movement activists, made public petitions twice within two weeks to ask Chen to resign and correct his radical strategy. The two petitions were very unusual and particularly challenging to Chen because most of the twenty thousand petitioners have been well known for their long term pro-DPP and pro-independence stance. In August, the DPP's previous chairman, Shih Ming-teh, announced that if he could receive NT$100 per person from one million Taiwanese within one month, he would organize a mass movement forcing Chen to resign. Within ten days, more than one million people donated, which was unprecedented in Taiwan's social movement history. The mass movement against Chen started in Taipei, Taiwan's capital city, in early September and soon spread to the whole island. Similar to the previous petitioners, most of the movement leaders had an outstanding history of supporting the DPP, the TIM or other social movements. They organized daily sit-ins and two large protests in Taipei with several hundred thousand participants, which became the most controversial issue in Taiwan's politics and also attracted attention from international media until the end of 2006 when the movement finally faded away.

Facing these challenges, Chen did not resign. Instead, he continued his radical strategy, trying to improve his credit as the TIM leader to make up for the lost credit as the President. This time he focused on two highly controversial issues: making a new constitution and promoting Taiwan's United Nations (UN) membership through referendum.

In late September 2006, having faced the strongest challenge from the mass movement, Chen hinted in a talk that the Constitution reform needed to consider Taiwan's territory issue, which implied another concrete step

[6] http://www.time.com/time/topten/2006/scandals/05.html, accessed on 6 April 2009.

toward Taiwan's *de jure* independence. About three weeks later, at the birthday party of a senior pro-independence activist, Chen reiterated his commitment to Taiwan's independence and declared that it was necessary to freeze the existing Constitution and make a new one called the Second Republic Constitution. Since then, Chen expressed his determination to create and then legalize the new constitution on different occasions. In March 2007, Chen's scholars finished the draft of the Second Republic Constitution.

The second controversial issue raised by Chen was pursuing Taiwan's UN membership. In 1971, mainland China replaced Taiwan as the legal representative of China in the UN. Since the early 1990s, Taiwan has tried annually to resume its UN membership but failed. In May 2007, Chen proposed to hold a referendum together with the presidential election in March 2008 to show the world Taiwanese's determination for joining the UN. The most controversial part of his proposal was that the referendum question asked the public if they agreed that Taiwan should "join," instead of "rejoin or return to," the UN with a new country name of Taiwan, instead of the Republic of China which was its current official name. Clearly, the question was asking the public if they supported Taiwan to join the UN as a new, independent country. Having learned from the counterproductive effect of their past aggressive reactions against Taiwan, this time the Chinese government denounced Chen's referendum proposal as usual, but without more extreme actions such as the military exercise. The US government now seemed to believe that Chen was a real "trouble maker" and explicitly asked him not to hold the referendum for Taiwan's UN membership. This time, Chen showed no compromise to the US government. In an interview with the US Republican delegation, he insisted on the point that Taiwan's future should be determined by the most democratic procedure, the referendum.

Chen's radical stance on the independence issues were summarized at two occasions in the last year of his second term. In March 2007, in his speech at the 25th anniversary ceremony of an important pro-independence organization, Formosan Association for Public Affairs, he declared "four wants and one without;" that is, "Taiwan wants independence; Taiwan wants the rectification of its name; Taiwan wants a new constitution; Taiwan wants development; and Taiwanese politics is without the question of left or right, but only the question of unification or independence,"[7] which literally broke his 2000 inauguration promise of "four noes and one without." In September 2007, the DPP's Party Member Representatives Meeting passed the Normal Nation Resolution which was proposed by Chen and specified the major tasks for the DPP in the future: "actively pursue name-rectification and promulgate a new Constitution, accede to the UN as an equal member, and implement transitional justice and policies aimed at nurturing a Taiwan-centric consciousness" (Normal Nation Resolution, English version, page 4).[8] This Normal Nation Resolution was called the DPP's "new pro-independence platform" and severely denounced by the Chinese government.[9]

As the 2008 presidential election came closer, Chen had successfully consolidated the TIM fundamentalists' loyalty to him through the radical strategy. He almost personified the TIM in the eyes of the fundamentalists — he seemed to be the most sincere, committed and capable leader of the TIM, and therefore, any challenge to him equaled the challenge to the TIM and the fundamentalist supporters. As the DPP's Chairman, he also dominated the DPP's presidential election campaign with the radical strategy until January 2008, when the DPP saw its disastrous defeat in the legislative election and then Chen had to resign from the chairman position. By then it seemed too late for the DPP and its presidential candidate, Hsieh Chang-ting, to make up for all the negative impacts caused by Chen and his government — specifically, his government's failure in mending the economy, his family's corruption and his radical strategy. Ironically, Hsieh had to continue the radical strategy and resorted to popular nationalistic sentiment again in his election campaign, otherwise he would disaffect the fundamentalists, whose nationalistic sentiment and expectation had been cultivated radically by Chen in recent years. However, the nationalism-oriented campaign did not work well this time because by then many previous moderate supporters had been disappointed by Chen's radical strategy in the nationalism clothing. Eventually, the DPP lost the 2008 presidential election with significantly decreased popular support.

[7] http://www.president.gov.tw/php-bin/prez/shownews.php4?Rid=12655, accessed on 7 April 2009.

[8] http://www.dpp.org.tw/upload/policy/20071029100043_link.pdf, accessed on 18 June 2015.

[9] http://news.xinhuanet.com/newscenter/2007-10/01/content_6821206.htm, accessed on 18 June 2015.

Data, Operationalization and Hypotheses

After we have a general understanding of the evolution of Chen's government strategies, we can start to examine the effect of the three factors, specifically, the government's economic performance, his family's corruption scandals and his radical movement strategy on Taiwanese people's party support. This examination should be conducted in a comparative context between the two administrative terms of 2000–2004 and 2004–2008 because the two terms provide a "natural experiment" for better understanding the role of the above three factors in people's support for the DPP. In general, the first administrative term of 2000–2004 may be treated as the control period, and the second term of 2004–2008 as the experimental period where three new factors were "added" to this period, that is, the DPP government's worse economic performance, Chen and his family's corruption scandals, and his radical movement strategy. In the following sections, I first operationalize these three factors at the individual level and then develop competing hypotheses according to the popular arguments and the movement government framework, and finally I examine these hypotheses with regression models.

The datasets to be used in the examination are the 2004 post-presidential election survey (i.e., TEDS2004P) and the 2008 post-legislators election survey (i.e., TEDS2008L[10]). The 2008 survey was conducted during the ending period of the DPP administration's second term, about one month before the presidential election in March 2008. The two datasets do not have a variable indicating each individual's evaluation of the DPP government's economic performance. However, they include each individual's assessment of his or her family's current economic fortune as compared to that in the last year, which includes three assessment categories: better off, no change and worse off. The popular argument suggests that the DPP government's poor economic performance made people less

---

[10] Data analyzed in this chapter were from Taiwan's Election and Democratization Studies, 2005–2008(III): Legislative Elections, 2008 (TEDS 2008L) (NSC 96-2420-H-002-025). The coordinator of multi-year project TEDS is Professor Chi Huang (National Chengchi University). TEDS2008L is a project on the legislative election in 2008. The principal investigator is Professor Yun-han Chu. More information is on TEDS website (http://www.tedsnet.org). The author appreciates the assistance in providing data by the institute and individuals aforementioned. The author is alone responsible for views expressed herein.

likely to support it. If this is valid, we should find evidence supporting the following hypothesis:

H3.1: Those who feel worse off about their family's economic fortune were less likely than those who feel better off or no change to have the DPP party identification (i.e., DPP ID) in both 2004 and 2008, even after controlling for their nationalistic sentiment. In other words, economically worse off people were less likely than others to support the DPP in both administrative terms, whether they had Taiwanese nationalistic sentiment or not.

However, if we find evidence supporting the following competing hypothesis H3.2, we may say that the above popular argument is not supported, and instead, the argument based on the movement government framework is supported; that is, Chen's radical movement strategy successfully reduced the negative impact of the government's poor economic performance on individuals' support for the DPP through enhancing their Taiwanese nationalistic sentiment:

H3.2: After controlling for individuals' nationalistic sentiment, although economically worse off people were less likely than others to have the DPP ID in 2004, they were not less likely than others to have the DPP ID in 2008. In other words, the negative effect of the DPP government's poor economic performance on individuals' support for the DPP was reduced to be insignificant by the radical movement strategy in 2008.

Similarly, regarding the effect of Chen's family corruption scandals on individuals' support for the DPP, we may develop two other competing hypotheses based on the following information. The two datasets do not have a variable indicating people's perceptions and opinions about the family's corruptions. Nevertheless, in the datasets, respondents were asked to rate Chen on a 0–10 scale based on how much they liked him: the higher the score, the more they liked Chen. In other words, this score may indicate the level of each individual's fondness of Chen. It is reasonable to believe that in 2008 Chen and his family's corruptions were among the most important factors determining how much each individual liked him. Therefore, this variable of fondness score may indicate indirectly how much negative influence his family's corruption scandals had on each respondent — a lower fondness score indicates higher negative impact by the corruption scandals on the individual. Therefore, if the family's corruption scandals reduced individuals' support for the DPP, the following hypothesis should be supported by evidence:

H3.3: Individuals' fondness of Chen was positively correlated with their support for the DPP in 2004 and 2008, even after controlling for their nationalistic sentiment. In other words, people who were less fond of Chen were less likely to support the DPP in both administrative terms, whether they had Taiwanese nationalistic sentiment or not.[11]

Based on the movement government framework, the competing hypothesis proposes that Chen's radical movement strategy may reduce the negative effect of his family's corruption scandals on individuals' support for the DPP, as stated in the following hypothesis:

H3.4: After controlling for individuals' nationalistic sentiment, people who were less fond of Chen were not less likely to support the DPP in 2008. In other words, the negative effect of the family's corruption scandals on individuals' support for the DPP was reduced to be insignificant by the radical movement strategy in 2008.

In the above four hypotheses, the effect of Chen's radical movement strategy is indicated by the individual's nationalistic sentiment, which in turn is measured by the two three-category variables that have been used in Chapter 2 to indicate whether an individual supports the TIM or not. To repeat, the first one is the individual's national identity, including Taiwanese, Chinese or dual identity (i.e., both Taiwanese and Chinese) and the second is his or her attitude about Taiwan-mainland China relations, including pro-independence, pro-unification, or pro status quo. Table 3.1 provides the sample means of the variables used in the analysis.

[11] We know that Chen and his family's corruption scandals occurred only in his second term; therefore, in 2004 models, the effect of fondness of Chen on individuals' support for the DPP cannot be interpreted as the effect of the family's corruption scandals.

Table 3.1 Sample Means of the Variables Used in the Analysis of Party ID/Support and Fondness of Chen, 2004 and 2008

Variables	2004 Mean	2008 Mean
Dependent Variable		
Party ID: "Which political party do you feel identified with?"		
1. Pro-independence parties: DPP and TSU	0.34	0.25
2. Neutral (ref.)	0.34	0.36
3. Anti-independence parties: KMT, PFP, and NP (ref.)	0.32	0.39
Independent Variable		
Family economic fortune under DPP administration		
1. Better off	0.10	0.07
2. The same	0.63	0.55
3. Worse off (ref.)	0.27	0.37
National identity: "Do you consider yourself to be Taiwanese, Chinese, or both?"		
1. Chinese	0.07	0.05
2. Both	0.46	0.46
3. Taiwanese (ref.)	0.47	0.49
Attitude about Taiwan's independence: "What's your opinion about Taiwan's future relation with mainland China?"		
1. Pro-unification	0.18	0.16
2. Pro-status quo	0.56	0.63
3. Pro-independence (ref.)	0.27	0.21
Fondness Score of Chen	5.43	3.12
Ethnicity		
1. Minnan (Hoklo)	0.75	0.78
2. Kejia (Hakka)	0.12	0.13
3. Mainlander (ref.)	0.12	0.10
Gender		
1. Female	0.50	0.50
2. Male (ref.)	0.51	0.50
Age		
1. 20–29	0.23	0.19
2. 30–39	0.22	0.22
3. 40–49	0.22	0.23
4. 50–59	0.14	0.18
5. 60 and above (ref.)	0.18	0.18
Education		
1. Lower (junior high or below)	0.39	0.35
2. Middle (senior high or vocational)	0.30	0.30
3. Higher (college or above) (ref.)	0.31	0.35
N	1823	1240

Data source: TEDS2004P, TEDS2008L.

Method and Results

In Tables 3.2 and 3.3, I use three-level nested multinomial logistic regressions to examine the above hypotheses. The dependent variable in the following models is Party ID, which includes three categories: the DPP ID, the neutral who have no party preference and the anti-independence party ID (i.e., the KMT, the PFP, or the NP ID), with the latter two categories as the reference groups. The four common control variables are gender (male as the reference), age (five age categories: 20–29, 30–39, 40–49, 50–59, 60 and above, with 60 and above as the reference), education (three categories: junior high and below, senior high and vocational, and college and above, with college and above as the reference) and ethnicity (three categories: Minnan, Kejia and Mainlander, with Mainlander as the reference). The starting model (i.e., the first constrained model) includes the four control variables and the variable of family economic fortune, which include three categories: Better off, no change and worse off, with worse off as the reference. We want to see whether economically worse off people were less likely than others to have the DPP ID.

The second constrained model adds the two variables of the individual's nationalistic sentiment to the starting model. The first nationalistic sentiment variable is the individual's attitude about Taiwan-mainland China relations, with the pro-independence attitude as the reference. The second one is the individual's national identity, with the Taiwanese identity as the reference. The second constrained model can show us how much the effect of family fortune on individuals' support for the DPP can be reduced by Chen's radical movement strategy; therefore, it examines hypotheses H3.1 and H3.2.

In the full model, I add the variable of fondness of Chen to the second constrained model. On one hand, the full model can show us if the effect of fondness of Chen is still significant after controlling for individuals' nationalistic sentiment (i.e., Chen's radial strategy) and examines hypotheses H3.3 and H3.4. On the other hand, it can help us comprehensively understand the effect of the three examined factors on Taiwanese people's support for the DPP.

As indicated by the starting models A1 and B1 in Tables 3.2 and 3.3, economically worse off people were indeed less likely than others to have

Table 3.2 Nested Multinomial Logistic Regressions of Party ID, 2004

	(A) DPP ID vs. Neutral ID			(B) DPP ID vs. Anti-Independence Party ID		
	Model A1	**Model A2**	**Model A3**	**Model B1**	**Model B2**	**Model B3**
Independent Variables	**Co-ef.**	**Co-ef.**	**Co-ef.**	**Co-ef.**	**Co-ef.**	**Co-ef.**
Ethnicity						
Minnan	0.967***	0.750*	0.717†	2.403***	1.819***	1.719***
Kejia	0.689*	0.589	0.643	1.832***	1.427***	1.444***
Mainlander (ref.)	—	—	—	—	—	—
Gender						
Female	–0.161	–0.104	–0.195	–0.293*	–0.454**	–0.522**
Male (ref.)	—	—	—	—	—	—
Age						
20–29	–0.142	–0.004	0.064	0.598*	0.694*	0.626†
30–39	0.162	0.403	0.536†	0.164	0.482†	0.583
40–49	0.126	0.392	0.614*	–0.140	0.162	0.237
50–59	0.093	0.318	0.464	–0.144	0.308	0.334
60 and above (ref.)	—	—	—	—	—	—
Education						
Lower (junior high or below)	–0.237	–0.230	–0.535*	0.884***	0.606**	0.178
Middle (senior high or vocational)	–0.138	0.220	–0.050	0.347*	0.415*	–0.042
Higher (college or above) (ref.)	—	—	—	—	—	—

Family's economic fortune						
Better off	**1.146*****	**0.861*****	**0.564***	**1.739*****	**1.392*****	**0.936****
No change)	**0.696*****	**0.526****	**0.399***	**0.798*****	**0.676*****	**0.413**†
Worse off (ref.	—	—	—	—	—	—
Attitude about Taiwan's independence						
Pro-unification	—	−1.743***	−1.296	—	−2.584***	−1.849***
Pro-status quo	—	−1.386***	−1.044	—	−1.832***	−1.257***
Pro-independence (ref.)	—	—	—	—	—	—
National identity						
Chinese	—	−0.150	0.282	—	−1.761***	−0.988*
Both Taiwanese & Chinese	—	−0.721***	−0.443**	—	−1.647***	−1.140***
Taiwanese (ref.)	—	—	—	—	—	—
Fondness of Chen	—	—	**0.517*****	—	—	**0.875*****
Intercept	−1.368***	0.042	−3.431***	−3.103***	−0.163	−5.259***
−2LL	946.314***	1595.245***	1871.086***	946.314***	1595.245***	1871.086***
N	1628	1522	1494	1628	1522	1494

Note: TEDS2004P.

†$p \leq 0.1$, *$p \leq 0.05$, **$p \leq 0.01$, ***$p \leq 0.001$.

Table 3.3 Nested Multinomial Logistic Regressions of Party ID, 2008

	(A) DPP ID vs. Neutral ID			(B) DPP ID vs. Anti-Independence Party ID		
	Model A1	Model A2	Model A3	Model B1	Model B2	Model B3
Independent Variables	**Co-ef.**	**Co-ef.**	**Co-ef.**	**Co-ef.**	**Co-ef.**	**Co-ef.**
Ethnicity						
Minnan	1.795**	1.201†	1.033	3.178***	2.766***	2.430***
Kejia	1.154†	0.664	0.562	2.151***	2.026**	1.880**
Mainlander (ref.)	—	—	—	—	—	—
Gender						
Female	–0.083	0.052	0.029	–0.179	–0.205	–0.234
Male (ref.)	—	—	—	—	—	—
Age						
20–29	–0.177	0.169	0.323	0.270	0.835*	1.147*
30–39	0.237	0.502	0.752*	0.129	0.759*	1.357*
40–49	0.230	0.620†	0.842*	–0.310	0.165	0.711†
50–59	0.215	0.283	0.292	–0.347	0.059	0.173
60 and above (ref.)	—	—	—	—	—	—
Education						
Lower (junior high or below)	–0.405†	–0.252	–0.462	0.850***	0.918***	0.405
Middle (senior high or vocational)	–0.486*	–0.429†	–0.699**	0.216	0.321	–0.201
Higher (college or above) (ref.)	—	—	—	—	—	—

Family's economic fortune						
Better off	**0.952****	**0.389**	**0.181**	**1.119*****	**0.189**	**−0.327**
No change	**0.462****	**0.302**	**0.196**	**0.459****	**0.254**	**−0.037**
Worse off (ref.)	—	—	—	—	—	—
Attitude about Taiwan's independence						
Pro-unification	—	−1.055***	−0.872*	—	−2.359***	−2.074***
Pro-status quo	—	−1.229***	−0.935***	—	−2.214***	−1.855***
Pro-independence (ref.)	—	—	—	—	—	—
National identity						
Chinese	—	−0.682	−0.150	—	−1.841***	−0.741
Both Taiwanese & Chinese	—	−0.900***	−0.711***	—	−1.535***	−1.103***
Taiwanese (ref.)	—	—	—	—	—	—
Fondness of Chen	**—**	**—**	**0.326*****	**—**	**—**	**0.707**
Intercept	−2.092**	−0.468	−1.815*	−3.826***	−1.275†	−3.629***
−2LL	740.340***	1179.804***	1331.325***	740.340***	1179.804***	1331.325***
N	1127	1017	969	1127	1017	969

Note: TEDS2008L

†$p \leq 0.1$, *$p \leq 0.05$, **$p \leq 0.01$, ***$p \leq 0.001$.

the DPP ID in both 2004 and 2008. However, after adding the variables of nationalistic sentiment, the second constrained models A2 and B2 in the two tables show different patterns in 2004 and 2008. Although the effect of family economic fortune remained significant in 2004, it became insignificant in 2008. Therefore, hypothesis H3.2 rather than H3.1 is supported by the above results.

In a sense, the above results indicate that Taiwanese people have become "irrational" in 2008 as compared to in 2004. We have heard increasing complaints from both pundits and ordinary Taiwanese about Chen's poor economic performance during his second term. Therefore, it is certainly reasonable to expect those economically worse off people to support the DPP less in 2008. However, the results show that Taiwanese people's nationalistic sentiment could make them overcome their concern about their families' economic fortune when they chose which party to support. In other words, as long as they had Taiwanese nationalistic sentiment, that is, as long as they were pro-independence and/or accepted Taiwanese identity, they were more likely than others to support the DPP, even if their families were economically worse off under the DPP administration in 2008. On the other hand, because Taiwanese people did not show this "irrationality" at the end of Chen's first term in 2004, it is reasonable to attribute the emergence of this "irrationality" to Taiwanese people's enhanced nationalistic sentiment which was successfully promoted by Chen's radical movement strategy during his second term.

This "irrationality" that was evoked by enhanced nationalistic sentiment can be more convincingly demonstrated by the following Table 3.4. It shows the percents of people having worse off family, DPP ID, and Taiwanese nationalistic sentiment (i.e., pro-independence or having Taiwanese identity) in different social groups in 2008.

Table 3.4 shows that while the three social groups, that is, those whose education was junior high or below, who lived in south Taiwan, and whose occupation/class status was farmer, had the highest percents of worse off family; surprisingly, they also had the strongest support for the DPP and strongest Taiwanese nationalistic sentiment. Similarly, among the five age groups, while the oldest group of 60 and above had the highest percent of worse off family, they also had the second strongest support for the DPP (i.e., only lower than the age group of 30–39 by 0.8%) and the strongest

Table 3.4 Percent of People Having Worse off Family, DPP ID and Taiwanese Nationalistic Sentiment,* and the Average Fondness Score of Chen in Different Social Groups, 2008

(Unit in the first three columns: % of people in each social group)

	Having Worse off Family	Having DPP ID	Having Taiwanese Nationalistic Sentiment	Average Fondness Score of Chen
Age				
20–29	28.4	25.1	54.7	2.93
30–39	33.8	27.5	50.2	2.74
40–49	41.5	21.7	43.6	2.82
50–59	35.8	24.4	48.2	3.45
60 and above	*48.4*	*26.7*	*64.1*	*4.05*
Education				
College and above	29.4	25.3	46.3	2.53
Senior high and vocational	38.5	22.5	47.4	3.13
Junior high and below	*45.4*	*27.5*	*60.5*	*3.88*
Residence Region				
North and Central	36.2	22.2	47.9	2.96
South	*39.8*	*30.6*	*59.2*	*3.46*
Class/occupation				
Upper-middle class	31.1	27.7	47.4	2.91
Lower-middle class	34.5	26.3	47.2	2.85
Workers	41.1	24.4	50.3	3.43
Farmers	*48.6*	*29.4*	*73.9*	*4.61*

*A person had Taiwanese nationalistic sentiment if he or she was pro-independence or considered him/herself as Taiwanese only.

Data source: TEDS2008L.

Taiwanese nationalistic sentiment. It is remarkable that how "irrational" these elders, lower educated, south Taiwan residents, and farmers were when their families were most severely hurt economically by the DPP administration's poor economic performance, but they still committed the strongest support to the DPP. Not accidently, these social groups also showed strongest Taiwanese nationalistic sentiment. Therefore, these social groups' counterintuitive and stronger support for the DPP may be explained by their stronger nationalistic sentiment. It was Chen's radical movement strategy that enhanced these social groups' nationalistic sentiment.

In contrast, 4 years ago in 2004, these most "irrational" social groups showed much less "irrationality." Table 3.5 replicates the above Table 3.4 with the 2004 data.

Table 3.5 shows that those people who were older than 60, whose education was junior high or below, who lived in south Taiwan and who were

Table 3.5 Percent of People Having Worse off Family, DPP ID and Taiwanese Nationalistic Sentiment* in Different Social Groups, 2004

(Unit: % of people in each social group)

	Having Worse off Family	**Having DPP ID**	**Having Taiwanese Nationalistic Sentiment**
Age			
20–29	20.6	35.8	52.4
30–39	25.7	35.1	48
40–49	27.3	31.6	47.5
50–59	30	35.1	60.2
60 and above	*35.4*	*29*	*58*
Education			
College and above	19.1	31.8	43.9
Senior high and vocational	26.2	35.8	47.6
Junior high and below	*34.8*	*33.4*	*63.2*
Residence Region			
North and Central	26.6	31.2	50.3
South	*28.4*	*38.1*	*56.8*
Class/occupation			
Upper-middle class	19.6	34.3	42.2
Lower-middle class	30.2	32.3	47
Workers	28.1	38.1	59.4
Farmers	*38.0*	*31.8*	*72.2*

*A person had Taiwanese nationalistic sentiment if he or she was pro-independence or considered him/herself as Taiwanese only.

Data source: TEDS2004P.

farmers were still the most unfortunate in terms of their families' economic fortune. Although they still showed the strongest Taiwanese nationalistic sentiment, except those living in south Taiwan, they did not show the highest support for the DPP. Actually, in 2004, the elders and farmers showed the lowest support and the lower educated showed moderate support for the DPP, which was "rational" because it was congruent with their families' miserable fortune under the DPP administration of 2000–2004. I argue that the lower radical level of Chen's movement strategy in his first term led to the lower level of "irrationality" in these social groups' party support.

In summary, the above nested regressions suggest that Taiwanese people's nationalistic sentiment has completely overcome their concern about their families' economic fortune in deciding their party support in 2008. Furthermore, for those people whose education was junior high or below, who lived in south Taiwan, who were farmers and who were 60 or above years old, their nationalistic sentiment was so strong that although their families' economic fortune was the worst under the DPP administration, they still showed the highest or relatively higher support for the DPP in 2008. In contrast, Taiwanese people in general and these four social groups particularly did not show such strong "irrationality" in their party support in 2004. These findings do not support the popular argument that the DPP government's poor economic performance reduced individuals' support for the DPP in 2008 but support my argument about the effect of Chen's radical movement strategy according to the movement government framework.

Now let us discuss the full models A3 and B3 in Tables 3.2 and 3.3 which show the effect of fondness of Chen on individuals' party support. The results indicate that even after controlling for individuals' nationalistic sentiment and their families' economic fortune, fondness of Chen still has a positive correlation with individual's support for the DPP. In other words, after controlling for the other two important determinants of party support, those who liked Chen less were still less likely to support the DPP. It seems that Taiwanese people's nationalistic sentiment did not overcome their dislike for Chen in deciding whether or not to support the DPP. In other words, even if an individual was pro-independence and had Taiwanese identity, the less he or she liked Chen, the less likely he or she would support the DPP. Therefore, the family's corruption scandals, as long as they could really reduce Taiwanese people's fondness of him, had an independent negative effect on individuals' support for the DPP. These results support hypothesis H3.3 and the popular argument and do not support hypothesis H3.4 and my argument about the positive effect of Chen's radical movement strategy based on the movement government framework. However, in the next chapter, I will show that Chen's radical movement strategy itself was another important factor in addition to his family's corruption scandals that made the previous moderate supporters dislike him and withdraw their support for the DPP in 2008.

Overall, the full models suggest that in 2004 the three factors had independent effects on Taiwanese people's support for the DPP, but in 2008 only individuals' nationalistic sentiment and their fondness of Chen had net effects on their support for the DPP. According to the movement government framework, the interpretation could be that during Chen's second term it was his radical movement strategy that significantly reduced the negative effect of his government's poor economic performance on popular support for the DPP through enhancing popular Taiwanese nationalistic sentiment. In Chapter 2, we have seen that individuals' dissatisfaction with the DPP government could reduce their support for the DPP. However, the findings here suggest that the DPP government's poor economic performance did not reduce individuals' support. Therefore, there must be something else about the DPP government that made people dissatisfied and withdraw support. Besides Chen's family corruption scandals as shown by the above findings, I argue that the DPP's radical movement strategy consolidated a smaller group of movement fundamentalists' support but alienated a larger group of moderates. The next chapter will present this argument in detail.

The Radical Strategy and Fondness of Chen

The above findings show that Chen's radical movement strategy was not able to completely overcome the negative effect of his family's corruption scandals on people's support for the DPP. We need to further discuss this finding to explore the role of Chen's radical movement strategy in Taiwanese people's party support. First of all, this finding does not necessarily mean that the corruption scandals had the same level of negative effect on different people's fondness of Chen. According to the movement government framework, it was highly possible that Chen's radical movement strategy reduced the corruption scandals' negative effect on many TIM supporters in terms of their fondness of him. In other words, being influenced by Chen's radical movement strategy, many TIM supporters might be more "immune" to his corruption scandals and still maintained stronger fondness of him, and this stronger fondness of Chen may turn into support for the DPP. In addition, we should notice that as early as 2002 and in his first term, Chen had given up the government-oriented strategy and started using movement-oriented strategy to consolidate and improve popular support for him, although not in the radical way as he did in his second term. Therefore, we should see that at the end of his first term, people with Taiwanese nationalistic sentiment (i.e., those TIM supporters) liked Chen more than others. If Chen's radical movement strategy could really make these people more "immune" to his corruption scandals which occurred in his second term, we should see that this positive correlation remained significant. Therefore, the following hypothesis should be supported by evidence:

H3.5: In 2004, individuals who were pro-independence or had Taiwanese identity liked Chen more; in 2008, this positive correlation between individuals' nationalistic sentiment and their fondness of Chen remained significant.

However, if Chen's radical movement strategy was not able to reduce the negative impact of his family's corruption scandals on movement supporters' fondness of him, we should see that the following hypothesis is supported by evidence:

H3.6: In 2004, individuals who were pro-independence or had Taiwanese identity liked Chen more; however, in 2008, this positive correlation between individuals' nationalistic sentiment and their fondness of Chen became insignificant.

Because "fondness of Chen" is an interval variable with values between 0–10, I use Ordinary Least Squares (OLS) linear regressions in the following Table 3.6 to examine the above hypothesis. The dependent variable is

Table 3.6 OLS Linear Regressions of Fondness of Chen, 2004 and 2008

Independent Variables	2004 Co-ef. (S.E.)	2008 Co-ef. (S.E.)
Ethnicity		
Minnan	0.258 (0.180)	0.464† (0.243)
Kejia	0.128 (0.226)	0.353 (0.293)
Mainlander (ref.)	—	—
Gender		
Male	0.076 (0.110)	0.051 (0.136)
Female (ref.)	—	—
Age	–0.005 (0.005)	0.011* (0.006)
Education		
Lower (junior high or below)	0.692*** (0.163)	0.652** (0.205)
Middle (senior high or vocational)	0.354** (0.136)	0.477** (0.163)
Higher (college or above) (ref.)	—	—
Family's economic fortune		
Better off	0.603** (0.206)	0.579* (0.270)
No change	0.423*** (0.132)	0.416** (0.145)
Worse off (ref.)	—	—
Attitude about Taiwan's independence		
Pro-unification	–0.769*** (0.191)	–0.374 (0.250)
Pro-status quo	–0.658*** (0.144)	–0.543** (0.192)
Pro-independence (ref.)	—	—
National identity		
Chinese	–1.000*** (0.248)	–1.491*** (0.346)
Both Taiwanese & Chinese	–0.526*** (0.131)	–0.625*** (0.157)
Taiwanese (ref.)	—	—
Party ID		
Anti-independence party ID	–3.819*** (0.165)	–3.293*** (0.194)
Neutral	–1.863*** (0.143)	–1.560*** (0.189)
DPP ID (ref.)	—	—
Constant	7.397*** (0.314)	4.187*** (0.402)
R^2	0.474***	0.433***
N	1481	969

Note: TEDS2004P, TEDS2008L

†$p \leq 0.1$, *$p \leq 0.05$, **$p \leq 0.01$, ***$p \leq 0.001$.

fondness of Chen with a higher fondness score indicating stronger fondness of him. I add all the control and independent variables used by the second constrained model in the previous Tables 3.2 and 3.3 to the 2004 and 2008 regression models; specifically, they are gender, age, education, ethnicity, family economic fortune, and the two variables of nationalistic sentiment. I also add the party ID variable to the models as a more rigorous control. The results show that in both 2004 and 2008, those pro-independence individuals and those with Taiwanese identity liked Chen more than others.[12] Therefore, the above hypothesis H3.5 rather than H3.6 is supported by these results. In general, the results support my argument that Chen's radical movement strategy made these TIM supporters more immune to his corruption scandals, and as a result, they remained strongly fond of him. The previous Table 3.4, which shows different social groups' level of nationalistic sentiment and their average fondness score of Chen in 2008, provides further evidence for my argument. It shows that the four "irrational" social groups, that is, those elders (i.e., 60 years old or above), less educated (i.e., junior high or below), south Taiwan residents and farmers, had the strongest nationalistic sentiment and liked Chen most in 2008. It seems the family's corruption scandals had the least negative impact on these social groups. Therefore, it is reasonable to argue that Chen's radical movement strategy made these four social groups more "immune" to both his government's poor economic performance and his family's corruption scandals.

In general, the examinations in this chapter show the positive effect of Chen's radical movement strategy on individuals' support for the DPP. But I propose that the radical movement strategy was a double-edged sword with both positive and negative impact on popular support for the DPP. Specifically, Chen's radical movement strategy successfully maintained movement fundamentalists' fondness of him but also disaffected many movement moderates and made them like him less. It was the lower support of these moderates that eventually reduced the overall social support for the DPP. In the next chapter, I will further analyze the characteristics

[12] I also used Poisson regressions with all the same independent variables to predict the individual's fondness of Chen, which showed the same results as the OLS regressions.

of Chen's radical movement strategy and show its double-edged sword effect on fundamentalists and moderates.

Summary

The purpose of this chapter is to critically examine the popular explanations of the lower social support for the DPP at the end of its second administrative term, and then generally examine an alternative explanation based on the movement government framework which emphasizes the impact of Chen's radical movement strategy on Taiwanese people's support for the DPP. The popular explanation suggests that Chen's poorer economic performance and his family's corruption scandals reduced popular support for the DPP, but based on the movement government framework, I propose that Chen's radical movement strategy might be able to significantly lessen the negative impact of these two factors on popular support for the DPP. After a detailed review of the evolution of Chen's strategies from concession to confrontation in its first term and finally to radicalization in its second term, I examine the effect of and the relations between the three factors in terms of their roles in determining individuals' support for the DPP. The results show that in 2008 Taiwanese people's nationalistic sentiment could make them overcome their concern about their families' economic fortune but could not make them overcome their dislike of Chen when they decided whether or not to support the DPP.

Since individuals' nationalistic sentiment, their families' economic fortune, and their fondness of Chen may indicate the impacts of Chen's radical movement strategy, his government's economic performance, and his family's corruption scandals on individuals, respectively, these results suggest that Chen's radical movement strategy could completely eliminate the independent negative impact of his government's poor economic performance on individuals' support for the DPP. Although the radical movement strategy was not able to completely remove the independent negative impact of the family's corruption scandals on individuals' support for the DPP, the further examination shows that it could make the TIM supporters more "immune" to the negative impact of these scandals because the examination shows that the TIM supporters still maintained their stronger fondness of Chen in his second term.

This chapter also shows that four social groups were more likely to be fundamentalists and were most influenced by Chen's radical movement strategy which made them support the DPP and like Chen most, although their families experienced the worst economic fortune under the Chen administration. Specifically, they were the elders of 60 years old or above, the lower educated of junior high or below level, the south Taiwan residents, and farmers. Overall, this chapter shows the inadequacy of the popular explanations about the declining popular support for the DPP because they overlook the role of Chen's radical movement strategy.

CHAPTER 4: THE MOVEMENT GOVERNMENT'S RADICAL STRATEGY: A DOUBLE-EDGED SWORD

Introduction

In the previous chapters, I have shown the misleading interpretation and the inadequate explanations about the changing popular support for the Democratic Progressive Party (DPP) during 2000–2008. In this chapter, I use the movement government framework proposed in Chapter 1 to provide and examine a complementary account. The movement government framework suggests that the DPP government is a typical movement government which is different from conventional democratic governments, in that it plays the dual roles of movement leader and national government. As a result, a strategic dilemma will trouble the DPP government as long as its movement supporters' expectation for pursuing Taiwan's independence contradicts the popular expectation for delivering good government performance. Facing such structural constraint, the DPP government tried different strategies to maintain and expand its support base, and these strategies have different impacts on the popular support. In the early period of its first administration from 2000 through 2002, the DPP government conceded on important independence issues and tried to establish a centrist government image, but did not see much benefit with this concession strategy. Since 2002, the DPP government gradually returned to its confrontational position on the independence issues and used the confrontation strategy to retain and expand the movement support. After Chen Shui-bian was re-elected in 2004, he radicalized the confrontation strategy, hoping to make up for his lost credit as the President by improving his credit as the Taiwan Independence Movement (TIM) leader. Finally, the extremely radical strategy alienated many moderate supporters, although it successfully maintained the support of movement fundamentalists.

From the perspective of the movement government framework, it was quite understandable for Chen to stick to the movement-oriented strategy during his second term. Since 2002, this strategy had been effective in promoting Taiwanese nationalistic sentiment and improving popular support for the DPP and finally helped Chen win the 2004 presidential re-election. Therefore, there was no reason for him to abandon this strategy in his second term. More importantly, we have seen in Chapter 3 that Chen not only continued this strategy, but also radicalized it, mainly because the radical movement strategy might help him escape from his family's corruption scandals. I propose that when the movement-oriented strategy was over radicalized, it generated positive impact on the movement fundamentalists but negative impact on the movement moderates. To better understand the impact of Chen's radical strategy on people with different social characteristics and political orientations, we need an in-depth anatomy of the strategy, especially, on its underlying rationale and characteristics. In this chapter, first I discuss the radical movement strategy's main characteristics, and then analyze the double-edged sword effect of this strategy on the movement fundamentalists and moderates.

The Anatomy of the Radical Strategy

The underlying rationale of Chen's radical strategy seems to build on two presumptions: First, the radical strategy can significantly enhance people's nationalistic sentiment; second, enhanced nationalistic sentiment can reduce people's concerns about the government's problems and his family's corruption scandals; therefore, the radical strategy is a good choice for the unsatisfactory government to maintain popular support. Indeed, popular nationalism has been one of the most reliable and effective popular sentiments used by many countries' political oppositions to fight against power holders, and after they take power, continually used by the new government to maintain power. The DPP's history as an opposition party and a new government during its first term had also shown that popular Taiwanese nationalism was one of its most effective appeals to maintain popular support. However, there are many different ways to make use of popular nationalism. Different strategies of using the nationalism show different characteristics and have different social impacts.

Naming black sheep

The most common characteristic and a prerequisite of the nationalism strategy is identifying or creating a common enemy for the nation — no enemy, no nationalism. Usually the enemy is a group of people outside the nation such as the Chinese government outside Taiwan. However, when it is believed that the nation's enemy includes both outsiders and insiders of the nation, like both the Chinese government and the *Kuo Min Tang* (KMT) in Taiwan, the nationalism strategy may become radical. This is the case of Chen's radical strategy. Since 1949 when the KMT was defeated in Chinese Civil War by the CCP and then fled to Taiwan, the Chinese government has been a natural enemy to Taiwan but with different connotations in different periods of time. During most of the time from 1949–2000, when the KMT held power in Taiwan, it depicted the Chinese government as Taiwan's enemy competing with the KMT government and even trying to eliminate it for the sole representation of China in the international community. Since 2000 when the DPP was in power, the Chinese government was Taiwan's enemy not because of the two governments' competition for representing the same China internationally, but because of the Chinese government's opposition against Taiwan's *de jure* independence of mainland China as a new and separate country. As I have discussed in Chapter 3, during the second half of Chen's first term, he successfully used the confrontation strategy to stimulate the Chinese government and then made use of the latter's aggressive reaction to mobilize popular Taiwanese nationalism. However, in Chen's second term, the Chinese government had finally learned its lesson and stopped reacting to Chen's provocation aggressively. Therefore, this outsider enemy had become much less available for Chen to make use of and he needed to identify a new enemy for the nation. The KMT was an ideal enemy of the nation for him not only because it was the largest opposition party in Taiwan but also because the KMT shared many commonalities with the Chinese Communist Party (CCP). For example, both of the parties had or has maintained an authoritarian regime for a long time, and consequently, have a negative political image for pro-democracy people; both of them originated in mainland China and pursued China's ultimate reunification, and therefore, opposed Taiwan's *de jure* independence of mainland China; and since 2000, both of them opposed the Chen government's close-door policy toward mainland China. As a result, it was not difficult for Chen to group the KMT and the Chinese government together as the nation's common enemy. In 2005, when the former KMT chairman, Lien Chan, visited the CCP and expressed the two parties' common stance on anti-independence, it seemed reasonable for Chen to label the KMT as the most dangerous inside enemy who was trying to sell Taiwan out to the Chinese government.

According to the logic of this strategy of naming black sheep,[1] if the KMT was the nation's black sheep because of its various similarities and connections with the Chinese government, it was "reasonable" to add Taiwan's mainlanders to this category of enemy as well. Mainlanders were those Chinese who followed the KMT to Taiwan during 1945–1949, and since then, they have dominated Taiwan's political, economic and cultural systems and became the privileged ethnic group in Taiwan. Most of them were loyal supporters of the KMT, had much stronger economic, cultural and emotional connections with mainland China than other ethnic groups did in Taiwan, and most strongly opposed Taiwan's *de jure* independence of mainland China. As the author of an editorial article in *The China Post* (5 March, 2009) noted, "[a]ccording to Taiwan independence demagogues, 'mainlanders' were responsible for the 28 February incident. Therefore 'mainlanders,' even those born after 28 February

[1] For a similar and more detailed case of naming black sheep in South Korea's domestic nationalism politics, see Shin, Gi-Wook. 2006. *Ethnic nationalism in Korea: Genealogy, politics, and legacy*. Stanford, Calif.: Stanford University Press.

1947, are 'Enemies of Taiwan' guilty of 'Mainlander Original Sin'."[2] Therefore, through the naming black sheep strategy, Mainlanders became Taiwan's black sheep with the "original sin" as well.

An illiberal and undemocratic strategy

The second characteristic of Chen's radical strategy was its illiberal and undemocratic nature on national agenda setting and implementation. Nationalism, especially in its radical and fundamentalist form, is usually not liberal, nor democratic, which always turn to be an advantage for politicians to manipulate it. In Chen's second presidency, to shift the public's attention away from his government's failure and his own corruption, he sanctified the goal of Taiwan's independence and the conduct of loving Taiwan, giving them the highest priority over Taiwan's economic development and other social issues. The message of this sanctification to the public was that nothing was more important than pursuing Taiwan's independence and loving Taiwan. The unspoken part of this message was that Chen and his government were the most genuine pursuers of Taiwan's sacred independence and were also the most sincere Taiwan lovers. The sanctification also justified Chen's close-door policy toward mainland China — although it might be detrimental to Taiwan's economy, it was a necessary way of protecting Taiwan's independence and loving Taiwan (Shi, 2007). In terms of how to pursue Taiwan's independence and love for Taiwan, implicitly, Chen contended that there was only one way for both, which was the way he and his government were doing it. In summary, the whole argument of this radical nationalistic strategy was this: Taiwan's independence was the highest national priority and the most sincere manifestation of loving Taiwan; Chen and his government's policies were the

[2] The author continued to compare "Mainlander Original Sin" with "Jewish Original Sin": "certain details about this tragedy are still unknown, but 'reasoning' that 'mainlanders' set out to kill the Taiwan-born back in 1947 and that this still holds true today based on what is known about 28 February is akin to some Christian Fundamentalists 'reasoning' that 'Jews killed Christ,' and that therefore 'Jews,' even those born long after Christ's crucifixion, are 'Christ killers' guilty of 'Jewish Original Sin.'" http://www.chinapost.com.tw/editorial/taiwan-issues/2009/03/05/198731/Ma-Ying-jeou:.htm accessed on 18 June 2015.

best way to achieve Taiwan's future independence and therefore they loved Taiwan most; anyone who challenged their policies were opposed to Taiwan's independence, were "China conspirators" (because China opposed Taiwan's independence, too), and therefore, did not love Taiwan.

In politics, a strategy that treats political rivals illiberally and undemocratically does not seem radical. However, the strategy becomes radical when a party uses the same illiberal and undemocratic argument against its own members and supporters. During Chen's second term, almost every part of the above radical argument was criticized not only by the KMT and its supporters but also by many DPP's moderate members and supporters. Chen and his government's reactions toward the friendly criticism from their own camp were not different in nature than those toward the KMT's criticism, that is, no matter which camp they were in, as long as they challenged Chen and his government's policies, they were "pro-China" (a somewhat mild label for opponents from the DPP camp) or "China conspirators" (a more severe label for opponents from the rival camp). The common attribute of "pro-China" people and "China conspirators" was that they did not love Taiwan. Following such an argument, the mass movement led by the former DPP chairman against Chen's family corruptions in September 2006 was labeled as "Chinese are bullying Taiwanese president" by Chen's supporters, which helped maintain the TIM fundamentalists' sympathy of Chen and finally enabled him to survive this mass challenge. Similarly, at the end of 2006, 11 former and incumbent DPP legislators, including Lin Cho-shui, who were well-known for their seniority and great contribution to Taiwan's democracy and independence movement, were labeled "Eleven Rebels" by the DPP's fundamentalist supporters because of their criticism of Chen's radical strategy, their moderate position on Taiwan's independence issues, and presumably, the damage to the DPP's solidarity brought by their criticism. Since then, these 11 DPP cadres' influential positions were quickly marginalized in the DPP, indicating the victory of Chen's radical strategy in the party.

Politicized society

The third characteristic of Chen's radical strategy was its tendency to politicize Taiwanese society. Since Chen was re-elected in 2004 through the confrontation movement strategy, he and the DPP seemed to believe that it was better for them to be a leader, rather than a follower, of the public opinion, which meant they needed to take all kinds of initiatives to educate the public to accept their policies, that is, influencing and leading the public opinion rather than following and being constrained by it. The success of their radical campaign strategy during the 2004 presidential election convinced them that it was possible to convert more and more Taiwanese to be pro-independence, and furthermore, to be pro-independence fundamentalists. What they needed to do was to provide extensive pro-independence education to Taiwanese society in not only political fields but also many other fields of Taiwanese's social life. When a variety of fields in the society were linked to a political objective through political education, the politicization of this society was unavoidable.

The most apparently politicized field in Taiwanese society was its social movement sectors. This does not mean that Taiwan's social movement sectors were apolitical before 2000, but means that when the pro-independence issue became the nation's highest priority and the most divisive issue in Taiwan's politics, most social movement organizations split up along pro- vs. anti-independence ideologies as well. Taiwan used to have unified and strong social movement organizations before 2000, but as the pro- vs. anti-independence debate permeated throughout the society, the social movement leaders, who shared common movement causes, often found themselves opposed to each other on the independence issues. Most importantly, as the whole society became constantly and intensively involved in debates and conflicts on the independence issues, the same debates and conflicts among the social movement leaders became more and more prominent, unbearable and unable to be reconciled. Therefore, many social movement organizations started either splitting up or losing those members who had opposed views on the independence issues. As a result, the influence of Taiwan's social movements had declined greatly.[3]

---

[3] The former and current social movement leaders and activists I interviewed during my fieldwork in Taiwan in 2006 and 2007 provided these observations.

Another noticeable politicized field was language use. Language has been an unfortunate object politicized first by the KMT explicitly since 1949 and then by the DPP implicitly since 2000. There are two major dialects of Chinese in Taiwan, Mandarin and Minnan (i.e., Taiwanese), which are the popular spoken languages of the two major ethnic groups in Taiwan, Mainlanders and Minnan (Hoklo) people, respectively. Mandarin, also called the national language, was the official language in mainland China since the early 1910s and brought by the KMT and Mainlanders to Taiwan in 1949. Since 1949, the KMT has treated Mandarin as the major symbol of a unified Chinese national culture and Minnan as that of a Chinese local culture. Therefore, to repress the resistance and independence tendency of Minnan people in Taiwan, the KMT had continued to use Mandarin as the national language and prohibited speaking Minnan in public. During most of the KMT regime, speaking Mandarin was a prerequisite for Minnan elite to secure their positions in political, economic and cultural fields, and for ordinary Taiwanese, it was also a fashionable symbol of being educated by and identifying with the privileged Chinese national culture. As the democracy and pro-independence movements became more and more popular in Taiwan since the 1980s, the movement activists often intentionally spoke Minnan dialect in public gatherings to attract Minnan people's participation, thus speaking Minnan gradually became a symbol of resistance and pro-independence. Since the DPP took power in 2000, although Mandarin continued to be Taiwan's national language, its popular status has declined greatly. On the other hand, Minnan dialect's status has improved significantly, largely because President Chen and other Minnan politicians spoke it purposely on many important public occasions. Gradually and implicitly, Mandarin and Minnan dialects have experienced reverse politicization. Minnan dialect has been called Taiwanese and become an important symbol of Taiwanese local culture, which was once repressed by the KMT but now liberated by the DPP. Now it was Mainlander politicians who needed to learn and speak Taiwanese (Minnan) to show their identification with Taiwan and to attract Minnan people's support. Currently it is also fashionable for ordinary people in Taiwan to speak Taiwanese. During Chen's second term, his radical strategy politicized language use to a greater extent — not being able to speak Taiwanese became unacceptable to many pro-independence people because they believed that indicated a lack of love for Taiwan. In such a politicized atmosphere, it was not rare that some Minnan business persons started refusing to do business with or recruit those Mainlanders who could not speak Taiwanese. What was even more common was that some Minnan taxi drivers refused to serve the people who could not speak Taiwanese. These cases indicated a dramatic change in Taiwan's society since the democratization because previously only the reverse might happen, that is, Minnan people who could not speak Mandarin would be discriminated by Mainlanders on various occasions.

Chen and his government's de-China campaign, which started as early as in his first term and became more radical in his second term, further politicized the society in a variety of ways. The purpose of this campaign was to separate Taiwan from mainland China more explicitly and reduce Chinese historical influence in Taiwan through cleaning out Chinese elements in political, economic and cultural fields. Some of these de-China actions were justifiable and not very controversial to the public such as reducing the contents about mainland China but increasing those about Taiwan in school textbooks. Under the KMT regime, the government had purposely increased the contents about mainland China to overweight those about Taiwan to a ridiculous extent in textbooks, which well served the KMT's political purpose but contradicted the educational goals in Taiwan. However, many other de-China actions such as rectifying the names of streets, stamps, historical buildings and state and private enterprises through deleting the China-related terms often were controversial and sometimes led to violent conflicts between de-China campaign advocates and opponents. Especially during Chen's second term, some radical de-China actions, like requiring important Taiwanese enterprises and institutes to replace "China" with "Taiwan" in their names and removing and then destroying the previous KMT leader Chiang Kai-shek's statues all over Taiwan, led to strong resistance from different social groups. In the repressive atmosphere created by Chen's radical strategy, the resistance of these groups was implicitly imposed political connotation, that is, the people who resisted the de-China campaign did not love Taiwan and were pro-China. A government usually does not want to see social resistance and conflicts. But in the case of Chen's government, these resistance and conflicts could help it identify "black sheep" (i.e., those who did not love Taiwan and were pro-China), and then, through the conflicts with these "black sheep", enhance the solidarity among its own fundamentalists. Therefore, Chen and his government might have welcomed these social conflicts.

A conflict-ridden Taiwan

From the above discussion, we can find that Chen's radical strategy also had a tendency to create conflicts not only in political fields but also in Taiwanese people's ordinary life. The radical strategy's techniques such as naming black sheep and the illiberal and undemocratic argument were first fully demonstrated through Congress debates, Chen and his government officials' public speeches, talk shows, and political commentaries on TV, newspapers and other media sources. The techniques were then quickly learned by TIM fundamentalists who found that such a strategy was straightforward, powerful, and especially, easy to use. The politicization of the society by the radical strategy also provided them with ample opportunities to use this strategy in their daily life. As we can realize from the above discussion of the strategy's characteristics, when the radical strategy spread from the political field to other fields, conflicts followed to these fields as well.

Besides the fields of social movements, language use, and those influenced by the de-China campaign, the ethnic relation was another field where conflicts between Mainlanders and Minnan people increased, following the spread of the radical strategy. Being named black sheep with the implicit "original sin", many Mainlanders experienced hostile treatments by the DPP politicians and Minnan people in their daily life. Some Mainlanders found the discriminative situation was unbearable and left Taiwan temporarily. One of my interviewees in Taiwan, who was a second generation Mainlander and frustrated by this naming strategy, left Taiwan for a foreign country in 2003 to escape from this depressive environment. However, after one year when he came back to Taiwan, he found the Mainlanders' situation even worse under Chen's radical strategy. In the street conflicts between Minnan people and Mainlanders during the de-China activities or other political gatherings, Minnan people often shouted to Mainlanders: "Out of Taiwan, go back to China, you Chinese!" Another more insulting term frequently used by pro-independence people for Mainlanders was "Chinese pig." They used this term not only in their sensational public gatherings but also in their private life.[4] Enraged by the insult and Chen's radical strategy, a government official who was a Mainlander wrote a series of criticisms anonymously in his blog, calling pro-independence people "rube Taiwanese" and Taiwan a "ghost island" during 2006–2007 when Chen's radical strategy reached its heyday.[5]

A Double-Edged Sword of the Radical Strategy

After we have a deeper understanding of the characteristics of Chen's radical strategy, we can start discussing the different impacts of this strategy on people with different social characteristics and political orientations. I propose that the radical strategy had a double-edged sword impact — it successfully consolidated the TIM fundamentalists' support, but disaffected many previous moderate supporters. In general, this argument does not contradict, but complement, the popular argument that Chen's poor economic performance and his family's corruptions had great negative impact on the popular support for the DPP. From the review of Chen's radical strategy, we can find that the strategy was his rational reaction to two structural constraints in his second term: first, the trouble of his government's poor performance and his family's corruption scandals; second, the strategic dilemma sustained by the conflicting expectations of the TIM's fundamentalists and moderates. Simply put, Chen tried to use the radical strategy, relying on the fundamentalists, to make up for his lost credit as the President by improving his credit as the TIM leader. However,

---

[4] One of my Minnan interviewees told me that his father often called Mainlanders Chinese pigs after getting drunk. His father became a very radical TIM fundamentalist during the DPP administration, which surprised him very much. The interviewee believed that this was mainly because of Taiwan's radical political atmosphere which was especially conveyed through pro-independence media during the DPP administration.

[5] In March 2009, this official was fired by the government due to these critical articles, although he received strong support from many Mainlanders. For details, please see http://www.onlineb2bsupport.com/taiwan-deplomatic-officers-blogposts-ignite-ethnic-controversy/ accessed on June 17, 2009.

the radical strategy brought Chen into a vicious circle: His poor performance in mending the economy and the fundamentalists' criticism of his concessions on the independence issues had pushed him to become more radical, but as he became more radical, the economic performance became worse due to the radical close-door policy. Meanwhile, he received more criticism from moderate supporters, all of which forced him to rely more on the fundamentalists and become even more radical to fight back the criticism from both moderate supporters and the opposition camp. Therefore, although my argument is built on and does not contradict the popular argument, it presents a more interactive process involving a differentiated category of the DPP's support base than the popular argument, and additionally, it emphasizes the contrary impacts of the radical strategy on the different constituents of the DPP's support base.

The evidence for the following discussion are mainly from the 2008 post-presidential election survey (i.e., TEDS2008P),[6] which was conducted by the Election Study Center at the National Cheng Chi University in Taiwan soon after the presidential election in March 2008.

Consolidated fundamentalists

The Taiwanese scholar Cheng (2007) found that around 2004 and 2005 the DPP's fundamentalist supporters had four major social characteristics in terms of age, education, ethnicity and occupation: they were usually over 50, less educated (mostly with junior high or below education level), Minnan people and farmers and workers. In Chapter 3, by comparing these people's identification with the DPP to other social groups' in 2004 and 2008, I found an "irrational" trend among those who were 60 years old or above, less educated (i.e., junior high or below), residents in southern Taiwan and farmers. In other words, during 2004–2008, these people became more

[6] Data analyzed in this chapter were from Taiwan's Election and Democratization Studies, 2005–2008(IV): the Survey of the Presidential Election in 2008 (TEDS 2008P) (NSC 96-2420-H-004-017). The coordinator of multi-year project TEDS is Professor Chi Huang (National Chengchi University). TEDS2008P is a project on the Presidential election in 2008. The principal investigator is Professor Ching-hsin Yu. More information is on TEDS website (http://www.tedsnet.org, accessed on 13 June 2015). The author appreciates the assistance in providing data by the institute and individuals aforementioned. The author is alone responsible for views expressed herein.

"irrational" on their support for the DPP because their families' economic fortune was most likely to be worse off in 2008, but they were still more likely than other social groups to support the DPP, and like Chen, while in 2004, they were not so "irrational." This increased "irrationality" was an apparent sign of increased loyalty and consolidation among the DPP's fundamentalists. In Chapter 3, I have proposed that Chen's radical movement strategy was the major factor contributing to these fundamentalists' consolidated support for Chen and the DPP.

Why are these groups of people more susceptible than others to Chen's radical movement strategy? To answer this question, we need to explore the key natures of these social groups and the radical strategy and see how the two sides' natures matched each other logically. The first nature of these four groups of people is that all of them were economically disadvantaged social groups in Taiwan. In highly modernized societies such as Taiwan, it is common that elders, less educated and farmers are economically disadvantaged; they usually have lower incomes and are more vulnerable than other social groups to economic fluctuation. People in southern Taiwan are also economically disadvantaged *vis-à-vis* those in northern and central Taiwan because of the concentration of sunset industries and the relatively less development in the south. On the other side, Chen's radical strategy in the economic field showed a strong nature of populism and economic nationalism, which was welcomed by disadvantaged groups in Taiwan. Specifically, the radical strategy contended that although the increased economic exchange between Taiwan and mainland China under the open-door policy would benefit Taiwan's business elite, it might be detrimental to ordinary Taiwanese, especially to those disadvantaged groups. For example, they argued that under the open-door policy more investments and plants would leave Taiwan for mainland China due to mainland China's cheaper labor cost, larger consumer market, and many other business advantages. Consequently, more ordinary Taiwanese would lose their jobs in Taiwan. As the unemployment rate goes up, it will become more difficult for those in the disadvantaged groups to find a job. The more advantaged groups, like those younger, better educated, sunrise industry workers, may go to mainland China to find even better jobs, but those disadvantaged groups can only stay in Taiwan and suffer the economic downturn. The open-door policy may also hurt Taiwan's farmers because cheaper Chinese agriculture products will pour into Taiwan and severely reduce Taiwanese farmers' income from selling their own products. Along this line of argument, it is necessary for the government to use the close-door policy not only to prevent Taiwan from being more dependent on mainland China economically but also to protect ordinary Taiwanese, especially those economically disadvantaged, from job and income insecurity.

The above four groups of fundamentalists are indeed more likely than other social groups to be convinced by such a populist and economic nationalism argument. As the following Table 4.1 shows, in the four social categories defined by age, education, residence region and occupation, the social groups of 60 years old or above, less educated (i.e., junior high or below), southern residents and farmers have the highest percent of people believing that both Taiwan and themselves would become worse off economically under the open-door policy, and at the same time, have the lowest percent of people believing that both Taiwan and themselves would become better off under that policy.[7] It suggests that these four social groups would be more likely than other social groups to oppose the open-door policy proposed by the opposition parties but support Chen's closed-door policy. Economically disadvantaged groups that already had the highest percent of families who underwent economic misfortunes might find Chen's close-door policy particularly attractive for protecting their endangered economic status.

There is one more piece of evidence showing why these four social groups were more likely to trust Chen's governmental promise and capability of protecting them. The following Table 4.2 shows the percent of people in each social group who chose "social welfare" as Chen's best achievement in his second term. We can see that the four fundamentalist groups, that is, those 60 years old or above, less educated, southern residences and farmers were more likely than other social groups to be satisfied with Chen's performance in social welfare. In other words, these economically disadvantaged people might have felt more strongly about

[7] The age group of 60 years old or above has the second-highest percent of people believing they will be better off under the open-door policy. The age group of 50–59 has the highest percent of that category.

Table 4.1 Percent of People in Each Social Group Possibly Accepting the Open-door Policy, 2008

(Unit: % of people in each social group)

	Will Taiwan be Better off Under the Open-Door Policy?			Will You be Better off Under the Open-Door Policy?		
	Better off	**Worse off**	**The Same**	**Better off**	**Worse off**	**The Same**
Age						
20–29	53.2	21.2	25.5	15.2	15.8	69
30–39	49.9	26.4	23.7	15.9	18.6	65.4
40–49	45.1	31.2	23.7	17.5	22.7	59.8
50–59	42	40.5	17.5	10.4	24.6	65
60 and above	*35.4*	*41.4*	*23.2*	*12*	*30.7*	*57.9*
Chi-square test	$n = 1579$, $\chi^2 = 46.326$, df = 8, $p < 0.001$			$n = 1635$, $\chi^2 = 29.743$, df = 8, $p < 0.001$		
Education						
College and above	62	20.1	17.9	20.5	11.9	67.7
Senior high and vocational	49.3	28.3	22.4	15.9	19.7	64.4
Junior high and below	*29.4*	*42.5*	*28.1*	*8.7*	*31.1*	*60.2*
Chi-square test	$n = 1576$, $\chi^2 = 97.934$, df = 4, $p < 0.001$			$n = 1634$, $\chi^2 = 63.684$, df = 4, $p < 0.001$		

(Continued)

Table 4.1 (*Continued*)

	Will Taiwan be Better off Under the Open-Door Policy?			**Will You be Better off Under the Open-Door Policy?**		
	Better off	**Worse off**	**The Same**	**Better off**	**Worse off**	**The Same**
Residence Region						
North and Central	50.9	26.1	23	16.9	18.1	65
South	*35.7*	*41.2*	*23.2*	*9.1*	*30.4*	*60.5*
Chi-square test	$n = 1579$, $\chi^2 = 41.775$, df = 2, $p < 0.001$			$n = 1637$, $\chi^2 = 40.080$, df = 2, $p < 0.001$		
Class						
Upper-middle class	53.9	27.7	18.3	17.7	17.5	64.8
Lower-middle class	53.8	22.4	23.8	18.8	15.9	65.3
Workers	34.8	36.9	28.3	9.7	27.6	62.7
Farmers	*23.5*	*50*	*26.5*	*8.0*	*37.5*	*54.5*
Chi-square test	$n = 1209$, $\chi^2 = 65.895$, df = 6, $p < 0.001$			$n = 1243$, $\chi^2 = 45.705$, df = 6, $p < 0.001$		

Data source: TEDS2008P.

Table 4.2 Percent of People in Each Social Group Choosing Social Welfare as the Chen Government's Best Achievement in His Second Term, 2008

(Unit: % of people in each social group)

	Social Welfare	Other Achievements
Age		
20–29	12.5	87.5
30–39	14.7	85.3
40–49	19.2	80.8
50–59	18.2	81.8
60 and above	*25.0*	*75.0*
Chi-square test	$n = 1592, \chi^2 = 17.992$, df = 4, $p = 0.001$	
Education		
College and above	9.7	90.3
Senior high and vocational	16.2	83.8
Junior high and below	*25.3*	*74.7*
Chi-square test	$n = 1591, \chi^2 = 36.783$, df = 2, $p < 0.001$	
Residence Region		
North and Central	15.3	84.7
South	*21.8*	*78.2*
Chi-square test	$n = 1591, \chi^2 = 10.147$, df = 1, $p = 0.001$	
Class		
Upper-middle class	12.8	87.2
Lower-middle class	14.1	85.9
Workers	22.0	78.0
Farmers	*35.1*	*64.9*
Chi-square test	$n = 1213, \chi^2 = 34.343$, df = 3, $p < 0.001$	

Data source: TEDS2008P.

the care provided by Chen's governmental social welfare programs, which would enhance their belief that the Chen government was a committed protector of disadvantaged groups. This enhanced belief in the government might make them more likely to accept the government's closed-door policy, a policy seeming to share the same nature of protecting the disadvantaged as social welfare programs.

The second key nature of Chen's radical strategy is its appeal to Taiwanese nationalistic sentiment. On the side of the four fundamentalist groups, almost all of them constantly showed the strongest Taiwanese nationalistic sentiment[8] since the mid-1990s. As Figures 4.1–4.4 show, except the age group of 60 or above in 1996 and 2004, all the other three groups of less educated, southern residents and farmers showed the strongest Taiwanese nationalistic sentiment in their respective social category from 1996 through 2008.

The age group of 60 or above showed the strongest nationalistic sentiment among all the age groups in 2000 and 2008, and the second strongest nationalistic sentiment in 2004. Therefore, these four groups of people were the ready receivers for a strategy mobilizing Taiwanese nationalistic sentiment. They were the richest soil for the tree of Taiwanese nationalistic sentiment to grow stronger. No wonder during 2004–2008 they became more "irrational" under the influence of Chen's radical strategy. A popular saying in the South during the DPP administration's second term characterizes this "irrationality" vividly. It says, "even if we are starving, we still support Chen!" (duzi e bianbian, yeyao ting A-bian! i.e., 肚子饿扁扁，也要挺阿扁！), meaning that although the fundamentalists

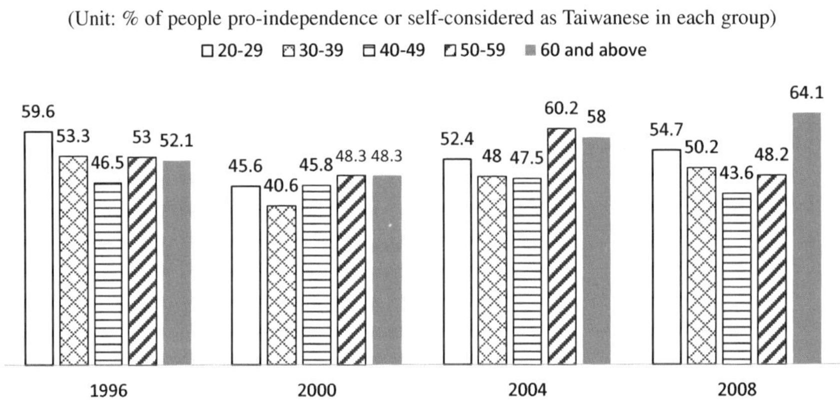

Figure 4.1 Level of Nationalistic Sentiment in Different Social Groups: By Age, 1996–2008

[8] As in Chapter 3, a person is defined as having Taiwanese nationalistic sentiment if he or she was pro-independence or considered him/herself as Taiwanese only.

(Unit: % of people pro-independence or self-considered as Taiwanese in each group)

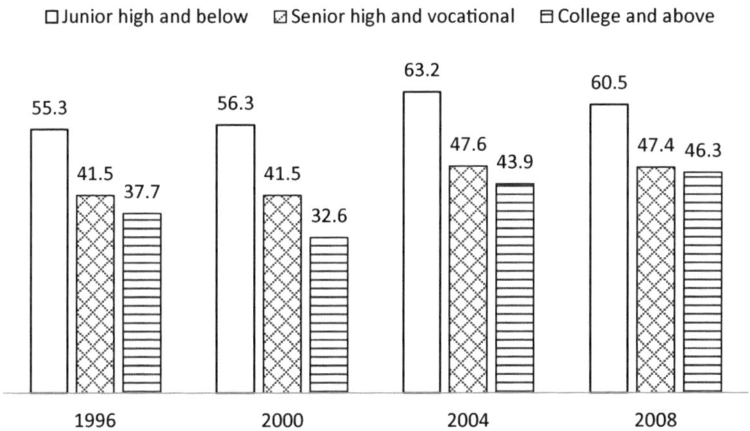

Figure 4.2 Level of Nationalistic Sentiment in Different Social Groups: By Education, 1996–2008

(Unit: % of people pro-independence or self-considered as Taiwanese in each group)

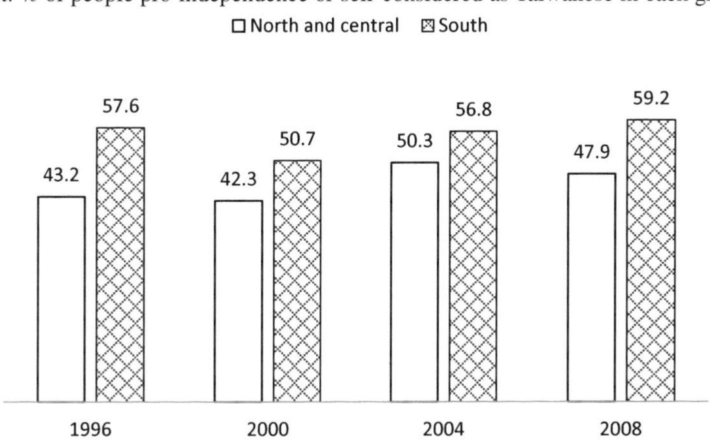

Figure 4.3 Level of Nationalistic Sentiment in Different Social Groups: By Residence Region, 1996–2008

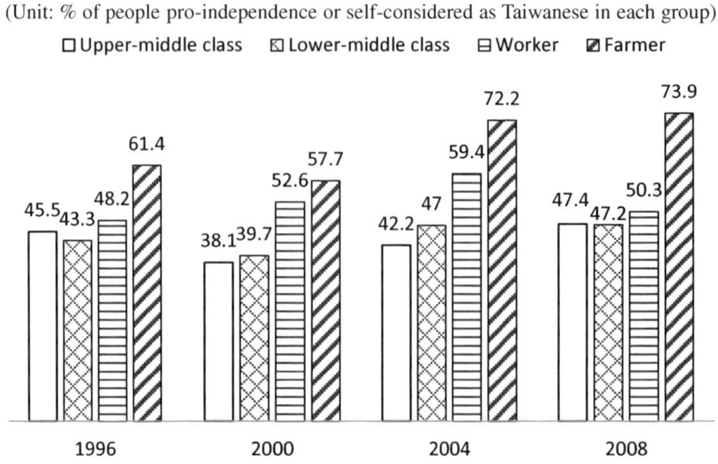

Figure 4.4 Level of Nationalistic Sentiment in Different Social Groups: By Class, 1996–2008

Data sources for Figures 4.1–4.4: The data are recoded from four datasets: Democracy, Political Parties and Taiwan's Mass Politics: Research on the Electorate in the 1996 Presidential Election (NSC 85-2414-H031-004-Q3), An Interdisciplinary Study of Voting Behavior in the Presidential Election in 2000 (NSC 89-2414-H-004-021-SSS), Taiwan's Election and Democratization Studies, 2004 (TEDS 2004P) (NSC92-2420-H-031-004) and Taiwan's Election and Democratization Study, 2005–2008(III): Legislative Elections (TEDS 2008L).

underwent economic hardship under Chen's presidency, they would not withdraw support of him.

An important purpose of the radical strategy was to transform popular nationalistic sentiment into support for Chen and his government. The formula of this transformation was first to simplify the meaning of Taiwanese nationalism into a single term, "loving Taiwan," and then monopolize the right of defining what conducts were "loving Taiwan." Chen and his government argued that only the genuine Taiwanese government could protect Taiwan from the Chinese government's annexation conspiracy. Therefore, if one loves Taiwan, one must support the Taiwanese government. They further argued that the KMT was not a genuine Taiwanese party because it had been a party of Chinese immigrants, and even now, Mainlanders were over represented in its leadership, so the KMT government would not be a genuine Taiwanese government.

The final conclusion of this formula is, if one loves Taiwan, they must support the DPP government, the most genuine Taiwanese regime. This whole formulation was simplified by the DPP as a nationalistic slogan: "If you love Taiwan, you must support Taiwanese/local regime." Table 4.3 shows the approval rate of this slogan in each social group. We can find that the four fundamentalist groups have the highest approval rate of this

Table 4.3 Percent of People in Each Social Group Agreeing or Disagreeing with the Statement: "If you love Taiwan, you must support local/Taiwanese regime." 2008

(Unit: % of people in each social group)

	Agree	Disagree
Age		
20–29	41.7	58.3
30–39	39.4	60.6
40–49	43.2	56.8
50–59	46.8	53.2
60 and above	*61.7*	*38.3*
Chi-square test	$n = 1671$, $\chi^2 = 36.938$, df = 4, $p < 0.001$	
Education		
College and above	30.4	69.6
Senior high and vocational	38.7	61.3
Junior high and below	*66.1*	*33.9*
Chi-square test	$n = 1668$, $\chi^2 = 138.798$, df = 2, $p < 0.001$	
Residence Region		
North and Central	40.9	59.1
South	*55.9*	*44.1*
Chi-square test	$n = 1671$, $\chi^2 = 32.462$, df = 1, $p < 0.001$	
Class		
Upper-middle class	30.5	69.5
Lower-middle class	42.5	57.5
Workers	54	46
Farmers	*76.4*	*23.6*
Chi-square test	$n = 1268$, $\chi^2 = 91.715$, df = 3, $p < 0.001$	

Data source: TEDS 2008P.

slogan. In light of this finding, these fundamentalists' "irrationality" in supporting the DPP becomes more understandable. Under the influence of the radical strategy, they tended to believe that even though their families experienced economic hardship under Chen's presidency, they could not stop supporting him and his government, since not supporting him would indicate they did not love Taiwan.

The four fundamentalist groups' stronger susceptibility to the radical strategy may also be strengthened by their weaker susceptibility to the negative consequences of the radical strategy. In other words, they were less likely than other groups to feel the negative consequences of the radical strategy, which made them easier to accept the radical strategy. The following Table 4.4 shows the percent of people in each social group who chose "ethnic relations" and "cross-strait relations" as the worst performance of Chen's government in his second term. We find that these four fundamentalist groups were less likely than other groups to be dissatisfied with Chen's government performance in ethnic relations and cross-strait relations. Since the previous discussion has shown that two of the major negative consequences of the radical strategy were deteriorated ethnic relations and escalated political conflicts between Taiwan and mainland China, if these four groups of people were less likely to feel these negative consequences, they were more likely to support the radical strategy.

Disaffected moderates

I have mentioned in the previous discussion that Lin Cho-shui, a well-known TIM theorist and senior DPP member, opposed Chen's radical strategy and later was alienated by the DPP's fundamentalists as one of the "Eleven Rebels." Lin (2006) believed that there had been three different lines of pro-independence throughout the DPP's history: the de-independence line, the moderate line and the radical line. In his view, the de-independence line's advocates were not really committed to pursuing Taiwan's complete independence of mainland China because of their fear of the overwhelming backlash from the domestic and international anti-independence forces, and therefore, held Taiwan's independence only as a bargaining chip in the domestic and international politics. He believed that Chen's concession strategy during

Table 4.4 Percent of People in Each Social Group Choosing Ethnic Relations and Cross-Strait Relations as the Chen Government's Worst Performance, 2008

(Unit: % of people in each social group)

	Ethnic Relations & Cross-Strait Relations	Other Issues
Age		
20–29	14	86
30–39	16.2	83.8
40–49	17.6	82.4
50–59	19.8	80.2
60 and above	*10.2*	*89.8*
Chi-square test	$n = 1616, \chi^2 = 10.547, \text{df} = 4, p < 0.05$	
Education		
College and above	20.4	79.6
Senior high and vocational	16.9	83.1
Junior high and below	*9.9*	*90.1*
Chi-square test	$n = 1612, \chi^2 = 18.752, \text{df} = 2, p < 0.001$	
Residence Region		
North and Central	18.8	81.2
South	*9.4*	*90.6*
Chi-square test	$n = 1617, \chi^2 = 22.844, \text{df} = 1, p < 0.001$	
Class		
Upper-middle class	21	79
Lower-middle class	18.3	81.7
Workers	10.3	89.7
Farmers	*6.1*	*93.9*
Chi-square test	$n = 1246, \chi^2 = 25.550, \text{df} = 3, p < 0.001$	

Data source: TEDS2008P.

2000–2002 was an application of this de-independence line. He also believed that since 2003, Chen's confrontational and then radical strategies were his opportunistic reaction to the unfavorable political environment, which tried to enhance the fundamentalists' support. Lin criticized the radical line for its oversimplification of pursuing Taiwan's independence to an all-in-one battle: rectifying the state name and making a new constitution for Taiwan. In contrast, he supported the moderate line which recognized many obstacles in pursuing Taiwan's complete independence and proposed to use gradual ways to achieve the independence goal. Following the moderate line, Lin also opposed Chen's close-door policy. As shown by the marginalization of the 11 moderate DPP cadres, including Lin in the DPP at the end of 2006, the moderate line was stigmatized and repressed by the DPP's leadership.

Chen's radical strategy was criticized not only by those moderate DPP cadres within the party but also by many pro-independence scholars, professionals and social movement activists, many of whom were not DPP members but well known for their long-term pro-DPP stance. During their public petitions for Chen's resignation in July 2006, many of the petition participants criticized Chen for his involvement in the corruption scandals as well as the illiberal and undemocratic nature of his radical strategy and the negative consequences caused by the strategy. For example, a popular political scientist and one of the 15 initiators of the first petition, Wu Rwei-ren, who was also a long-term pro-independence and pro-democracy scholar and activist in Taiwan, called for a more liberal and more democratic pro-independence strategy in his speech at the first public petition meeting. At the second public petition meeting, he asked political leaders to pay more attention to the negative impact of their mobilization strategy on Taiwan's ethnic relations. Wu and many other petition participants believed that the pro-independence movement could only prevail with its previous liberal and democratic nature, and on the other side, an illiberal and undemocratic nationalism movement, which was promoted by Chen's radical strategy, would lead Taiwan to a dead end and produce significant undesirable social consequences such as the politicization of the society and deteriorated ethnic relations. Wu seemed to especially detest Chen's strategy of naming black sheep. He often mocked it in his critical public speeches, saying that since he was well-known for his long-term pro-independence stance, those black sheep finders would not be able to use his criticism of Chen as the evidence to name him another pro-China black sheep.[9]

---

[9]The author attended two of his public speeches in 2007 and 2008 and heard his criticism of Chen's radical strategy and mockery of naming black sheep at both occasions.

The criticism of Chen's radical strategy by the above moderate DPP cadres, previous pro-DPP scholars, professionals, and social movement activists found an echo in people who were relatively younger (i.e., 20–39 years old), better educated (i.e., college or above), northern and central Taiwan residents and the middle class (including both upper-middle and lower-middle classes). By comparing the above social groups to fundamentalists, who were parts of disadvantaged social groups (i.e., the older, less educated, southern Taiwan residents and farmers), it is not difficult to understand why these moderates disliked Chen's radical strategy. First of all, as the previous Table 4.1 shows, a higher percent of the fundamentalists supported the close-door policy because more of them believed that the close-door policy would protect their disadvantaged economic fortune from becoming worse; in contrast, a higher percent of the moderates, who were generally privileged social groups and would benefit from the open-door policy, disliked the closed-door policy because it would significantly reduce the opportunities and benefits brought by the open and frequent exchanges between Taiwan and mainland China. Additionally, Table 4.1 also shows that a much higher percent of the moderates (actually, most of them) believed that Taiwan would become better off under the open-door policy. These findings suggest that the moderates should be more likely than the fundamentalists to believe that the close-door policy was detrimental to both themselves and Taiwan, and therefore, to oppose the close-door policy which was a key component of Chen's radical strategy.

Similarly, previous Tables 4.2–4.4 and Figures 4.1–4.4 show the moderates' completely opposite patterns as compared to the fundamentalists' on a variety of attitudes related to the radical strategy, which generally suggests that while the fundamentalists were the most likely to support the radical strategy, it is the moderates that were the least likely to do so. In other words, they were the most likely to oppose Chen's radical strategy. Specifically, Table 4.2 suggests that while the fundamentalists were the most likely to believe Chen's promise and capability of protecting disadvantaged groups through its close-door policy, the moderates should be the least likely to believe so because, while the highest percent of the fundamentalists chose social welfare as Chen's best achievement, the lowest percent of the moderates did so. Figures 4.1–4.4 indicate that while the fundamentalists had the strongest nationalistic sentiment since 1996, which made them the most susceptible to Chen's nationalistic mobilization, the moderates were the social groups with the weakest nationalistic sentiment since then, which should make them the least susceptible to such mobilization.[10] Table 4.3 shows that while the fundamentalists were the most likely to accept the core argument of Chen's radical strategy, "if you love Taiwan, you must support Taiwanese/local regime," the moderates were the least likely to accept it. Finally, Table 4.4 suggests that while the fundamentalists were the least likely to "feel" the negative impact of Chen's radical strategy on the ethnic relations in Taiwan and the cross-strait relations between Taiwan and mainland China, the moderates were the most likely to "feel" such negative impact because the lowest percent of the fundamentalists, but the highest percent of the moderates, chose "ethnic relations" and "cross-strait relations" as Chen's worst performance.[11] Therefore, it suggests once more that the moderates should be more likely than the fundamentalists to oppose the radical strategy.

A complete argument about the double-edged sword effect of the radical movement strategy

The above two sections provide some strong evidence suggesting that while the fundamentalists tended to support Chen's radical strategy, the moderates tended to oppose it. My ultimate argument according to the movement government framework is that the fundamentalists' support of Chen's radical strategy turned into a vote for the DPP in the 2008 presidential election, and in contrast, the moderates' opposition of the radical strategy turned into their lower support of the DPP in the election. In other words, Chen's radical strategy was a double-edged sword, which consolidated the fundamentalists' support, but disaffected the moderates at the same time. To make this argument complete and more convincing, I need

[10] Except for the younger group (i.e., 20–39 years old) whose Taiwanese nationalistic sentiment was relatively weaker than farmers' sentiment, but stronger than some others' since 2000.

[11] Except for the younger group (i.e., 20–39 years old) who were more likely than the fundamentalist group (i.e., 60 years old or above) to choose these two issues as Chen government's worst performance, but less likely than the other age groups to do so.

to present two more pieces of evidence. First, I need to find the evidence showing that individuals' attitude about the radical strategy was correlated with their voting decision in the 2008 presidential election; second, there should be evidence showing that the moderates were indeed less likely than the fundamentalists to vote for the DPP in the 2008 election. Together with the previous evidence about the fundamentalists and the moderates' different attitudes about the radical strategy, the three pieces of evidence provide the three necessary components of my argument: (1) people who opposed the radical strategy were less likely than those who supported it to vote for the DPP in 2008; (2) the moderates were more likely than the fundamentalists to oppose the radical strategy; and (3) the moderates were less likely than the fundamentalists to vote for the DPP in 2008.

From the previous discussion, we have seen that people's attitudes about three issues, that is, the open-door policy, the highly nationalistic slogan, "If you love Taiwan, you must support the local/Taiwanese regime," and Chen's government performance on ethnic relations and cross-strait relations, can indirectly indicate their attitudes about the radical strategy. Therefore, a binary logistic regression of individuals' voting decisions by these three indicators may reveal their (and indirectly, the radical strategy's) independent effect on people's voting decision. The following Table 4.5 shows the results of such a regression model. Specifically, the dependent variable in the following model is binary: vote for the DPP vs. the KMT, with vote for the KMT as the reference and the control variables include gender, age, education and ethnicity. The interested independent variables include the three attitude indicators with opposing the radical strategy as the references: (1) attitude about the open-door policy with three categories, opposition (because the individual believed his/her family would be worse off under the open-door policy), neutral (because the individual believed the open-door policy would have no impact on his/her family's economic fortune) and support (because the individual believed his/her family would be better off under the open-door policy), with support as the reference; (2) attitude about the slogan, "If you love Taiwan, you must support local/Taiwanese regime," including two categories, agree and disagree, with disagree as the reference; and (3) the indicator of how susceptible the individual was to the negative impact of the radical strategy, including two categories, "susceptible"

Table 4.5 Binary Logistic Regression of Individual Voting Decision: Vote for the DPP vs. the KMT (ref.), 2008

Independent Variables	Co-ef.	Odds Ratio
Ethnicity		
Minnan	2.511***	12.320
Kejia	2.034***	7.644
Mainlander (ref.)	—	—
Gender		
Male	0.569***	1.767
Female (ref.)	—	—
Age		
20–29	0.296	1.344
30–39	0.243	1.275
40–49	0.353	1.423
50–59	0.720*	2.055
60 and above (ref.)	—	—
Education		
Lower (junior high or below)	–0.177	0.838
Middle (senior high or vocational)	–0.285	0.752
Higher (college or above) (ref.)	—	—
Attitude about the open-door policy		
Opposition	2.785***	16.193
Neutral	1.338***	3.810
Support (ref.)	—	—
Attitude about the nationalistic slogan of unconditionally supporting local/Taiwanese regime		
Agree	1.696***	5.454
Disagree (ref.)	—	—
Susceptibleness to the radical strategy's negative impact		
Not susceptible	0.388†	1.474
Susceptible (ref.)	—	—
Intercept	–5.947***	
–2LL	969.133***	
N	1075	

Note: TEDS2008P.

†$p \leq 0.1$, *$p \leq 0.05$, **$p \leq 0.01$, ***$p \leq 0.001$.

(because the individual chose ethnic relations and cross-strait relations as the Chen government's worst performance) and "not susceptible" (because the individual chose other issues as the Chen government's worst performance), with "susceptible" as the reference.

The regression results generally support my argument that people who opposed the radical strategy were less likely than those who supported it to vote for the DPP in 2008. Specifically, the results show that those who believed their families would become better off under the open-door policy, and therefore, those who opposed the close-door policy were less likely than others to vote for the DPP. Those who did not accept the nationalistic slogan were less likely than those who accepted it to vote for the DPP, and those who were more susceptible to the negative impact of Chen's radical strategy were less likely than those who were less susceptible to it to vote for the DPP in 2008.[12]

The last piece of evidence we need to find is that the moderates were indeed less likely than the fundamentalists to vote for the DPP in 2008. The following cross-tables of individuals' voting decisions by their age, education, residence region and class/occupation present such evidence. Specifically, Table 4.6 shows that the younger group of 20–39 years old, the better educated of college-or-above level, the northern and central Taiwan residents, and the lower-middle and upper-middle classes were indeed less likely than the elders of 60 years old or above, the less educated of junior high-or-below level, the southern Taiwan residents and farmers to vote for the DPP in 2008, respectively.

Therefore, I have found the evidence to support the three necessary components of my argument about the double-edged sword effect of Chen's radical movement strategy. To repeat, the three components are: 1) people who opposed the radical strategy were less likely than those who supported it to vote for the DPP in 2008; 2) the moderates were more likely than the fundamentalists to oppose the radical strategy; and 3) the moderates were less likely than the fundamentalists to vote for the DPP in 2008.

If we compare my above argument to the popular argument, we can see how the movement government framework helps us develop the

[12] Please note the significance level of this variable's effect is < 0.1, not as good as those of the other two variables' which are < 0.001.

Table 4.6 Percent of People in Each Social Group Voting for the DPP or the KMT in the 2008 Presidential Election

(Unit: % of people in each social group)

	Vote for the DPP	Vote for the KMT
Age		
20–29	37.8	62.2
30–39	30.9	69.1
40–49	34.6	65.4
50–59	44.4	55.6
60 and above	*40.1*	*59.5*
Chi-square test	$n = 1440$, $\chi^2 = 13.098$, df = 4, $p = 0.01$	
Education		
College and above	30.7	69.3
Senior high and vocational	33	67
Junior high and below	*47.2*	*52.8*
Chi-square test	$n = 1439$, $\chi^2 = 30.502$, df = 2, $p < 0.001$	
Residence Region		
North and Central	30.8	69.2
South	*51.1*	*48.9*
Chi-square test	$n = 1441$, $\chi^2 = 54.770$, df = 1, $p < 0.001$	
Class		
Upper-middle class	33.1	66.9
Lower-middle class	29.7	70.3
Workers	46.3	53.7
Farmers	*50.5*	*49.5*
Chi-square test	$n = 1103$, $\chi^2 = 29.002$, df = 3, $p < 0.001$	

Data source: TEDS2008P.

argument about the double-edged sword effect of the radical movement strategy. First of all, as we have seen in the previous chapters, the popular argument emphasizes the negative effect of Chen's poor economic performance and his family's corruption scandals on popular support for the DPP. From the perspective of the movement government, such an argument is inadequate because in explaining the changing popular support for the DPP, it only pays attention to the DPP government's governmental role and overlooks its movement role, and especially, does not consider the dynamic relations between the two roles. In contrast, the movement government framework provides a systematic way to investigate how the DPP government and President Chen Shui-bian used different strategies to deal with the strategic tension and dilemmas between the government's two roles, and how these strategies influenced different social groups' support for the DPP. Second, the popular argument tends to view the DPP's support base as a homogeneous group that reacted to the President and his government's performance in the same way. The movement government framework distinguishes not only between the DPP government's proponents and opponents, but also between its moderate supporters and fundamentalist supporters, and then suggests investigating the different reactions of these two support groups towards the DPP government's performance and strategy. Finally, the popular argument is a simplistic "stimulus-reaction" model: The DPP government's poor performance, including Chen's family corruption scandals, was the stimulus, and the public reacted to this negative stimulus with decreased support for the DPP. The movement government framework provides a much more sophisticated and interactive model. The framework suggests that the relations between the movement government and different social groups are highly interactive and dynamic. On the one hand, expectations and reactions from some groups can constrain the government's behavior; on the other hand, the government also shows a strong agency to educate some social groups and mobilize their support. Furthermore, there are many factors contributing to the movement government's strategy adoption such as the government's economic performance, international support, and so on. In the next chapter, I will further discuss the implications of the movement government framework for better understanding state–society relations.

Summary

This chapter applies the movement government framework to explain why the popular support for the DPP declined greatly during Chen's second term of 2004–2008. The argument centers on the double-edged sword effect of Chen's radical movement strategy on popular support for the DPP. The radical strategy was Chen's rational reaction to two major constraints: first, the troubles of his government's poor economic performance and his family's corruption scandals; second, the strategic dilemma sustained by the conflicting expectations of the TIM's fundamentalists and moderates. Simply put, Chen tried to use the radical strategy, relying on the fundamentalists to make up for his lost credit as the President by improving his credit as the TIM leader. The radical movement strategy generates opposite impacts on people with different social characteristics: while the radical strategy successfully consolidated the fundamentalists' support, it disaffected many previous moderate supporters who were younger, better educated, living in north and central Taiwan, and middle class, which finally led to the significant decline of the DPP's overall support base.

CHAPTER 5: CONCLUSION AND IMPLICATIONS

The purpose of this chapter is to briefly review the movement government framework proposed in Chapter 1, then discuss how the framework helps inform the analysis of the lower popular support for the DPP, and on the other hand, how the case study of the DPP government may sophisticate the framework as well, and finally, discuss how this case study and the movement government framework may contribute to the literature of state-movement relations theoretically and the DPP's future development empirically.

Differences between Movement Governments and Conventional Democratic Governments

Movement governments are those new democratic governments that are established through popular democratic elections by the political parties that have developed from significant social and political movements. The 20th century has witnessed many such governments, like those in "South Korea, Taiwan, Iran, South Africa, Venezuela and Bolivia" (McAdam and Tarrow, 2009:15). It is expected that movement governments would emerge in more and more authoritarian countries through democratic movements in the future. Because of movement governments' origins in and long-term connections to the movements, they usually keep their commitment to the movement's cause and continue their role as the movement leader even after they take control of the government. Therefore, the first and most important difference between the movement government and the conventional democratic government is that the former plays the dual roles of government and movement simultaneously, while the latter is only expected to be a government and has no obligation to officially lead certain movements.[1] This difference of dual roles vs. a single role is the primary reason for conceptually separating movement governments from conventional democratic governments. It also leads to the differences between these two types of governments in terms of the strategic constraints they face and the strategies they might use to deal with these constraints.

Being a government and the leader of a movement at the same time might seem to benefit the new government in terms of expanding its support base. As McAdam and Tarrow (2009) argue, however, in many cases the dual roles impose significant strategic constraints on the government and damage its electoral performance because of the inherent tension between the role of government and that of the movement in electoral politics. The two authors suggest that

> Electoral politics turns on a centrist, coalitional logic . . . Extreme views and preoccupation with single issues are antithetical, in this view, to the electoral 'project.' Movements, on the other hand, tend toward narrow — sometimes extremist — views and an uncompromising commitment to single issues. (McAdam and Tarrow, 2009:21)

In other words, as a government, it is generally expected to perform as a centrist moderator in social conflicts and to perform well economically

---

[1] I thank Prof. Doug McAdam for his clarification on the difference between movement governments and conventional democratic governments in terms of their connections to movements. In his comments on this chapter, he correctly pointed out that "in point of fact most conventional political parties include active movement wings that have to be accommodated in some way. So in the US the Republican Party includes the Christian right and the pro-life movement. Democrats include environmentalists, feminists, etc. The constraints that these movement wings impose on conventional governments are certainly less severe than the ones imposed on movement governments by the movements that spawned them, but … conventional governments are not entirely free of movement pressures." Prof. Andrew Walder also raised the same point in his comments on the previous versions of this work. I agree with both of them.

and socially. In contrast, as a movement leader, it is usually expected by movement supporters to remain a contentious challenger on movement issues and to deliver movement performance, which often fails to meet the expectations of mainstream voters.

When the conflict between the two roles becomes apparent, the movement government faces a strategic dilemma in maintaining social support. The dilemma is that, regardless of which role and which support base it chooses to favor, it would have to downplay the other role, alienating the other support base. For example, if the movement government chooses to behave like a centrist government at the expense of movement goals, thus maintaining popular support for its government role, movement supporters would be likely to withdraw their support for the government, and vice versa. Therefore, the movement and its supporters constrain the movement government and create dilemmas for it. A conventional democratic government certainly faces constant strategic constraints and sometimes finds itself in dilemmas as well, but the nature of these constraints and dilemmas is different from that of the movement government. Without previous ties and a strong commitment to the movement, the conventional democratic government has much more freedom to be a moderator in dealing with various conflicts between the government and the movement. Therefore, the movement and its supporters usually play a much smaller role in the constraints and dilemmas of the conventional democratic government.

Corresponding to the different constraints and dilemmas noted above, the strategies used by the movement government to deal with their constraints and dilemmas typically differ from those used by the conventional democratic government as well. Because the movement government usually has a number of movement activists and supporters in its key administrative positions, it has a tendency to use movement-oriented strategies to deal with the constraints imposed by role conflicts. In other words, they tend to emphasize movement goals at the expense of government goals and to mobilize the movement base for needed support. Many other factors such as poor government performance, the high level autonomy of the movement and the hostile international environment may enhance the movement government's tendency to act more like a movement. In contrast, the conventional democratic government usually does not particularly rely on the movement and its supporters to deal with the challenges it faces.

In short, the movement government may be distinguished from the conventional democratic government by its dual roles and persistent role conflicts, the constant strategic constraints and dilemmas caused by role conflicts, and finally, its tendency to mobilize the movement to deal with various challenges.[2]

The Case of the DPP Government and the Limitations of the Movement Government Framework

Does the movement government framework provide any real additional insights in analyzing the electoral politics in the so-called "movement states" such as "South Korea, Taiwan, Iran, South Africa, Venezuela and Bolivia" (McAdam and Tarrow, 2009:15). This is one of the challenging questions for the movement government framework. Here I summarize the previous chapters to show how the movement government framework helps inform the analysis of the lower popular support for the Democratic Progressive Party (DPP) and how this case study may further sophisticate the framework.

If the popular arguments that describe and explain the DPP government's case are accurate and adequate, it is unnecessary to propose a new framework and then develop an alternative explanation based on it. The movement government framework is proposed because the popular interpretation and explanation of the lower support for the DPP government are either misleading or inadequate. For example, a popular interpretation is that the lower support for the DPP government indicates parallel declining support for the Taiwan Independence Movement (TIM), and the popular explanation attributes the lower support for the DPP to the DPP

[2] Based on my discussion about the differences between the two types of governments, Prof. Doug McAdam raises an important hypothesis that "movement governments are inherently more fragile and likely short-lived than conventional governments." Although this study does not test this hypothesis, future researchers may collect data to examine it.

government's poor economic performance and President Chen Shui-bian family's corruption scandals. In Chapters 2 to 4, I showed that this interpretation is misleading and the popular explanation is inadequate. The main reason for their problems is that they fail to understand the complex relations between the DPP's dual roles as both government and movement. The popular interpretation views the two roles as the same, with the same support base; the popular explanation only emphasizes the DPP's government role and ignores its movement role and therefore cannot see the double-edged sword effect of the DPP government's radical movement strategy. Both of these accounts treat the DPP government as a conventional democratic government and pay little attention to its movement role. In contrast, my argument about the radical movement strategy and its consolidating effect on fundamentalists and disaffecting effect on moderates is informed by the movement government framework, which places the dynamic relations between the DPP's government role and its movement role in the center of analysis.

From the perspective of the movement government framework, the DPP government is a movement government facing constant strategic constraints and dilemmas due to the persistent conflicts between its government and movement roles. The strategy it uses to deal with these constraints and dilemmas has a great, sometimes different, impact on different support bases. Right after the DPP took power in 2000, to pacify the strong international and domestic oppositions and further expand support base, President Chen Shui-bian tried to build up a centrist and moderate government image through conceding on important movement issues. However, this concession strategy not only failed to mollify the oppositions but also hit the TIM and disappointed many movement supporters. Therefore, emphasizing its government role and downplaying its movement role through the government-oriented strategy failed to convert opponents and would possibly lose old proponents. From 2002–2004, Chen replaced the concession strategy with the confrontation strategy through creating controversial and confrontational independence issues against the Chinese government. This movement-oriented strategy and later the presidential election campaign, which was also highly confrontational to the Chinese government, successfully mobilized Taiwanese people's nationalistic sentiment and increased the popular vote for the DPP in the 2004 election.

Therefore, at the end of the DPP government's first term, emphasizing its movement role and relying on its movement supporters seemed to be an effective strategy for increasing popular support.

However, when this movement strategy became more and more radical during the DPP government's second term, it generated opposite impact on movement fundamentalists and moderates and finally led to lower support for the DPP. As we have seen in Chapter 3, if President Chen was not troubled by a series of corruption scandals involving the key officer in his office and his own family members, he might not have needed to radicalize the movement strategy to such an extreme extent for securing support. Chapter 4 shows that this radical movement strategy successfully consolidated the movement fundamentalists' support for Chen and the DPP, but disaffected many more moderates, which finally led to the decline in the DPP's overall support base.

We can see in Chapters 2 to 4 that a better understanding of the DPP government's dual roles, its movement strategies, and the reactions from different supporters toward these strategies is necessary for a sophisticated explanation of the lower support for the DPP. The movement government framework conceptualizes these elements and provides a basic analytic framework to make this explanation possible. On the other hand, this case study of the DPP government also reveals some limitations of this structuralistic framework. The framework proposed in Chapter 1 is aimed to present a more dynamic and interactive process between the government and its support base, but in general, it is still a structuralized framework. The main "structures" in this framework include the movement government's dual roles, the strategic constraints and dilemmas imposed by role conflicts, and the different components of the government's support base, all of which usually are stable and provide constraints or opportunities for the movement government to act upon. The most dynamic and agentic element in this framework, the government's three strategies, that is, the government-oriented, the movement-oriented and the shifting strategies, basically are determined by some structural factors such as the strategic constraints, the government's performance in managing economy and social affairs, the level of international support, and so on.

However, the evolution of the DPP government's strategy from concession to confrontation and finally to radicalization during 2000–2008 shows that to a large extent the change from one strategy to another was not determined by these structural factors. In other words, these structural factors such as the strategic constraints and dilemmas, the government's performance, and the level of international support did not change dramatically, but the government's strategy changed greatly. These changes were initiated by President Chen prior to any significant changes in "structures." The major reasons for him to change the strategy from concession to confrontation in 2002 and from confrontation to radicalization in 2005 were mostly personal. In the first case, he needed to secure the support within the party when the Chinese government tried to humiliate his government in the international community, and in the second case, he wanted to consolidate the movement fundamentalists' loyalty to him to help resist the legal accusation of his family's corruptions after he stepped down in 2008. Here we see the limitation of the movement government framework. The framework does not distinguish between the President and the government because it presumes that the President shares the same political interests and goals with his government which is to improve popular support for the DPP. Under this presumption, the interaction between the government/President and various structural factors and its outcomes are fairly stable and predictable. But the case here shows that President Chen did not always share the same interests with his government and the DPP. When Chen and his family members were involved in corruption scandals, as suggested by many DPP's moderate supporters, the best way for the government and the DPP to retain popular support would be Chen's voluntary resignation. However, although facing strong resignation appeals from within and without the DPP, Chen was determined to finish his presidency and use all his power to radicalize the movement fundamentalists to prepare his political struggles after he stepped down in 2008. It is hard to believe that Chen did not see the damage brought by his radical movement strategy to the DPP; he, nevertheless, became more and more radical because he had put his personal interests above the DPP's. Factors such as corruption scandals and the President's personal characteristics are highly contingent and find no position in the structuralized movement government framework. But in reality, they may turn to be the most important factors determining the movement government's fate.

Regarding the corruptions, I need to spend more time to explain its complex role in determining the popular support for the DPP. Corruptions of the government, especially President Chen and his family members' corruption, as suggested by the popular argument, would certainly hurt the popular support for the DPP. This study does not argue against the negative influence of these corruptions on the DPP government's fate. Nevertheless, this study calls for attention to how Chen and his government strategically dealt with the corruptions and suggests that the strategy they used had significant impact on the popular support for the party. We have seen that the radical movement strategy could successfully minimize the negative impact of the corruptions on movement fundamentalists, but at the same time, it alienated many moderates. I suspect that if Chen had not used the radical strategy but resigned as expected by many moderates, the DPP would not have lost so badly in the 2008 elections. However, it was extremely difficult, if not entirely impossible, to distinguish the net effect of the strategy used to deal with the corruption from that of the corruption itself. This study has shown multiple evidences to support the argument that the radical strategy had great negative impact on moderates, but we still cannot definitely say how much of this impact was solely caused by the strategy and not by the corruption itself. This is why I tend to call the argument of this study an explanation complementary, instead of an explanation completely alternative, to the popular explanations.

From this study's narrative account about the evolution of the DPP government's strategies, readers may have the impression that it was the corruption scandal that pushed President Chen to become more and more radical through time. However, although the corruption scandal was an important contributing factor to Chen's radicalization, it only provided necessary motivation for Chen to radicalize. There are other important factors enabling him to realize this motivation, which are not discussed in this study. For instance, according to the law in Taiwan, President Chen has some substantial power that is unusual in most democratic regimes. He had the right to nominate the Premier who then nominated the Cabinet members mainly according to the President's advice as well. He could also dismiss the Congress, which made the Congress extremely difficult to effectively restrain his political decisions. Moreover, since 2000, the DPP's party system has become less and less democratic. As a result, it imposed less and less constraints on Chen's political behaviors when he was the party chairman. Chen's unchecked power as the President and the DPP leader had enabled him to radicalize even though facing strong challenges from within and without the party.

In terms of motivations and goals underlying either the President or the movement government's strategy, there is another limitation in the movement government framework. Basically, the framework presumes that the ultimate motivation and goal for the President or the government to adopt certain strategies is to secure the party's political power through maintaining popular support and achieving electoral victories. The above discussion mentions the possibility that President Chen's motivations and goals might be at odds with the party's under certain conditions, which is not presumed by the movement government framework. Similarly, neither does the framework presume that the President or the government may be mainly motivated by the movement principles and goals while trying to choose which strategy to use. The framework basically depicts the movement government as a highly rational and election-driven actor who tries to use everything possible, including the movement, to secure electoral victories and political power. Is it possible that in some cases the movement is not a secondary goal and instrument for the government to secure power, but the foremost priority and urgent goal that the political power needs to serve? If this is the case, it is quite understandable that President Chen and his government seemed to ignore the possible damage caused by their radical movement strategy to the party's electoral performance. In other words, because they have chosen the movement principles and goals as their first priority, they determined to use the radical movement strategy to promote the movement even at the expense of government performance and the party's popular support. This possible scenario is not explored in this study, mainly because the movement government framework, on which this study is based, does not take it into account. However, future studies of the DPP government and other movement governments should try to avoid presuming the government and its leader as the actor being motivated solely by narrow self-interest or a desire to stay in power.[3]

[3] I thank Prof. Doug McAdam for pointing out different possible assumptions about government leaders' underlying motivations for their political behaviors. He also suggests that future researchers collect subjective information on preferences and motivations and incorporate these subjective data into their accounts of government actions.

Implications for the Literature on State-Movement Relations[4]

In their recent paper, McAdam and Tarrow (2009) review the long-term practice in the studies of elections and movements by political scientists and sociologists who generally conceptualize elections and movements as two distinct political phenomena (i.e., elections as the institutional form of politics vs. movements as the non-institutional form of politics) and completely separate the studies of the two subjects. They criticize the political scientists' studies of elections without movements and the sociologists' studies of movements without elections, and urge the election and movement scholars in both disciplines to pay more attention to the "reciprocal links between elections and movements" (McAdam and Tarrow, 2009:11). Among the five processes that they suggest to characterize these reciprocal links, the first one is "movement seizures of power," and they call the states that experience this process "movement states." Due to space constraint, their paper only briefly mentions the important political phenomena of movement states in less than one page and regrets that "both social movement scholars — who eschew the study of states — and political scientists — who generally disdain the study of movements — have been slow to recognize its significance" (McAdam and Tarrow, 2009:15). As we have seen in previous chapters, this study is aimed to contribute to the study of movement states (i.e., movement governments) through providing a general framework to analyze the reciprocal links between governments and movements and a case study within this framework.

After spending four chapters to propose the framework and study the case of a movement government, it seems unnecessary to repeat here that my study supports McAdam and Tarrow's main argument "that social

[4] I thank Prof. Gi-Wook Shin for reminding me of this study's possible implications for the studies in several other fields; for example, state–society relations in East Asia, ethnic nationalism and conflicts in the former Soviet Union, and even the revolutionary mass-movement regimes such as China and North Korea. Here I only focus on the implications for the general studies of state-movement relations.

movements and elections are not discrete and separate phenomena, but are mutually constitutive forms of politics that often interact to shape the prospects for both short and longer-term social/political change" (2009: 2). This argument is especially supported by the study of movement governments because the "mutually constitutive" nature of movements and elections is most apparent in the case of movement governments. In other words, the movement government, like the DPP government, intentionally brings the movement into the institutional politics such as elections, mixing institutional and non-institutional politics together, and taking advantage of the movement to achieve victories in elections.

Besides a general framework of movement governments, what else can this case study contribute to a better understanding of state-movement relations? The study of the DPP government suggests that the state-movement relations are not simply antagonistic, as suggested by the literature on state-movement relations, or symbiotic, as suggested in Chapter 1, but highly contingent and situational. Under some conditions such as when the government and the movement are facing a common "enemy," the two political forces may start sharing a common ground and the relations between them become symbiotic. For example, when Chen skillfully used some confrontational issues to trigger the Chinese government's aggressive reactions such as military exercises, the Chinese government became the common enemy to both the DPP government (which is supposed to represent the general public) and the TIM. Then the symbiotic relation between them was legitimized and they received broader popular support. Under some other conditions such as when the government's goal contradicts the movement's, it is hard for them to find a common ground, and therefore, their relations become antagonistic. For example, an important goal of the DPP government was to mend Taiwan's economy as soon as possible, which required closer and more open economic relations between Taiwan and mainland China; however, the TIM had a goal of preventing Taiwan's economic dependence on mainland China to avoid the Chinese government's strong influence in Taiwan, which required carefully supervised economic relations with mainland China. The two goals were antagonistic to each other and it was impossible for the government and the TIM to have a harmonious relation in this case.

Implications for the DPP's Future Development

What can the DPP learn from this study? First of all, if the DPP continues Chen's radical movement strategy after they lost power in 2008, they should understand, as suggested by the findings in this study, that it would be extremely difficult for them to retain the support from those young and middle-aged, better educated, residents in north and central Taiwan, and middle class, although those older, less educated, south Taiwan residents and farmers would continue their support for the party.

It seems that the DPP has realized this problem and tried to correct its radical strategy. In the party chairperson election soon after the DPP lost the 2008 presidential election, Tsai Ing-wen, a senior female scholar of law and democracy and also an experienced former official in the Chen administration, defeated the famous pro-independence fundamentalist, Koo Kuan-min, which showed that the majority of the DPP members did not want to continue the radical movement strategy.

Second, the TIM is not necessarily a liability for the DPP to expand support base. This study shows that not like the declining popularity of the DPP, the Taiwanese nationalistic sentiment generally had been increasing during 2000–2008, which provides the opportunity for the DPP to continue its nationalism strategy. But the findings in this study also show that the old radical nationalism strategy, which was highly contentious, ethnically divisive, illiberal and undemocratic, and tended to politicize the whole society, alienated the movement moderates. Therefore, the DPP needs a more liberal and democratic nationalism strategy that can promote ethnic harmony and reduce social conflicts. Only with such a new strategy can the DPP win back the moderates' support.

Finally, this chapter has shown that the unchecked power of President Chen Shui-bian was one of the most important factors determining the DPP's radical strategy. Although this study does not discuss why Chen's power was so strong and not constrainable, it is clear that the DPP needs to reform its party system to avoid the emergence of another democratic "dictator" in the party.

PART II

TAIWAN INDEPENDENCE MOVEMENT OUT OF POWER: 2008–2012

CHAPTER 6: TWO YEARS IN OPPOSITION: TAIWAN'S DEMOCRATIC PROGRESSIVE PARTY MOVES FROM DEFEAT TO REVIVAL?

The DPP's Quick Recovery from the 2008 Electoral Defeats

When the Democratic Progressive Party (DPP) was trounced by the opposition Chinese Nationalist Party (or Kuomintang, i.e., KMT) in both the legislative and presidential elections in early 2008, its eight-year administration from 2000–2008 was widely believed to have failed in almost every field. The DPP, losing power and resuming its previous position as the largest opposition party in Taiwan, was in disarray and severely troubled by corruption scandals, factional conflicts and over-radicalization of its pro-dependence stance. To revive the party, the first task for the DPP was to elect a new party leader who has a completely different public image from its previous notorious leader, Chen Shui-bian. Tsai Ing-wen, a former government official with a rational, moderate, clean and able public image was elected Chairwoman of the DPP, the party's first elected top female leader. The immediate challenge to Tsai was to tackle the party's embarrassing relationship with former president Chen Shui-bian. While Chen is the largest contributor to the DPP's electoral catastrophe and has been accused of severe corruption by the prosecutors, he still has a large following of loyal supporters. Tsai dealt with Chen's corruption cases carefully without alienating the radicals. Furthermore, Tsai initiated a number of substantial reforms in the party to dissociate itself from Chen's negative legacy, constrain major faction leaders' influence and improve the party's connection with its social base. The reforms have greatly helped the DPP recover from the electoral defeat.

Meanwhile, the DPP tried to check the KMT's various policies and mobilize popular support through three ways: initiating new legislations and resisting the KMT's initiatives in the Legislative Yuan (i.e., the congress), organizing large scale street protests and mobilizing mass petitions for referendum. These institutional and non-institutional political actions demonstrated the DPP's political commitment and power, and most importantly, won many previous supporters. On the KMT side, the Ma Ying-jeou administration failed to improve Taiwan's economy by the end of 2009. The new administration was also severely criticized by the public for its ineffective handling of some important national issues such as the August 8 flood. Increasing popular dissatisfaction with Ma's administration boosted the support for the DPP. The party scored consecutive victories in both the national legislative by-elections and the local governor elections in 2009 and early 2010. With these electoral victories, the DPP managed to emerge from the shadow of the Chen Shui-bian corruption scandals.

Although the DPP seems to be on the right track and is recovering its traditional support base, it will have a tougher time in the remaining two years before the next presidential election in early 2012. The Ma administration's weak spot, the declining Taiwan economy, is gradually recovering and expected to grow faster after the Economic Cooperation Framework Agreement (ECFA) with mainland China became effective on 12 September 2010. The DPP has opposed ECFA for its potential negative impact on Taiwan's political and economic independence from mainland China and domestic social equality. The debate on ECFA between the DPP and the KMT fully demonstrates the two parties' divergent vision and strategic thinking about cross-strait relations and Taiwan's future development agenda in an era of deepened globalization.

Tsai Ing-Wen and the Two Pro-Independence Factions in the DPP

The DPP's first move towards revamping the party was to elect a new Chairperson. Tsai Ing-wen was elected in May 2008. Tsai's career path is distinct from all former DPP Chairpersons who were opposition leaders or long term activists for democracy under the KMT's one-party rule before 2000. Tsai actually worked for the post-90s KMT regime and since 2000 for the DPP/Chen Shui-bian administration in various positions including some important ones, such as Minister of Mainland Affairs Council and Vice Premier.[1] Unlike most of the DPP's former Chairpersons who were deeply involved in the party's factional politics, Tsai did not join the DPP until 2004. Therefore, she has much less connection with any factions in the party and is in a more neutral position to mediate factional conflicts.

The difference between Tsai Ing-wen's and Chen Shui-bian's career path and public image is even more distinct. Tsai grew up in a wealthy and influential family and obtained a PhD in Law from the London School of Economics and Political Science (LSE). She was first known to the public as a Professor in International Law, and had worked as the appointed official of different positions in the central governments of the KMT and the DPP since the early 1990s before she became the DPP's Chairwoman. Chen was from an extremely poor family and graduated from National Taiwan University with a BA in Law. He first worked as a lawyer before becoming an influential activist in the opposition and democracy movement. Chen once served as the elected national legislator and the mayor of Taiwan's capital city, Taipei, before he was elected President in 2000. After an eight-year presidency, Chen Shui-bian has an extremely negative public image: Corrupt, radical, arbitrary and opportunistic.[2] In contrast, Tsai Ing-wen's public image is one of being clean, moderate, rational, able and reliable.[3]

In terms of education, career path and personality, Tsai Ing-wen has many commonalities with Ma Ying-jeou, Taiwan's new President as well

---

[1] See Tsai Ing-wen's Resume, *China News Service* (*CNS*), 18 May 2008, http://www.chinanews.com.cn/tw/twyw/news/2008/05-18/1254148.shtml, accessed on 18 June 2015.

[2] See, for example, Lin Cho-shui. 2009. Li Shi Ju Chang: Tong Ku Zhi Zheng Ba Nian (*Theatre of History*: *Eight Years Regime of Suffering*). Taipei Xian Zhong He Shi: INK; John F. Copper. 2008. *Taiwan's Failed President. Asian Affairs: An American Review*. 34: 4 (Winter) 179–192; John F. Copper. 2009. The Devolution of Taiwan's Democracy during the Chen Shui-bian Era. *Journal of Contemporary China*. 18(60), June. 463–478.

[3] See, for example, Tsai Ing-wen Joining the Election for DPP Chairperson, the Green Camp Legislators Said She Has a Big Chance, *China Network Television*, 19 April 2008, http://news.cctv. com/taiwan/20080419/100014.shtml, accessed on 6 July 2010.

as the KMT's star leader. To rebuild the DPP's public image catastrophically damaged by Chen and to counter Ma's popularity in Taiwan, Tsai was an ideal candidate for the DPP's new Chairmanship. In March 2008, Tsai defeated her major competitor, Koo Kwang-ming, with 58% of vote in the DPP's election for Chairperson. Koo was a senior pro-independence fundamentalist who supported former President Chen Shui-bian's radical pro-independence strategy. He and his campaign team believed that a moderate pro-independence line would further alienate supporters.[4]

In general, there have been two major factions — the radical and the moderate — on Taiwan's independence issues in the DPP. The radical line was promoted by the Chen Shui-bian faction which became dominant in the party in Chen's second administrative term of 2004–2008. The radicals have a strong sense of urgency in pursuing Taiwan's complete (*de jure*) independence from mainland China, and therefore, adopted radical strategies in dealing with important independence issues domestically and internationally. They view mainland China only as a threat and enemy to Taiwan, and to avoid Taiwan's economic and political over-dependence on mainland China, they prefer adopting a close-door policy toward it. These radical strategies had become Chen's political instrument to consolidate fundamentalists' personal loyalty to him and to persecute challengers within the party.

The moderates in the DPP have been mainly supported by the New Tide Faction in recent years. Members of the New Tide Faction seem to be both idealists and pragmatists. They are committed to the vision of Taiwan's future independence, but have a clear understanding of the tremendous difficulties of pursuing this goal. They oppose the use of radical ways to address these difficulties, and particularly, dislike the political manipulation of independence issues for personal gains in politics. In terms of cross-strait relations, they share the radicals' worry of mainland China's effort to incorporate Taiwan through economic means, but do not think that completely isolating Taiwan from mainland China is a rational choice. Instead, they suggest gradual, careful and transparent exchanges

[4] Chen Shimeng Strongly Supports Koo Kwan-ming for DPP Chairperson and Severely Criticizes the Moderate Line, *ifeng.com*, 25 April 2008, http://news.ifeng.com/taiwan/1/1/200804 /0425_2937_509284.shtml, accessed on 6 July 2010.

between the two sides of the Taiwan Strait.[5] Koo's defeat in the election for the DPP's Chairperson suggested that the majority of the DPP members rejected a continuation of the radical stance and looked forward Tsai Ing-wen to reforming the DPP and leading it out of defeat with a moderate line. Nevertheless, the election result also implied that a large number of DPP members are still sympathetic toward Chen, supportive of his radical line and suspicious of Tsai's leadership. As a result, although Tsai was generally on the side of the moderates, she had to tread carefully so as not to alienate the radicals within the party.

Tsai's first serious challenge after taking office was to deal with the embarrassing relation between the DPP and Chen Shui-bian, who was under investigation for corruption soon after he stepped down from the presidency. As Chen still has the strong support of radicals within the party, Tsai faced a dilemma of cutting off the party's connections with him while retaining the radicals' support for the party. The DPP expelled Chen from the party according to party regulations and indicated its respect for the legal investigation and prosecution of him. The party also organized a series of self-criticism meetings to repress the unconditional support for Chen, and most importantly, cultivate a favorable atmosphere for reforms in the party. On the other hand, Tsai defended the Chen administration's contributions in developing Taiwan's economy, establishing a better social welfare system, and particularly, promoting Taiwanese nationalistic sentiment.[6] She also protested the extended pre-trail detention of Chen, believing it was a violation of Chen's human rights.[7] Particularly, she visited Chen twice, while he was in custody, showing her care for him to the

[5] Lin Cho-shui's two books on DPP provide detailed discussion of these two pro-independence lines. Lin, Zhuoshui. 2006. *Gong Tong Ti*: *Shi Jie Tu Xiang Xia de Taiwan* (*Community*: *Taiwan in the global context*). Xin Dian: Zuo An Wen Hua; 2009. *Li Shi Ju Chang*: *Tong Ku Zhi Zheng Ba Nian* (*Theatre of History*: *Eight Years Regime of Suffering*). Taipei Xian Zhong He Shi: INK.

[6] Proceedings from the 13th National Party Congress, *DPP Official Website*, 20 July 2008, http://www.dpp.org.tw/index_en/, accessed on 6 July 2010.

[7] The joint statement calling for the reform of the detention system, implementation of human rights in the administration of justice and an immediate end to the detention of former President Chen, *DPP Official Website*, 25 June 2009, http://www.dpp.org.tw/index_en/, accessed on 6 July 2010.

public. To most radicals and moderates in the party, Tsai's handling of Chen's case was sensible and acceptable. Therefore, Tsai successfully maintained the general solidarity of the party, which was necessary for her to implement a series of reforms to minimize the impact of Chen's negative legacy on the DPP.

Erasing Chen's Negative Legacy with Reforms in the DPP

Corruption is one of Chen's negative legacies in the party as not only Chen and his family members, but also many other DPP members serving important positions in his administration, were jailed for corruption. To keep corruption practices at bay, the new leadership under Tsai significantly enhanced the independence and power of the party's Anti-corruption Committee through a revision of the party's Constitution.[8] Another negative legacy from Chen was the dominance of the radicals in the party. The radicals controlled the party mainly through the party's nomination procedure for various elections in Taiwan, such as elections for national legislators, city mayors and county magistrates. Traditionally, whether a candidate would be nominated was determined by his or her performance in two "exams," that is, the public opinion surveys and the party primary election. Those who received higher popular support in the two "exams" are more likely to be nominated by the party.

The two "exams" had been manipulated by the radicals to ensure their candidates' better performance. According to the party's regulation revised by them before the legislative election in early 2008, if a respondent to the public opinion polls was a KMT supporter or sympathizer, he or she would be excluded from the polls. Therefore, only opinions from those who explicitly support the DPP would be counted in assessing the candidates' popularity. This so-called "pan-blue[9] exclusion clause" had

---

[8] Proceedings from the 13th National Party Congress, 2008-07-20, *DPP Official Website*, 20 July 2008, http://www.dpp.org.tw/index_en/, accessed on 6 July 2010.

[9] The supporters and sympathizers of the KMT and its ally parties are called pan-blue and those of the DPP and its ally parties pan-green in Taiwan because the background colors of the two major parties' party flags are blue and green, respectively.

greatly improved the radical candidates' chance of receiving higher approval rates in the public opinion polls. In party primary elections, the radicals had used a large group of "dummy members" to manipulate election results. "Dummy members" were a group of nominal DPP members employed by some major faction leaders in the party to boost the electoral performance of their own candidates. The DPP has been troubled by this dummy member issue for a long time and every new chairperson is expected to address the problem.

Not long after the DPP's defeat in the presidential election and even before Tsai was elected the DPP's new Chairwoman, the DPP leadership had to abolish the highly controversial "pan-blue exclusion clause" to pacify the opposition from the moderates. After Tsai took office, the new leadership promoted some important reforms to prevent major faction leaders from using dummy members in DPP elections. A long term practice for the radicals and other faction leaders to maintain dummy members was to pay membership fees for them. The new leadership under Tsai has prohibited any DPP members from such practices. In addition, under the new regulation, all members are required to submit their membership dues directly to the party headquarters instead of its local branches, putting the membership issue under closer supervision by the party's top leadership. The DPP has anticipated about 50% membership (150,000) reduction caused by these new rules.[10]

An even more radical reform was the exclusion of the party primary election from nomination procedures for some positions. For example, in January 2010, the DPP developed a new nomination procedure, independent of the party's conventional nomination regulation, to identify the best candidates for the 2010 elections of mayors and councilors in the five special municipalities. These elections are extremely important for the DPP because the five special municipalities cover about 60% of Taiwan's population and the election results will have significant implications for the DPP's presidential election in early 2012. For the nomination of

[10] Submitting Membership Fee on behalf of Others Banned, DPP May Lose 150,000 Members, *ChinaReviewNews.com*, 19 February 2010, http://www.chinareviewnews.com/doc/1012/3/4/8/101234871.html?coluid=7&kindid=0&docid=101234871, accessed on 18 June 2015.

mayor candidates in the two DPP strongholds, Kaohsiung and Tainan, and all the local councilor candidates in the five special municipalities, the nomination procedure did not include the party primary election. In other words, those who receive the highest approval rate in the public opinion polls would automatically become the party's nominated candidates in these areas. This nomination procedure has been severely criticized by the radicals in the party.[11]

Signs of Revival with Consecutive Electoral Victories

In addition to various reforms within the party, the DPP has continued its three conventional ways of mobilizing previous supporters: Initiating new legislations and resisting the KMT's initiatives in the Legislative Yuan, mobilizing large scale street protests and organizing mass petitions for referendum on important national issues such as ECFA. Although being the absolute minority party (less than one-fourth of the seats) in the Legislative Yuan since early 2008, the DPP legislators have been good at resisting, sometimes violently, the KMT administration and legislators' various initiatives. The DPP under Tsai also did not waste any opportunity in mobilizing large scale protests against the Ma administration's policies. Finally, the DPP have continued its tradition of creating referendum issues to publicize its political arguments. For example, the DPP rallied one hundred thousand people to sign the petition for holding the referendum on ECFA. All these political mobilizations have demonstrated the DPP's political commitment and power to the public, and to a large extent, recovered its support base.

In contrast, the Ma administration, although enjoying a high popularity at the beginning, had been troubled by the decline in economic growth, high unemployment rate and serious mishandling of some important national issues by the end of 2009. Statistics show that Taiwan's economic growth rate had been constantly negative since Ma took office until the last quarter of 2009, while unemployment rate had been high and

[11] Senior Pro-independence Fundamentalist Koo Kwang-ming Asking for Re-holding the Party Congress, *ifeng.com*, 26 January 2010, http://news.ifeng.com/taiwan/1/201001/0126_351_1525896. shtml, accessed on 6 July 2010.

increasing during the same period.[12] As the DPP pointed out, the Ma administration's economic performance in 2008 and 2009 was worse than the Chen administration's. In early August 2009, southern Taiwan experienced its largest flood in half a century, causing 677 deaths. The Ma administration was criticized severely by the public for its ineffective handling of the rescue, which finally led to the dismissal of the entire cabinet. All these factors have contributed to the DPP's four consecutive electoral victories in both the national legislative by-elections and local governor elections in 2009 and early 2010. Now the DPP holds over one-fourth of the seats in the Legislative Yuan, a number that allows it to initiate some important motions such as impeaching the President.[13] Even the KMT had to admit that the DPP had got rid of the shadow of Chen Shui-bian.[14]

These electoral victories and the DPP's new image have significantly improved the popular support for Tsai within and outside the party. In the DPP's Chairperson election in May 2010, Tsai defeated her competitor, a senior pro-independence fundamentalist, with 90% of votes. This shows that most DPP members approved of Tsai's reforms and leadership and is also a reflection of its solidarity.

Proposing a New Agenda for Taiwan but More Challenges Ahead

After the DPP's recovery, Tsai started to organize a series of conferences, seeking input from the public to develop DPP's 10-year Manifesto, a specific policy agenda for Taiwan's next 10 years. As the major opposition party, the DPP has shown its capability in attacking

[12] Quarterly National Economic Trends May 2010, Directorate General of Budget, Accounting and Statistics, Executive Yuan, R.O.C. http://www.dgbas.gov.tw/ct.asp?xItem=27213&ctNode=3363, accessed on 18 June 2015.

[13] However, it is still nearly impossible for these motions to be passed in the Legislative Yuan, because the "threshold" (the number of supporting legislators required) for the passage is much higher than the number of one-fourth seats.

[14] Ma Ying-jeou, Taking Actions, Thoroughly Reforming, KMT Official Website, 9 December 2009, http://www.kmt.org.tw/hc.aspx?id=32&aid=4160, accessed on 6 July 2010.

the Ma administration's policies in a variety of fields, such as cross-strait relations, economic development, democratic consolidation, human rights protection, international relations and social welfare programs; nevertheless, to persuade the public that the DPP can bring a better Taiwan to them, the DPP needs to show how these areas could be managed differently. The ECFA debate between the DPP and the KMT throughout 2008–2009 clearly demonstrated the two parties' divergent vision and strategic thinking about the future of Taiwan. In general, Tsai and the DPP have been attacking ECFA for its potential negative impacts on Taiwan's national security and social equality. The DPP has argued that ECFA will eventually threaten Taiwan's national security because it will lead to Taiwan's economic integration with mainland China, followed by Taiwan's political integration with it, as expected by the Chinese government. According to Tsai's argument in her debate with President Ma on ECFA issues, the DPP would rather choose a safer way for Taiwan's economic opening: open Taiwan to "the world," especially developed economies such as the US, before approaching mainland China. This is in contrast to KMT's proposed ECFA scheme of opening to mainland China first, and then going to "the world" through mainland China.[15]

The DPP is worried that ECFA will slow down or even stop Taiwan's gradual pursuit of its complete independence from mainland China. Therefore, although the DPP has abandoned the radical way of pursuing Taiwan's independence, it has not compromised on its vision of the *de jure* independence of Taiwan. In the DPP's 10-year Manifesto, this uneasy mixture of pragmatism and idealism would resurface. Another major concern raised by the DPP in its argument against ECFA is its potential negative impact on Taiwan's social equality. The DPP believes that ECFA will only be beneficial to a few large enterprises and privileged groups; Taiwan's small and middle enterprises (SME), the majority of ordinary workers and the young will gain little or even suffer from a bankrupt in business and a decline in real wages caused by ECFA. It believes that income inequality will significantly widen in

[15] Transcript of Ma Ying-jeou and Tsai Ing-wen's ECFA Debate, http://docs.google.com/View?id=dgv9n52c_6164pdj9ct, accessed on 18 June 2015.

Taiwan as a result. The DPP cites post-CEPA Hong Kong to support its argument, emphasizing Hong Kong's deteriorated social inequality as a result of CEPA.[16]

Progressivism (i.e., protecting ordinary people's interests) is the DPP's traditional commitment to Taiwan, as indicated by the "Progressive" in its name. Before the DPP took power in 2000, the public image of the DPP was a pro-ordinary people party, in contrast to that of the KMT as a pro-rich people party. At the end of the DPP's eight years administration, this distinction of progressiveness between the two parties had somewhat blurred. Nevertheless, in 2008 disadvantaged social groups such as farmers and workers were still more likely than others to vote for the DPP in the presidential election, mainly because the DPP administration had established a relatively better social welfare system in Taiwan.[17] Through debating on ECFA issues with the KMT and emphasizing its care for Taiwan's social inequality, the DPP has been trying to re-establish this distinction of progressiveness between it and the KMT in the public's mind. This progressive commitment is expected to occupy an important position in the DPP's 10-year Manifesto.

Although the DPP seems to be on the right track for its revival, the remaining two years of 2010 and 2011 before the presidential election in early 2012 will be much more challenging because the Ma administration's performance in reviving the economy has become much better in 2010; moreover, Taiwan's economy is expected to be significantly improved after ECFA became effective on 12 September 2011. Especially, if the public do not see those negative consequences of ECFA claimed by the DPP before the next presidential election, or if the public is persuaded by the fact that Taiwan gains more than it suffers from ECFA, the ECFA issue would finally lose its mobilizing power for the DPP. These scenarios are quite possible because most of the negative consequences of ECFA, such as endangered national security and widened social inequality, would only emerge in the long run, especially when the two governments across the strait have been alert to these potential problems and decided to proactively address them. For example, the Chinese government has

[16] *Ibid.*

[17] See Chapters 4 and 10 of this book.

promised to minimize ECFA's negative effects on the disadvantaged groups in Taiwan[18] and the Ma administration has also decided to compensate these groups' loss brought by ECFA.[19]

At the DPP's recent Party Congress Meeting in July, the non-mentioned of the DPP's 10-Year Manifesto has also cast doubts on the revival of the DPP. The manifesto, which Tsai has put much effort and high expectation of and promised to pass it in this Party Congress Meeting, was not discussed during the meeting. Many have expected Tsai and the New Tide Faction to further transform and revive the DPP with this policy agenda. However, it seems that although the DPP has achieved new power balance, its policy agenda setting for Taiwan is still unclear. As Tsai has promised that the 10-year Manifesto would be the general party platform for the year-end five special municipalities election, its non-mentioned in the Party Congress Meeting has cast a shadow on these elections which are believed to be extremely important for the DPP in the 2012 presidential election. Besides the manifesto, the absence of three important southern local executives who lost the party's nomination for the year-end elections is a sign that dissatisfaction within the party remains to be solved. Without their support, the DPP's supposedly easy victory in the two southern special municipalities, Tainan and Kaohsiung, would not be guaranteed. Pacifying these local executives will be another urgent challenge for the DPP.

The results of the election of the party's power center, Central Standing Committee, however affirm the demise of the Chen Shui-bian faction in the party. The moderate New Tide Faction emerged the biggest winner. Since Tsai is closer to the New Tide Faction, it seems that in terms of the party's power structure, the radicals have finally been marginalized and the moderates have consolidated their power of further reforming the DPP and attracting more moderate supporters. About three weeks after the

---

[18] Guotaiban Wang Yi, *zhuren jieshou Taiwan meiti zhuanfang* (Interview with Wang Yi, Minister of Taiwan Affairs Office of State Council), http://www.chinanews.com.cn/tw/news/2010/03-31/2200729.shtml, accessed on 18 June 2015.

[19] President Ma Holds Press Conference to Discuss Signing of ECFA, http://english.president. gov.tw/Default.aspx?tabid=491&itemid=21920&rmid=2355, accessed on 27 July 2010.

DPP's Party Congress Meeting, one of the three earlier mentioned local executives, Kaohsiung County Magistrate Yang Chiu-hsing, quit the DPP and started to run as an independent candidate to compete with candidates from the DPP and the KMT for the position of mayor of the new Kaohsiung Special Municipality. After the content of ECFA was published and the Legislative Yuan passed the ECFA, Yang started to support ECFA in public, impacting negatively on the DPP.[20] It seems that the ECFA issue has started to lose its mobilizing power for the DPP, making the DPP's revival efforts in the coming 2 years more difficult.

[20]Yang Chiu-hsing: Without ECFA, Taiwan Will Become Philippines, *NowNews.com*, 18 August 2010, http://www.nownews.com/2010/08/18/320-2637587.htm, accessed on 18 June 2015.

CHAPTER 7: TAIWAN'S 2010 MUNICIPAL ELECTIONS

The Ma Administration's Mid-Term "Exam" Concluded with Positive Implications

The three-in-one elections (i.e., elections of municipal mayors, city councilors and ward chiefs) in Taipei and four to-be-created special municipalities concluded on 27 November 2010. As the elections covered over 60% of Taiwan's population and almost all the strategically important large cities for the 2012 presidential race, they are believed to be both the Ma administration's mid-term "exam" and a prelude to the coming national legislative elections and the presidential election in early 2012. In the elections, the Kuomintang (KMT) maintained its three mayoral seats in Taipei, Sinbei and Greater Taichung in northern and central Taiwan, and the Democratic Progressive Party (DPP) successfully defended its two mayoral seats in Greater Tainan and Kaohsiung in the south. The DPP garnered 400,000 more votes than the KMT in the five mayoral elections and its shares in the five municipal councils increased significantly as well. These results clearly indicate that the DPP is on track to regain its credibility lost in its 2008 presidential election. Although there are different and even conflicting interpretations to the election results, it is generally believed that the elections have mostly positive implications for the two major parties' reform efforts, democracy in Taiwan, and future cross-strait relations between Taiwan and mainland China.[1]

The election results conveyed both positive and negative signals to the two parties at the same time. In other words, none of them completely won or lost the elections, providing good lessons and strong motivation for each of them to learn and grow. This is a strong sign that Taiwan is stepping into a more mature two-party system.[2] Since it took power in 2008, the KMT had been losing seats in both the national legislative by-elections and the county/city governor elections. Moreover, the public opinion polls from various sources before the elections showed the high possibility of a DPP's victory in Taipei, the KMT's stronghold and a strategically important city for the presidential race in 2012. Therefore, the KMT's victory in Taipei by a 12% margin was a better-than-expected result and boosted its confidence in a possible win in the next presidential election. However, the KMT's significantly less total number of votes and worse-than-expected performance in Greater Taichung, Tainan and Kaohsiung imply that tremendous challenges lay ahead in its presidential race in 2012.

For the DPP, it not only amassed more votes than the KMT, but also obtained the same number of seats (130) as the KMT in the five municipal councils, a marked achievement that boosted its confidence in its bid for the 2012 presidential election. However, the DPP's defeats in Taipei and Sinbei provided an opportunity for the pro-independence fundamentalists to attack DPP Chairwoman Tsai Ing-wen's unconventional moderate campaign strategy in northern Taiwan. One of the major challenges that DPP thus faces is in developing a China policy that can accommodate the divided northern and southern voters and their respective representatives within the party — the factions of moderates and hardliners. For both domestic and foreign observers, the elections also demonstrated

[1] For example, see A Win–Win Election in Taiwan, Charles E. Morrison, 6 December 2010, http://online.wsj.com/article/SB10001424052748703814404576000960804097334.html., accessed on 15 June 2015.

[2] Taiwan's Political System Maturing: U.S. Scholars, 28 November 2010, http://focustaiwan.tw/news/aipl/201011280015.aspx, accessed on 18 June 2015.

noticeable progress in Taiwan's democratic consolidation.[3] The DPP has deviated from its conventional ideology-driven and conflict-oriented campaign strategy and adopted a moderate and peaceful approach to attract younger and swing voters. Vote-buying, a long practiced strategy of the KMT that always stirred serious conflicts in previous elections, was effectively prohibited and did not become an issue in the elections. As a result, the election campaigns of both sides looked "cold," low profile and much less disturbing to the society than before. Although a deadly election-eve shooting incident in a KMT councilor candidate's rally shadowed the next-day elections, the two parties refrained from making use of it to mobilize their supporters.

The election results and the DPP's avoidance of the Economic Cooperation Framework Agreement (ECFA) issue in its campaigns suggest that the Ma administration's mainland China policy has finally become more of an advantage than a controversy for the KMT. It is expected that the Ma administration will continue its current mainland China policy cautiously to enhance cross-strait economic relations on the one hand, and to keep away from a pro-China image on the other.

KMT's Lackluster Victory

The national economic situation has become much more favorable to the KMT this year before the elections. Taiwan has weathered the worldwide financial crisis and its estimated GDP growth rate in 2010 is 9.98%, a 21-year record high.[4] The unemployment rate in October, as promised by the Ma administration, finally dropped below 5% (i.e., 4.92%) for the first time in 23 months.[5] However, these shining numbers did not reduce the pressure on the KMT's uphill election campaign against the reviving DPP.

[3] *Ibid.*

[4] Taiwan's GDP Growth Expected to be 21-year High, 19 November 2010, http://overseas.caing.com/2010-11-19/100200093.html., accessed on 5 December 2010.

[5] Taiwan`s Unemployment Rate Drops Below 5% in October, 23 November 2010, http://www.cens.com/cens/html/en/news/news_inner_34442.html., accessed on 18 June 2015.

In the DPP's two southern strongholds: Greater Tainan and Kaohsiung, the KMT demonstrated little determination to win the elections from the very beginning. The three special municipalities, Taipei, Sinbei, and Greater Taichung in northern and central Taiwan, have been the KMT's long term strongholds. As long as the voters' turnout rate is high enough in each of them, the likelihood of a KMT victory seems very promising. However, the KMT's consecutive defeats in the 2009 county/city governor elections and 2010 national legislative by-elections indicated that the pan-blue voters were much less willing than the pan-green ones to participate in the elections.

While the KMT campaigned vigorously to encourage its supporters' turnout, the DPP smartly changed its traditional conflict-oriented campaign strategy which usually provoked higher participation from both camps. DPP's moderate and peaceful election campaigns successfully promoted the popularity of its two mayoral candidates, Su Tseng-chang (苏贞昌) in Taipei and Tsai Ing-wen (蔡英文) in Sinbei. One week before the elections, various public opinion polls showed that it would not be a surprise if Su wins Taipei and Tsai gets a small-margin loss in Sinbei. Unexpectedly, a dramatic and deadly shooting incident in the election-eve secured the KMT's victories in Taipei and Sinbei. As one of the victims in the incident, Sean Lien (连胜文), is the son of honorary KMT Chairman Lien Chan, more pan-blue supporters came out to cast their sympathetic votes for the KMT candidates. Finally, the average turnout rate in the five elections was 72.7%, much higher than the widely anticipated 65%.

Although the KMT finally won three of five mayoral seats, Table 7.1 reveals that as compared to the 2005/2006 governor elections in the same areas, the popular support for the KMT has actually declined in four of the five places (except Taipei). In contrast, the DPP increased its vote shares in four of them (except Greater Kaohsiung where there is little change in popular support for the DPP).

The local election history from the day the KMT took power in 2008 also shows the same trend. Figure 7.1 indicates that while the KMT's vote share dropped from 58.45% in the 2008 presidential election to 47.88% in the 2009 county/city governor elections to 44.54% in current

Table 7.1 KMT's and DPP's Vote Shares (%) in Five Municipal Governor Elections: 2005/2006 and 2010

	2005/2006	2010	Change (2005/2006–2010)
Taipei			
KMT	53.81	55.65	1.84
DPP	40.89	43.81	2.92
Sinbei			
KMT	54.87	52.61	–2.26
DPP	44.3	47.39	3.09
Greater Taichung			
KMT	59.02	51.12	–7.90
DPP	39.07	48.88	9.81
Greater Tainan			
KMT	44.98	39.59	–5.39
DPP	48.54	60.41	11.87
Greater Kaohsiung			
KMT	45.59	20.52	–25.07
DPP	53.67	52.8	–0.87
Independent (Yang Chiu-hsing)[6]	—	26.68	—

Data source: Central Election Commission, ROC (Taiwan), http://www.cec.gov.tw/, accessed on 18 June 2015.

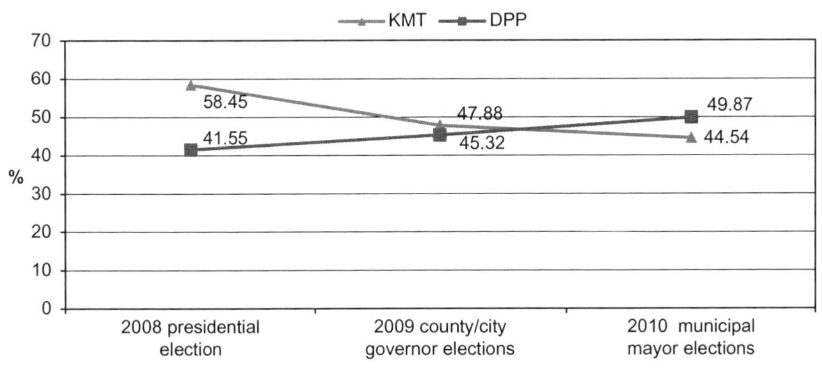

Figure 7.1 KMT's and DPP's Vote Shares: 2008–2010

Data source: Central Election Commission, ROC (Taiwan), http://www.cec.gov.tw/, accessed on 18 June 2015.

[6]Yang was the former DPP member and Kaohsiung County Commissioner.

municipal elections, the DPP's vote share increased from 41.55% to 45.32%, and finally, to 49.87%, which was 5.3% higher than the 44.54% of the KMT. Over the past two years, in total the DPP has amassed about 48.21% of the votes, more than the KMT's 45.76% in all the local elections.[7]

It is a puzzle to many why the KMT's popular support has been declining when the Ma administration has successfully revived Taiwan's economy through enhancing economic exchanges with mainland China. The KMT's exceptionally high vote share in the 2008 presidential election could largely be attributed to people's extreme dissatisfaction with then-president Chen Shui-bian's corruption. As Chen has since been prosecuted and sentenced to jail, the Chen factor has lost its mobilizing effect on popular support for the KMT. Furthermore, people's voting decision could be swayed by different considerations in national and local elections. While national factors such as KMT's mainland China policy could significantly influence people's vote in national elections, local factors such as the local governor's performance largely determines voters' decision in local elections. Unfortunately, KMT's local governors generally fared much worse in performance than their DPP counterparts. A survey conducted in July and August 2010 on people's satisfaction with their local governor's performance shows that of the 25 local governors, the DPP governors' rankings improved greatly when compared to those of last year and all top six governors are from the DPP; in contrast, the KMT governors' rankings dropped dramatically, with the KMT taking all last 12 rankings.[8]

Moreover, as many have pointed out, higher economic growth numbers do not necessarily indicate ordinary people's satisfaction with their economic situation. While the Ma administration used various growth numbers to suggest that Taiwan's economy is recovering, some scholars argued that Taiwan's higher GDP growth has little impact on improving

---

[7] KMT, DPP Neck-to-neck in Council Elections, 29 November 2010, http://www.chinapost.com.tw/taiwan/national/national-news/2010/11/29/281743/KMT-DPP.htm, accessed on 18 June 2015.

[8] Survey of People's Satisfaction Level with 25 County/city governors: Green Rise, Blue Decline, Popular Opinion Changes, http://www.cw.com.tw/survey/2010city/article.jsp, accessed on 18 June 2015.

livelihood issues such as unemployment of ordinary folks.[9] Particularly, the early fruit of Taiwan's recovering economy was mainly enjoyed by the upper class, and it will take some time for the effects of these benefits to trickle down to the grassroots.[10] The declined mobilization power of the KMT's grassroots organizations, especially its local party branches, also contributed to its lower popular support.[11] A KMT's local party branch head interviewed by the author told a revealing case. His party branch had about 300 KMT members. After receiving the mobilization order from the party's central headquarters, he called for a membership meeting. To his big surprise, only five members showed up in the meeting.

Additionally, the KMT has a serious problem in attracting younger voters,[12] probably because it is a really old and conservative party — it has been established for over 100 years and the average age of its members is the oldest among all the major parties in Taiwan.[13] During the elections, both the KMT and the DPP used Facebook to attract young supporters. All the five DPP mayor candidates recruited more Facebook fans than their KMT rivals (Table 7.2). For instance, while Su Tseng-chang's Facebook account had over 100,000 fans, his KMT competitor Hau Lung-pin's only got over 10,000. At the KMT congress meeting in August, even young

[9] A Study of Economic Factors' Impact on Taiwan's Politics, 21 June 2010, http://www.cassits.cn/zjlt/news_0083.html; High Unemployment Rate Caused by Triangle Trade, 26 July 2010, http://www.libertytimes.com.tw/2010/new/jul/26/today-s1.htm; Why Don't People Have No Feeling about Economic Recovery? 29 October 2010, http://tw.myblog.yahoo.com/ jw!3WucA0uGBR2iZ_41ENM-/article?mid=1770&prev=1774&l=f&fid=6, accessed on 5 December 2010.

[10] Taiwan Mayoral Race Sets Stage for Presidential Election in 2012, 30 November 2010, http://www.channelnewsasia.com/stories/eastasia/view/1096442/1/.html, accessed on 5 December 2010.

[11] Regional Divide, "Yeltsin Effect" Concerns after Taiwan Elections, 29 November 2010, http://focustaiwan.tw/news/aipl/201011290027.aspx, accessed on 18 June 2015.

[12] Huang Chongyan: KMT Losing Young Voters Significantly, 7 August 2010, http://www.nownews.com/2010/08/07/11490-2633793.htm, accessed on 5 December 2010

[13] Chinese KMT, 26 September 2010, http://big51.chinataiwan.org/twrwk/twdq/zhd/200910/t20091028_1123943.htm, accessed on 5 December 2010. A KMT member told the author jokingly that in the KMT 60-year-old members were still called "young talents (青年才俊)."

Table 7.2 Number of Mayoral Candidates' Facebook Fans

	Candidate	Number of Facebook Fans	Ratio between Numbers of DPP and KMT Fans
Taipei	Su Tseng-chang (DPP)	109,635	—
	Hau Lung-pin (KMT)	12,842	8.5
Sinbei	Tsai Ing-wen (DPP)	71,531	—
	Chu Li-lun (KMT)	15,493	4.6
Greater Taichung	Su Jia-chyuan (DPP)	25,562	—
	Hu Chi-keung(KMT)	8,331	3.1
Greater Tainan	Lai Ching-te (DPP)	10,729	—
	Kuo Tien-tsai(KMT)	3,895	2.8
Greater Kaohsiung	Chen Chu (DPP)	56,912	—
	Huang Chao-shun(KMT)	7,805	7.3

Data source: Candidate's Facebook account at facebook.com on 4 December 2010.

KMT party members complained that the party was losing younger generation voters.[14]

DPP's Cheerful Defeat

The hottest topic about the DPP during and even after the elections was its new campaign strategy. The DPP was known to be extremely good at mobilizing supporters in elections capitalizing on conflict-oriented issues, such as Taiwan's independence and ethnic issues. However, in these five elections, especially in Taipei, Sinbei, and Greater Taichung, the DPP completely avoided these old issues and tried a fresh campaign line which was moderate and peaceful. It was believed that the DPP's new line was designed particularly for northern and central Taiwan's urban voters who were better educated and less sensitive to emotion-provoking issues. The DPP also believed that the younger generation, women and swing voters

[14] KMT's Party Congress Meeting: No Discussion on Proposals, Party Representatives Treated as Extra, 8 August 2010, http://www.libertytimes.com.tw/2010/new/aug/8/today-fo7.htm, accessed on 18 June 2015.

should find the new campaign strategy especially attractive. Moreover, because DPP Chairwoman Tsai Ing-wen's popular personal image is moderate, intelligent and peaceful, the DPP needs to try a line that suits her style to prepare for her possible presidential race in 2012.

The new campaign line emphasized "governance ability" (治理能力) which was widely believed to be the Ma administration and the KMT local governors' weak point. Naturally, this emphasis led to popular discussions about local economic and social issues and why the current local governments failed to solve these problems. This real life focus, unlike furious ideological debates in previous elections, had benefited ordinary folks indirectly. For example, in response to high housing prices which had become a hot topic in both camps, the Ma administration launched the social housing policy in Taipei and Sinbei soon before the elections.[15] The DPP's new campaign strategy also took a dramatic change from an ideology-driven and combative image to a pragmatic, peaceful and entertaining one. It stopped attacking ECFA, used pink instead of its conventional pro-independence color green as the theme color in its campaign materials in Taipei and Sinbei, and held many street concerts to attract neutral voters who are usually non-party rally goers.

The DPP also significantly reduced its traditional emphasis on large scale rallies in its mobilization of supporters. Instead, it organized small groups and gatherings to hold face-to-face and more meaningful dialogues between DPP leaders and potential supporters. For example, a major type of small mobilization organizations for Tsai Ing-wen was Friends of Little Ing, established voluntarily by supporters with 10 members in each of them. Several Friends of Little Ing could together invite DPP leaders to have a meeting with them. The number of these "direct sales" style organizations grew rapidly.[16] The new strategy was a good attempt especially for Tsai Ing-wen in Sinbei and Su Jia-chyuan (苏嘉全) in Greater Taichung. This was the first time for Tsai Ing-wen to run for an elective position in Taiwan, and Su Jia-chyuan was parachuted to Greater Taichung only six months before

---

[15] Ma Ying-jeou: Promoting Social Housing Not for Elections, 16 November 2010, http://taiwan.dwnews.com/news/2010-11-16/57098375.html, accessed on 18 June 2015.

[16] Direct-sales Propaganda, Friends of Little Ing Becomes A Sharp Weapon to Beat the Blue, 11 October 2010, http://vote2010.chinatimes.com/election/content.aspx?cat=6&art=3278, accessed on 5 December 2010.

the election. Their election performance, especially Su Jia-chyuan's, was much better than expected. Although finally defeated by KMT's star politician and 9-year incumbent mayor Hu Chi-keung (胡志强), Su Jia-chyuan greatly increased popular support for the DPP in Greater Taichung from 2005's 39% to about 49% in this election (Table 7.1). This is a sign that the DPP's support base is expanding northward from its strongholds in the south. Su Jia-chyuan has since become the new heavyweight in the DPP for his outstanding contribution to this support base expansion.

Before the election-eve shooting event, it was widely believed that Su Tseng-chang had a good chance of defeating Hau Lung-pin (郝龙斌) in Taipei. However, although Su managed to increase the vote share from four years ago, he still lost the election by the largest margin among all DPP mayoral candidates (Table 7.1). The shooting event was believed to be of significant help to Hau, while the over-concentration of mainlanders in Taipei is the main structural reason for any DPP candidate's failure in Taipei's mayoral election. Additionally, unlike other DPP candidates, Su's campaign platform lacked concrete policy proposals. The DPP's victories in Greater Tainan and Kaohsiung were expected by everyone, but its impressive increase in vote share in Greater Tainan (12% increase) and the over-50% vote share in Greater Kaohsiung were still a surprise to many. Before the election, many had speculated that the extremely popular Kaohsiung County Commissioner Yang Chiu-hsing (杨秋兴), who quit the DPP and run as an independent, would share DPP's supporters with the DPP candidate Chen Chu. But the result proves otherwise: DPP supporters in Greater Kaohsiung had a stronger identification with the party than with the candidate — few left Chen for Yang. In contrast, KMT's supporters were less loyal to their party, deviating from KMT candidate Huang Chao-shun (黄昭顺) to support Yang. The city councilor elections are also a testimony to the progress made by the DPP. The KMT used to dominate city councils no matter which party won the mayoral seats. But this time the DPP's vote shares and seats in all the five councilor elections increased significantly. Its average vote share is only 3.3% less than that of the KMT (the DPP's 35.34% vs. the KMT's 38.6%), while the number of its total councilor seats is on par with that of the KMT at 130.

Overall, the election results indicate that the DPP has consolidated its dominance in southern Taiwan and is now targeting the north. It has revived significantly from its defeat in 2008 to compete with the KMT on an equal footing in the 2012 presidential race.

Future Challenges to the Two Parties

The DPP's new "middle of the road" strategy faces serious challenge from the party's hardliners who are mostly senior pro-independence radicals. They had expected the DPP to win at least one of the mayoral seats in Taipei and Sinbei; the defeats in the two cities made them believe that the new campaign strategy did not work well. The hardliners' social base is mainly in southern Taiwan. In the five elections, it was the DPP's landslide victory in the south, where the new strategy was not popular, that finally enabled the party to beat the KMT in total votes. Therefore, there is good reason for the hardliners to argue that although the new strategy may be attractive to voters in northern urban areas, it may not be a good choice for mobilizing farmers and production workers in the south, especially when the old strategy still works well in the south.

The election of Chen Chih-chung (陈致中) was taken as a case for the hardliner's argument. Chen is the son of former president Chen Shui-bian (陈水扁), a councilor candidate in Greater Kaohsiung and a key member of the newly established radical pro-independence political alliance, Alliance for One-Country-on-Each-Side. He was a pro-independence radical who was implicated in his father's corruption crimes and troubled by a prostitution scandal before the election. His election by record high votes was concluded by some that southern Taiwan had a distinct local culture from the north and might not welcome the DPP's moderate strategy. The radical pro-Chen Shui-bian and pro-independence Alliance for One-Country-on-Each-Side grabbed 33 councilor seats in the elections.[17] Many of these councilors were elected by highest or second highest votes in their respective district. It indicates a strong grassroots support for a possible radical line, which is a potential threat to the DPP's new strategy.

---

[17] Small Parties Reshuffle, Alliance for One-Country-on-Each-Side Won, Taiwan Solidarity Union Bubbled, 28 November 2010, http://gb.chinareviewnews.com/doc/1015/2/2/2/101522232 html?coluid=0&kindid=0&docid=101522232&mdate=1128113924, accessed on 5 December 2010.

Nevertheless, DPP Chairwoman Tsai Ing-wen who was behind this new strategy enjoyed majority support in both the DPP's leadership group and the public opinion survey.[18] It is obvious for her that in the 2012 presidential race, the DPP cannot avoid cross-strait issues such as ECFA again. Especially, it must present a China policy that is different from the KMT's and acceptable to major faction leaders in the party. To build a favorable discourse for her China policy, Tsai has donated 66% of her election subsidy (US$657,900) to establish a think tank to help create "a peaceful and stable framework for interacting with China."[19] This shows her preference for a moderate and pragmatic China policy in the future.

If the trend of declining popular support for the KMT remains, the KMT will no doubt lose many seats in the national legislative election prior to the presidential election in early 2012. However, this does not mean that the KMT has little hope of maintaining power. It is still possible that the Taiwanese people elect DPP candidates as local governors, city councilors and national legislators, but keep the KMT in power for an open and stable relation with mainland China. The Ma administration will continue its cautious mainland China policy to facilitate a full recovery of Taiwan's economy and reduce unemployment, while keeping away from a pro-China image. However, it remains to be seen whether the Ma administration can change the popular impression that ECFA will mostly benefit the north, urban areas, upper class and a very limited number of enterprises. In addition, the KMT has started to tackle its problems concerning the party's local branches and younger voters. Right after the elections, the KMT has planned to reshuffle local party branch and headquarters' executives across the island. It is reported that to prepare for the 2012 presidential election, some 20 college or graduate school graduates will be included in the campaign team.[20]

---

[18] Tsai Favored to Continue as DPP Head, 2 December 2010, http://www.chinapost.com.tw /taiwan/national/national-news/2010/12/02/282174/Tsai-favored.htm.

[19] DPP Chairwoman Donates Vote Subsidy to Set up Think Tank, 30 November 2010, http://focustaiwan.tw/news/a/201011300031.aspx, accessed on 18 June 2015.; Taiwan Opposition Proposes China Dialogue, 30 November 2010, http://ibnlive.in.com/generalnewsfeed/ news/taiwan-opposition-proposes-china-dialogue/518336.html, accessed on 5 December 2010

[20] KMT to Shuffle Local, Department Chiefs: Party Secretary-General, 28 November 2010, http://focustaiwan.tw/news/aipl/201011280030.aspx, accessed on 18 June 2015..

CHAPTER 8: TAIWAN'S 2012 PRESIDENTIAL AND LEGISLATIVE ELECTIONS[1]

Ma's Stability Card Defeats Tsai's Social Justice Card

On 14 January 2012, Taiwan had its first two-in-one presidential and legislative elections. President Ma Ying-jeou of the Kuomintang (KMT) won the re-election with 51.6% of the votes. The other two presidential candidates, main opposition Democratic Progressive Party (DPP) Chairwoman Tsai Ing-wen and People First Party (PFP) Chairman James Soong, received 45.63% and 2.77% of the votes, respectively.[2] In the legislative election, the KMT won only 64 of the seats, down from 81 in 2008. Nevertheless, it managed to garner over 50% of seats (about 57%), while the DPP successfully increased its seats to 40 from 27 in 2008. Two small parties, pro-unification PFP and pro-independence Taiwan Solidarity Union received 3 seats respectively.[3]

After a tough election campaign and a very close race against Tsai, Ma's comfortable winning margin of 6% is unexpected. Speculation had it that Ma would win the re-election by a much smaller margin. Observers tend to believe that Ma's successful mainland China policy is the largest contributor to his victory. Based on unprecedentedly improved cross-strait

[1] This chapter was originally published in *East Asia: Developments and Challenges*, 2012 Edited by Yongnian Zheng, Liang Fook Lye. World Scientific Publishing. pp. 115–132.
[2] http://www.cec.gov.tw/zh_TW/IDX/indexP1.html, accessed on 16 January 2012.
[3] *Ibid.*

relations in his first term, Ma has successfully convinced the majority of Taiwanese that only his administration has the ability to maintain cross-strait stability, a necessary condition for Taiwan's economic revival under current bleak world economic conditions.

Ma's campaign was also better organized. He was able to create a sense of crisis during the campaign, driving many marginal voters, some young middle class and James Soong's potential voters to support the KMT. He made his supporters believe that only he is capable of sustaining a stable cross-strait relationship that is beneficial to the majority of the people in Taiwan. The concurrence of the presidential and legislative elections had also impacted positively on Ma's election campaign. The municipal elections result in 2010 clearly demonstrated the KMT's weakness of grass-roots mobilization as compared to the DPP's. This two-in-one format compelled the KMT's legislative candidates to mobilize stronger grass-roots support for both themselves and Ma.

The threat of a large split in voters caused by the PFP candidate Soong on the KMT camp did not materialize as he only received 2.77% of the votes. Moreover, the KMT took advantage of this potential threat to enhance its inactive supporters' sense of urgency for voting. The KMT's legislator-at-large candidates list was also an effective answer to the DPP's criticism of the KMT's disregard of social justice issues. Compared to the DPP's nomination list which includes some candidates with corruption records, the KMT's has more representatives of disadvantaged social groups and reform-oriented scholars. A large number of overseas Taiwanese, mostly from mainland China, returned to vote for the KMT. They were especially concerned about the possible setback in cross-strait relations if Tsai was elected president.

Tsai was mainly defeated by her dubious China policy based on a confusing "Taiwan consensus" after her rejection of the "1992 consensus." Although she made a series of concessions on cross-strait issues such as Economic Cooperation Framework Agreement (ECFA) during her election campaign, the majority of Taiwanese still doubted her ability in maintaining improved cross-strait relations if elected. With an apparent disadvantage in cross-strait issues, Tsai hit hard on social justice issues such as income inequality and unemployment, and ordinary people's livelihood issues to gain support. This is Ma's weakest area as his administration has yet to prove itself on many of these issues. The mainland Chinese and American governments showed their preference for Ma before the election. Especially for the Chinese government, Ma's electoral victory will mean that it is on the right track for its current Taiwan policy.

Ma will continue to work with the mainland Chinese government to further improve cross-strait relations. However, the possibility of political and security talks between the two sides in the near future is slim. Ma's peace agreement proposal during his election campaign was unpopular with the mass, indicating that the majority of Taiwanese were not ready for political talks with mainland China.

Important Background to the 2012 Elections

General context

In the 2008 presidential election, Ma Ying-jeou's unprecedented landslide victory was driven by popular dissatisfaction with President Chen Shui-bian and his administration in four areas: corrupt practices of Chen, his family members and his close government officials; disappointing economic development supposedly caused by his close-door China policy; increasing "ethnic" conflicts as a result of his radical pro-independence and ethnically divisive policies, and finally, Taiwan's deteriorating international relations, especially with the US, caused by Chen's provocative pro-independence policies.

Therefore, the Taiwanese people have been expecting the Ma administration to perform much better in these areas. In general, Ma's report card did not disappoint his supporters: Ma and his administration have no serious corruption scandals; Taiwan's economy has survived the 2008 world financial crisis and the ECFA with mainland China is expected to boost Taiwan's economic revival; "ethnic" tension in Taiwan has declined visibly, while Taiwan's relations with the US has improved. While these general performances seem to greatly favor Ma's re-election, his re-election campaign was much more difficult than what most observers had expected. This requires a much deeper analysis of Taiwan's economic, political and social developments from 2008 to 2011.

Economic context: Economic uncertainty, and weak recovery, but better economic prospects with the Mainland

During his 2008 presidential election campaign, Ma Ying-jeou set 633, representing 6% GDP growth rate, US$30,000 per capita GDP, and 3% or less unemployment rate, as his administration's goals for Taiwan during his term. His performance yielded mixed results four years later. Table 8.1 provides a comparison of the Ma administration of 2008–2011 and the Chen administration of 2004–2007 on some key economic indicators. The results do not always favor Ma.

First, it is obvious that Ma has not achieved any of his 633 goals. In the past four years, the annual averages of the GDP growth rate, per capita GDP and unemployment rate were 3.54%, US$18,147 and 4.9%, respectively. These numbers suggest that there is still a long way to go for Ma to reach his goal of 633. Especially under current world economic

Table 8.1 Comparison of Key Economic Indicators between Ma's and Chen's Presidency

	Year	GDP Growth Rate (%)	Per Capita GDP (US$)	Unemployment Rate (%)	Real Wage Index of Non-Agriculture Workers (2004 = 1)
Chen administration	2004	6.19	15,012	4.44	1.00
	2005	4.70	16,051	4.13	0.99
	2006	5.44	16,491	3.91	0.99
	2007	5.98	17,154	3.91	0.99
	2004–2007 Average	5.58	16,177	4.10	—
Ma administration	2008	0.73	17,399	4.14	0.96
	2009	−1.81	16,353	5.85	0.92
	2010	10.72	18,588	5.21	0.96
	2011	4.51	20,246	4.40	N.A.
	2008–2011 Average	3.54	18,147	4.90	—

Data source: Directorate General of Budget, Accounting and Statistics, Executive Yuan, R.O.C.

uncertainties, political pundits and the public now tend to believe that 633 are overstretched and unaccomplishable goals even in Ma's second term of 2012–2015.

Compared to the Chen administration of 2004–2007, the Ma administration only performed better on per capita GDP growth. During Ma's first term, Taiwan's per capital GDP grew by 16.4% from US$17,399 in 2008 to US$20,246 in 2011. This is higher than the Chen administration's 14.3% increase. In terms of GDP growth, the Chen administration maintained a fairly stable growth rate, ranging from 4.7% to 6.19%, and an annual average of 5.58%. In contrast, the world financial crisis of 2008 had impacted Taiwan negatively, registering extremely slow and negative GDP growth in the first two years of the Ma administration (0.73% and −1.81% in 2008 and 2009, respectively). It was only in 2010 that the Taiwanese economy rebounded soundly at a two-decade high of 10.72%. However, the rebound was short-lived. In 2011, Taiwan's economic growth dipped to 4.5%. Overall, Taiwan's economy had experienced its worst economic setbacks during Ma's first term of office. With an average annual growth rate of 3.54%, Ma's economic performance is no better than Chen's (5.58%).

In terms of employment and real wage index, the Ma administration also did not perform better than Chen's (see Table 8.1). The average unemployment rate was 4.9% during Ma's 2008–2011, 0.8% higher than that during the Chen administration (4.1%). The real wage during the Ma administration declined by 4%–8% from the 2004 level, while it only declined by 1% during the Chen administration. As unemployment and real wage decline impact the masses more directly and strongly than any positive impact of GDP growth, the economy has been criticized by the DPP as a "recovery unfelt by people" (无感复苏). This has also prompted the DPP to run its election campaign around social justice and class issues.

Although Ma Ying-jeou's performance in economic indicators is not particularly outstanding as compared to Chen Shui-bian's, his effort in improving cross-strait relations has been substantial and visible. As a result, cross-strait relations have been peaceful, active, mutually beneficial and the best ever in history. The signing of the ECFA is considered by the Ma administration as one of the most important contributors to

Taiwan's economic revival. However, most Taiwanese are ambivalent about improved cross-strait relations in general, and ECFA in particular. While appreciating the positive outcomes of stable and peaceful cross-strait relations, such as economic gains and mutual understanding between the people in Taiwan and mainland China (the KMT perspective), the Taiwanese are also concerned about the potential negative consequences brought about by more frequent interactions in various fields between the two sides (the DPP perspective). Both parties have won sizable supporters for their respective stance.

Political context: DPP's revival in local elections

In Taiwan, because of the high frequency of various elections at different levels, election results are the best indicator of the island's changing political landscape. Figure 8.1 indicates that since 2008 when Ma was elected president with a record high vote share, the most significant change in Taiwan's politics had been the ever increasing popular support

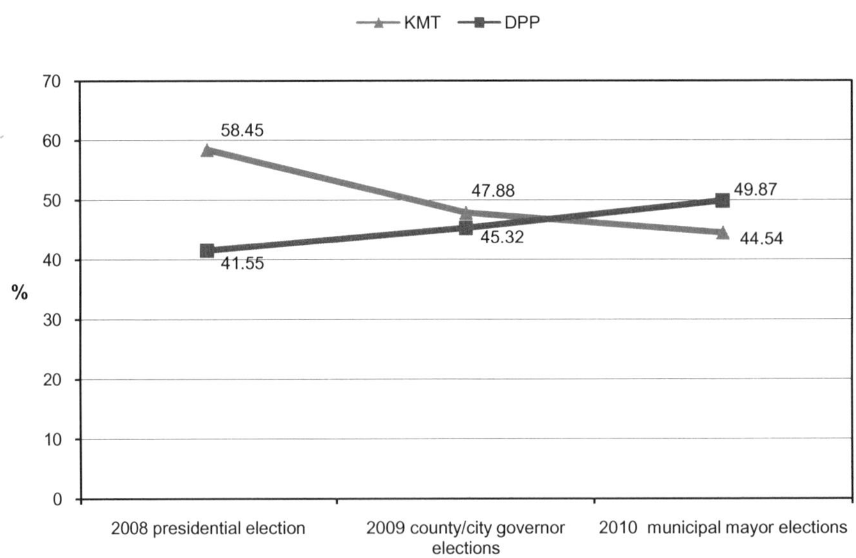

Figure 8.1 KMT's and DPP's Vote Shares: 2008–2010

Data source: Central Election Commission, ROC (Taiwan), http://www.cec.gov.tw/.

for the DPP in contrast to the declining vote for the KMT as evident in the two major local elections in 2009 and 2010. This demonstrates people's increasing dissatisfaction with the local governance of the KMT, which undoubtedly has a negative impact on their evaluation of the Ma administration at the national level.

For the DPP, under the leadership of Tsai, the party has successfully emerged from the shadow of Chen Shui-bian's corruption scandals and the DPP's disastrous electoral defeats in 2008 to finally compete with the KMT on an equal footing in local elections by the end of 2010. Tsai has managed to transform the party's radical, emotional and incompetent public image to one which is moderate, rational and competent. The transformation has largely been a success as shown by the DPP's rising popular support. In contrast, although Ma Ying-jeou has won due credit for improving cross-strait relations, his administration has been viewed by many as incompetent in local governance and indifferent to ordinary people's livelihood difficulties. For example, his administration's mishandling of the 8 August 2009 flood was criticized severely by the public and led to the Premier's resignation and the reshuffling of the Cabinet. In another widely criticized case, the new Premier and also the vice presidential candidate, Wu Den-yih, once commented at a conference that unpaid leave was a great invention which deserves a Nobel Prize in Economics.[4]

Social context: Rising Taiwanese nationalism

Apart from Economics, Taiwanese nationalism has a big part to play in Taiwan's politics and elections. Since its founding, the DPP has been the largest promoter and beneficiary of rising Taiwanese nationalism. The Chinese government's Taiwan policy is largely aimed at containing Taiwanese nationalism and its tendency to pursue Taiwan's independence in either moderate or radical ways. The Chinese government hopes that ECFA and working with the Ma administration to improve cross-strait relations will help win the Taiwanese people's hearts. But a series of

[4] http://www.ttv.com.tw/news/view/?i=09201001201048 2DEB106229479AB9F9112 65A0746 D805F0, accessed on 16 January 2012.

public opinion surveys conducted by the National Chengchi University's Election Study Center suggest otherwise.

The surveys show that during the Chen administration of 2004–2007, on average, about 43.5% of people in Taiwan identify themselves as Taiwanese only rather than Chinese only or both Chinese and Taiwanese, and about 20.5% of the respondents are pro-Taiwan's independence and not pro-unification or pro-status quo. During the Ma administration (until June 2011), these two indicators of Taiwanese nationalism went up to 51.7% and 22.4%, respectively.[5] Rising Taiwanese nationalism contributed to the popular disapproval of Ma's proposal for a peace agreement between Taiwan and mainland China in October 2011. In general, the DPP stands to gain from rising Taiwanese nationalistic sentiments than the KMT. Especially in previous presidential elections, the DPP had been extremely adroit at mobilizing supporters based on nationalistic issues. However, in this election the DPP replaced its highly provocative campaign strategy with a relatively low profile and defensive strategy on nationalistic issues. Tsai's preference for moderate campaign strategies is one reason, while the DPP's obvious disadvantage in cross-strait relations is another.

International context: Tension and cooperation between China and the US

The most important international development for this election is America's return to Asia. The DPP believes that Taiwan will play an important role in the US' "return to Asia" strategy to contain China's rise. Consequently, the DPP regards this as a good opportunity for Taiwan to balance cross-strait relations with American power. Specifically, Tsai proposes building bilateral cross-strait relations within a multilateral framework with other world powers such as the US and Japan.[6] The KMT on the other hand holds a more realistic and balanced view about

---

[5] Recoded and then recalculated from http://esc.nccu.edu.tw/modules/tinyd2/index.php?id=3, accessed on 16 January 2012.

[6] http://www.bbc.co.uk/zhongwen/trad/chinese_news/2011/06/110619_taiwan_china_tsai.shtml, accessed on 18 June 2015.

Sino–American relations. They tend to believe that cooperation, rather than tension, is the main theme of Sino–American relations. As the US needs China's cooperation on Iran and North Korea issues, a peaceful and stable cross-strait relation suits American interests better as it will reduce conflicts between China and the US.

Campaigns and Platforms

Platforms of the three candidates

In general, the 2012 presidential and legislative elections demonstrate that Taiwan's democracy and electorates have attained another level of maturity. Compared to previous presidential elections, the campaign strategies of the three participating parties are more rational, practical and positive. Consequently, the negative impact of post-election social divisiveness as experienced in previous elections is almost non-existent in this election.

DPP candidate Tsai gave up the party's traditional campaign strategy of mobilizing emotional support through a play on nationalistic and ideological issues. Tsai's moderate campaign strategy worked well in the 2010 Sinbei mayor election, laying out DPP's specific policy agenda the 10-year platform, to the public. Ma Ying-jeou's campaign was policy-oriented as well. His campaign was based on the delivery of results of his administration's past policies, a belief which would make his future policy proposal of 10 Golden Years more credible than Tsai's. A general comparison of their platforms shows more commonalities than differences. Both platforms emphasize the importance of sustainable economic development, environment protection, social justice and maintaining peaceful and active cross-strait relations.[7]

Nevertheless, after the two candidates' frequent policy debates and other campaign activities, the public saw substantial differences in the two camps' platforms. Ma seemed to prioritize economic development over social justice, while Tsai proposed the opposite and appealed to the "three

---

[7] http://10.iing.tw/, http://www.nownews.com/2011/09/29/301-2745692.htm, accessed on 16 January 2012.

middles": The middle and lower middle classes, residents in middle and south Taiwan, and small and middle enterprises (SMEs). Ma's policy agenda emphasized his biggest achievement in the past three years: ECFA and the significantly improved cross-strait relations. Ma repeatedly reminded the Taiwanese that only his administration could maintain long term stable economic relations with mainland China, which is the most important condition for Taiwan's future economic revival. Ma argues that Tsai could not do the same as she refused to accept the "1992 consensus," the consensus of "one China, different interpretations (一中各表)" agreed between Taiwan and mainland China in 1992. Most importantly, the Chinese government has reiterated that the "1992 consensus" is the necessary prerequisite for the implementation of ECFA and future improvement of cross-strait relations. Therefore, with the implicit but strong support of the Chinese government, Ma's mainland China policy was his largest campaign advantage. If most Taiwanese accept this argument, Tsai's China policy would obviously become her largest disadvantage.

Tsai tried to minimize the negative impact of this disadvantage in her campaign by attacking the Ma administration on its incompetence in solving ordinary people's livelihood issues. These issues mainly include high unemployment rate especially among the youth, real wage and stock market decline, income inequality, high and still rising housing price, etc. To counter the "1992 consensus," Tsai proposed the "Taiwan consensus" as the cornerstone of her China policy. She defined "Taiwan consensus" as the democratic process to achieve a consensus in Taiwan which would provide a more legitimate basis for the new administration's China policy. The outcome of this democratic process however will not be known until this democratic process, such as a referendum, is held. The "Taiwan consensus" seemed to be a good strategy for Tsai to escape from her disadvantaged position on cross-strait issues. In reality, however, it did not address the public's concern about whether her China policy can further improve or even maintain current cross-strait relations.

To allay the fears of swing voters about her China policy, Tsai gradually shifted from her complete rejection of ECFA to one of acceptance. She also promised that the current amicable cross-strait relations would be maintained under her future administration. This promise however lost ground when the Chinese government insisted that a good cross-strait relation would only be possible if Tsai accepts the "one China principle/framework." Throughout the election campaign, Tsai enjoyed much less public trust and support than Ma on cross-strait issues. However, her criticism of the Ma administration's incompetence in addressing ordinary Taiwanese's livelihood issues received a strong echo from the public, especially from social science scholars and various underprivileged groups.

Academic surveys since the 1990s have shown that the KMT has generally been viewed by most Taiwanese as a conservative (status quo oriented) and rightist party representing the rich and powerful, while the DPP is a progressive (reform oriented) and leftist party representing the interests of the ordinary people. During the Chen administration of 2000–2008, this popular distinction between the two parties became somewhat less prominent because of Chen and his close associates' corrupt relations with some powerful Taiwanese business persons. Nevertheless, in the 2008 presidential election, various underprivileged classes, such as the elderly, lower-middle class, less-educated, southern Taiwan residents, workers and farmers, were more likely than others to vote for the DPP. Two major characteristics of these classes explain their stronger support for the DPP. First, since the 1990s these classes have displayed stronger Taiwanese nationalistic sentiments than other social groups. Second, since 2000 they have shown a stronger tendency to believe that they were more victims than beneficiaries of improved economic exchange between Taiwan and mainland China. The DPP's nationalistic and leftist policy agenda seems more appealing to them.

The election campaigns of the two camps have revealed their biggest strengths and weaknesses. It was Ma's "importance of better cross-strait relations" vs. Tsai's "importance of social justice." James Soong, the presidential candidate of PFP, tried to borrow both Ma's and Tsai's strengths for his own use. His platform has an equal emphasis on cross-strait relations and Taiwan's social justice. He furthered the KMT's stance on cross-strait relations by explicitly proposing Taiwan's unification with mainland China. Meanwhile, he emphasized policies favoring the interests of the "three middles," a Tsai stance.

Major campaign events and fluctuating popular support

In the early period of the election campaign, public opinion polls conducted by different Taiwanese media showed Ma's large lead of over 10% against Tsai. Although the Taiwanese media have been famous for their polls' inaccuracy and bias, it is usually believed that a 10% margin would guarantee Ma's re-election. However, James Soong's unexpected participation in the election significantly reduced the possibility of a Ma re-election. Early polls showed that Soong generally enjoyed 10% support, and most of his supporters were from the KMT's pan-blue base. His participation had hence negatively impacted on Ma's chances than on Tsai's. Ma's leading margin against Tsai went down to around 6% after Soong's participation. This narrow margin made Ma's re-election extremely difficult. As a result, Soong became the critical minority in the election. Many observers believed that if Soong obtained over 5% of votes, Tsai would defeat Ma in the election.

Another major negative turning point for Ma's popular support was his proposal in October of a peace agreement with mainland China. The intention of this peace agreement, as explained repeatedly by Ma, is to institutionalize current peaceful cross-strait relations and guarantee peace across the strait. Based on his substantial achievement in improving cross-strait relations, Ma expected this proposal to work in his favor. However, as the KMT has been viewed as a pro-China and pro-ultimate-unification party by most Taiwanese, this proposal triggered the public's suspicion of Ma's promotion of unification in his next term. Under the DPP's attack and public pressure, Ma quickly compromised by proposing new conditions, such as referendum support, for such an agreement. After this event, Ma's lead in various opinion polls plummeted to an insignificant leading margin. In November, to reverse the declining support trend, the KMT released the legislator-at-large candidates list, which was a happy surprise to the public. Compared to the DPP's list, the top nominees on the KMT list included more representatives of disadvantaged social groups and reform-oriented scholars. In contrast, the DPP's nomination list was a disappointment. The list included some nominees with corruption records and fewer representatives of the disadvantaged groups. An interesting phenomenon was that both the KMT and the DPP lost credit on their supposedly advantage position: the cross-strait relations for the KMT and the social justice issues for the DPP. This complicated the race between the two candidates and made it an extremely close race.

In October 2011, the DPP capitalized on a warning issued by the Control Yuan for its possible violation of the law on donation to political parties when it accepted piggy banks from three-year-old triplets. The DPP cleverly used this warning to launch a "three little pigs" campaign to distribute free piggy banks first, and then collect them back full of small donations from the ordinary people. This two-month small donation drive was a big success for the DPP. It collected 143,000 piggy banks worth NT$201 million.[8] It also effectively consolidated its image as the genuine representative of "three little pigs" (ordinary people) in its fight against the "big bad wolf" (the coalition of the KMT and powerful business conglomerates).

On the external front, the US government's attitude toward Ma and Tsai was closely watched by the Taiwanese public. The US government showed its disapproval of Tsai as early as in September 2011 during Tsai's visit to Washington. *Financial Times* reported that after Tsai met with US administration officials, a senior official said "[s]he left us with distinct doubts about whether she is both willing and able to continue the stability in cross-strait relations the region has enjoyed in recent years."[9] In the months thereafter, the US government demonstrated its preference for Ma through a series of actions, such as arms sales to Taiwan, high level delegations' visit to Taiwan, nomination of Taiwan to its Visa Waiver Program, and finally, two days before the election, the ex-AIT (American Institute in Taiwan) director Douglas Paal's supportive remarks on Ma's "1992 consensus" in Taipei.[10]

In the roundup of the last 10 days of the election, a series of final public opinion polls showed that James Soong still received about 5% support, while Ma led Tsai by about 6% in some opinion surveys, and Tsai enjoyed the same level of support in some others.

---

[8] http://focustaiwan.tw/news/aipl/201201060036.aspx, accessed on 18 June 2015.

[9] http://www.ft.com/cms/s/0/f926fd14-df93-11e0-845a-00144feabdc0.html#axzz1jQBIoPVG, accessed on 16 January 2012.

[10] http://focustaiwan.tw/news/aipl/201201140009.aspx, accessed on 18 June 2015.

Post-Election Challenges for Ma and the DPP

Compared to the 2008 presidential and legislative elections, the vote share for Ma Ying-jeou and the number of legislative seats for the KMT in this election decreased by about 7% and 15%, respectively. This makes the second term of the Ma administration more challenging.

Ma is likely to have gained a much stronger sense of urgency in solving many ordinary people's bread-and-butter issues after the DPP's challenges in this election. However, Taiwan's difficult economic prospect as a result of global economic uncertainties will make these issues even harder to tackle. The global economic slowdown would seriously impact Taiwan's economy. Unemployment will rise and youth unemployment, in particular, is likely to become a flashpoint.

Long viewed as a pro-rich and pro-powerful, pro-capitalist, elitist and conservative party, the KMT is not expected to change its developmental mentality in the foreseeable future. In other words, the highest priority in Ma's second term will still be economic development rather than wealth redistribution. Essentially, solving the social justice issues raised by the DPP requires a redesign of Taiwan's wealth redistribution systems. Although the Ma administration may increase the social welfare budget in the second term, it will not be willing and able to complete some more important systematic reforms such as taxation reform disfavoring the rich. Therefore, it is expected that social justice will be a contending issue again as the DPP's major challenge to the KMT in the 2016 presidential election.

Rising Taiwanese nationalism will impose additional constraints on the Ma administration because of the KMT's pro-China image. Although Ma's mainland China policy was the largest contributor to his victory in this election, it will remain a double-edged sword for his administration. Ma should have learned from the significant decline in his popularity following his peace agreement proposal during the election campaign. Therefore, in the early years of his second term of office, Ma will have to tread carefully especially on sensitive cross-strait issues to avoid arousing the suspicions of many Taiwanese and the unease of the American government. In her visit to the US in February 2012, Taiwan's Mainland Affairs Council Minister Lai Shin-yuan emphasized that "it is not very likely for Taiwan and mainland China to embark on any political talks in the absence of a high level of consensus at home and mutual trust between the two sides."[11] This is a clear message from the Ma administration to the Taiwanese public, and the American and Chinese governments that rising Taiwanese nationalism will continue to restrain its mainland China policies.

Despite his hesitance on cross-strait political talks, Ma is likely to continue with the KMT policy of improving economic relations with mainland China as the most effective way to revive Taiwan's flagging economy in the current global economic slowdown. However, stronger popular support for Ma's mainland China policy does not mean the Taiwanese public would be blind to the negative domestic impacts of Taiwan's increasing economic dependence on mainland China. As Tsai had pointed out in her election campaign, these impacts mainly include rapidly increasing Taiwanese investments to mainland China at the expense of domestic investments, delayed industrial upgrading, rising income inequality and so on. Therefore, the Ma administration will also have to work hard to minimize these negative impacts. In particular, he needs to show that his mainland China policy can eventually help address Taiwan's social justice issues, issues which the KMT will be the most vulnerable to criticisms in the 2016 presidential election.

The DPP's defeat in the presidential election does not indicate the end of its road to revival. On the contrary, the increased number of legislative seats it has won suggests that popular support for the DPP is expanding. Although the majority of Taiwanese do not feel ready to appoint the DPP to office, they have empowered it with other important positions. The DPP is becoming a much stronger opposition against the Ma administration after this legislative election. Without doubt, the largest challenge for the DPP in this election is its China policy. If the Ma administration maintains its relatively stable performance without obvious failures in the second term, the DPP may well stay as a local power after 2016 without a new China policy. Tsai Ing-wen, in her speech after the election, has suggested

[11] http://www.wantchinatimes.com/news-subclass-cnt.aspx?cid=1101&MainCatID=&id=20120202000055, accessed on 18 June 2015.

that the DPP thoroughly review its China policy.[12] Although it is unlikely that the DPP will accept the "1992 consensus," this election result may prompt the DPP to take a more pragmatic stand on specific cross-strait issues in the future. On the other hand, although Tsai resigned as DPP Chairperson to take responsibility for the electoral defeat, her moderate line on cross-strait relations and the DPP's new priority on social justice issues are likely to continue in the party. With significantly increased legislative seats, the DPP will need to maintain its commitment to social justice issues through legislative actions.

Both the KMT and the DPP will face a leadership succession problem and intra-party politics will continue to influence both parties' development in the next four years. For the DPP in particular, its newly elected Chairman, Su Tseng-chang needs to maintain the DPP's popularity. There are also many DPP members who would like to see Tsai retake the helm and run for the presidential election again in 2016. For the KMT, Ma has repeated his determination to introduce further reforms to the party. His relatively smooth re-election has improved the creditability of KMT's Ma-King mechanism (*ma jin ti zhi*), which has also been the largest promoter of intra-party reforms. However, some KMT politicians consider the Ma-King mechanism an indication of Ma's over-reliance on King Pu-tsung on many important issues. For example, one of King's major reform efforts was to cut off the KMT's long term "black gold" ties with local factions in central and southern Taiwan. Consequently, local factions were said to have stopped garnering votes for the KMT in elections, leading to a drop in votes for the Party in the 2010 municipal elections. KMT candidates for future local and national elections may want to work towards building the party's conventional connections with local factions in a quest for more votes. Therefore, how long Ma and King can persist with their disconnection with local factions is still a question. Finally, the nine-in-one local elections in 2014 will be a mid-term report card for both the KMT and the DPP. Taiwan's political landscape for the 2016 presidential election will become clearer by then.

[12] http://udn.com/NEWS/NATIONAL/NATS9/6846979.shtml, accessed on 16 January 2012.

CHAPTER 9: THE CHINA POLICY OF TAIWAN'S DEMOCRATIC PROGRESSIVE PARTY SINCE 2012: THE UNFINISHED LAST MILE

Three Lines of China Policy in the Democratic Progressive Party (DPP)

On the evening of 14 January 2012, the (DPP) presidential candidate Tsai Ing-wen (蔡英文) announced her defeat in the presidential election and declared to her supporters that they were already close to their destination and had only one last mile to complete.[1] Observers and key DPP members were soon aware that the stumbling block to "the last mile" in this election was the DPP's vague, overly conservative and defensive China policy. It was responsible for the swing in votes away from the DPP in favor of the incumbent Kuomintang (KMT) candidate Ma Ying-jeou. Compared to Tsai's, Ma's mainland China policy is clear and liberal, and he has improved cross-strait relations significantly in his first term of presidency.

The DPP's China policy is in direct opposition to the KMT's as it absolutely rejects the "one-China principle." Both the Chinese Communist Party (CCP) and the KMT believe that they have achieved a consensus in their 1992 dialogue in HongKong. The two sides have accepted the

[1] http://blog.renren.com/share/287286312/11124746336, accessed on 18 June 2015.

"one-China principle" with different interpretations of "China" by each side. The CCP interprets "China" as the People's Republic of China (PRC), while the KMT's interpretation is the Republic of China (ROC). In its meetings with the CCP since 2005, the KMT has not only explicitly showed its acceptance of the "one-China principle," but also claimed that the party opposed any effort to pursue Taiwan's independence. Therefore, the so called "1992 consensus" and anti-independence have become the basis for the CCP and KMT to improve cross-strait relations.

The CCP has announced repeatedly that as long as the DPP does not pursue independence for Taiwan and accepts the "one-China principle," it is willing to talk to the DPP officially on any economic, political and social matters.[2] The DPP has however never accepted this pre-condition for talk, and insisted that the talk should be conducted without any pre-condition. As a result, the two parties have never met officially. On the other hand, the DPP believes that the rejection of the "one-China principle" is its core party spirit, a unifying force that binds different factions promoting different China policy lines. Since 2012 three major lines of China policy, namely, radical, moderate and pragmatic, have emerged in the DPP.

The radical line is supported by most pro-independence fundamentalists in the party. They pursue *de jure* independence for Taiwan and a new set of national institutions, such as the constitution, the country name, the national flag and anthem and most importantly, the official recognition of Taiwan by the international community as an independent country. They view mainland China as the largest threat to their independence dream rather than as an opportunity to develop Taiwan economically. Consequently, they oppose most pro-China activities even if they could improve cross-strait relations and are of tremendous economic benefit to Taiwan. The radical line's leading figures include former president Chen Shui-bian (陈水扁) and the party's heavyweight Yu Shyi-kun (游锡堃). The DPP's Party Charter added Normal Nation Resolution in 2007, an official endorsement of the radical line.

The moderate line, which has dominated the DPP since 2008, emphasizes Taiwan's *de facto* independence. It thus argues that there is no

[2]http://csis.org/files/publication/1203qchina_taiwan.pdf, accessed on 18 June 2015.

necessity for Taiwan to seek independence or a completely new constitution, country name and so on. They see mainland China as both a political threat and an economic opportunity: A political threat when mainland China's unification effort is jeopardizing Taiwan's *de facto* independence and an economic opportunity when it is instrumental to Taiwan's economic revival. Politically, to safeguard Taiwan's *de facto* independence, they propose a very careful and politically defensive China policy. Economically, to capitalize on mainland China's economic strength, it recommends that the party adopt a more flexible China policy. The moderate line is represented by leading figures such as the former (May 2012–May 2014) DPP Chairman Su Tseng-chang (苏贞昌) and former Chairwoman and 2012 presidential candidate Tsai Ing-wen. The Resolution on Taiwan's Future, which was incorporated into the Party Charter in 1999, is the official representation of the moderate line.

The pragmatic line has been controversial among DPP key members since 2012. Like the moderate line, the pragmatic line accepts Taiwan's current *de facto* independence and does not radically pursue future *de jure* independence for Taiwan. Supporters of this line believe that a good China policy is one that will send the DPP to power in the next presidential election. This implies significantly downplaying of mainland China's political threat to Taiwan's *de facto* independence as well as prioritizing its China policy on maintaining or further improving the economic opportunity brought by mainland China. The major leader of this line is Frank Hsieh Chang-ting (谢长廷), former chairman of the DPP, former premier of the DPP administration in 2005–2006, and the DPP presidential candidate in 2008. His current stance is to propose a China policy that may be tolerated by mainland China, even if it violates the Party Charter implicitly.

The initial atmosphere right after the electoral defeat in early 2012 was very much in favor of the DPP seriously reflecting on its China policy and making substantial policy adjustment. However, the DPP, with its new Chairman Su Tseng-chang, later chose to slow down the adjustment process, an important but not so urgent task for the DPP. Pragmatically speaking, the major role of the China policy is to serve the party's next presidential election campaign in mid-2015 which is still two years away. Nevertheless, since 2012 the core supporters of the DPP have started to follow general public opinion in approving the KMT's mainland China policy. A delay in China policy adjustment may alienate more previous supporters of the DPP.

Loss of Core Supporters on China Policy Since 2012

After the defeat in the 2012 presidential election, the pressure for the DPP to adjust its China policy comes from its not only moderate and pragmatic members, but also traditional support base. The DPP's largest support base is Taiwanese nationalists who have supported the DPP in each national election since the 1990s. In the studies of Taiwan's electoral politics, researchers usually pose two survey questions to identify Taiwanese nationalist:

(i) Do you consider yourself to be Taiwanese only, Chinese only or both Taiwanese and Chinese?
(ii) What is your opinion about Taiwan's future relation with mainland China, that is, are you pro-independence, pro-unification or pro-status-quo?

If the respondent chooses "Taiwanese only" for the first question, he or she is most likely a Taiwanese nationalist. Those who choose "pro-independence" for the second question are Taiwanese nationalists. As the DPP is the largest promoter of Taiwanese nationalism in Taiwan, it is natural for Taiwanese nationalists to support the party.

The second largest support base for the DPP is the disadvantaged groups in Taiwan, including the elderly (60-year-olds or older), the lower educated (junior-high-or-below education), southern Taiwan residents, blue collar workers and farmers. Prior to the DPP's 2000 presidential election win, these disadvantaged groups were more likely to vote for the KMT. However, during the DPP administration of 2000–2008, in particular since 2004, they had become more likely to vote for the DPP in presidential elections.[3]

[3] Dongtao Qi, 2013. Globalization, Social Justice Issues, Political and Economic Nationalism in Taiwan: An Explanation of the DPP's Limited Revival during 2008–2012. The *China Quarterly*, Vol. 216, pp. 1018–1044.

The support of the disadvantaged for the DPP could be attributed to first the large number of nationalists in the group. Compared to a much smaller nationalist component in the advantaged (Figure 9.1), this naturally translates into the group's stronger support for the DPP.

Second is the improvement in social policies during the DPP administration of 2000–2008, which benefited the disadvantaged population greatly by significantly increasing social welfare budget. Figure 9.2 illustrates that the average social welfare budget during the eight years of the DPP administration (2000–2008) was 18.2% of the central government's total budget, much higher than the 12.4% in the previous seven years of the KMT administration (1993–1999), by 5.8%.

Third is the belief that with the DPP's close-door China policy, their livelihood would be safeguarded against capital flight to mainland China and competition from cheap Chinese goods. Table 9.1 shows that shortly after the 2008 presidential election, 26.7% of the disadvantaged believed that they would be worse off; while 11.2% believed they would be better off under the open-door China policy. In contrast, only 13.8% of the advantaged believed they would be worse off.

As Taiwanese nationalists and the disadvantaged groups make up the core support base of the DPP, its China policy is a reflection of their

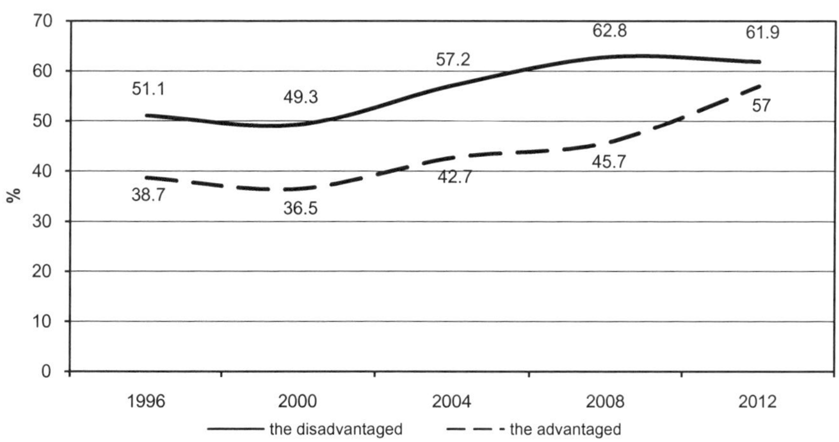

Figure 9.1 Percentage of Nationalists in Two Social Groups: 1996–2012

Source: Qi Dongtao, Globalization, Social Justice Issues, Political and Economic Nationalism.

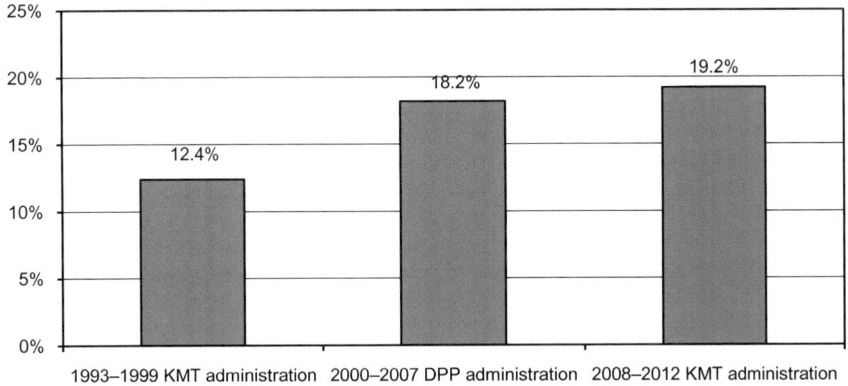

Figure 9.2 Average Percentage of Social Welfare Budget in Taiwanese Central Government's Total Budget during Different Administrations, 1993–2012

Data source: Hou-Sheng Chan, Yijiazi yilai Taiwan shehui fuli zhengce de yanbian (Sixty Years Evolution of Social Welfare Policy in Taiwan), paper presented at Shehui fuli moshi — cong chuancheng dao chuangxin yantaohui (Social Welfare Models: From Traditions to Innovations), Beijing, 15 to 19 April 2011, p. 9; Executive Yuan, Budget Plan of the Central Government (2012), p.32.

Table 9.1 Will You be Better Off, Worse Off, Or the Same Under the Open-Door China Policy? (2008)

(Unit: % of people in each social group)

	Better Off	Worse Off	The Same
The disadvantaged	11.2%	26.7%	62.1%
The advantaged	20%	13.8%	66.2%

Data source: TEDS2008P.

interests and sentiments. Indeed, the DPP's China policy has always been a mixture of political and economic nationalism. Its political nationalism component is to defend Taiwan's political independence from mainland China, which is the major concern of Taiwanese nationalists. On the other hand, its economic nationalism component attempts to protect the economic interests of the disadvantaged groups. To do this, the DPP believes in adopting a defensive, conservative, or even close-door China policy.

After its presidential defeat in 2008, the DPP has greatly moderated its China policy, but without substantially deviating from its two major cornerstones: The political and economic nationalism. Therefore, the DPP has continued to lambast the Ma administration on its China policy. To the DPP, the Ma administration's open-door China policy, represented by the Economic Cooperation Framework Agreement (ECFA), is too liberal and too hasty, and lacks transparency. It believes that the ECFA will increase Taiwan's economic dependence on mainland China, leading unavoidably to political dependence and eventually jeopardizing Taiwan's *de facto* independence. From the DPP perspective, the economic over-dependence will not only exacerbate capital flight from Taiwan to mainland China, but also increase the share of Chinese products and investment in Taiwan. This may delay Taiwan's industrial upgrading, increase competition for small and medium enterprises, raise unemployment rates and widen income inequality in Taiwan. While large businesses and high skilled labor will gain more from this process, the disadvantaged groups may have to accept lower salary or even lose their jobs.

The Ma administration has addressed these concerns by focusing only on improving economic, social and cultural exchanges and delaying official political talks with mainland China. To aid the disadvantaged groups, it has further increased its social welfare budget by 1%. The average social welfare budget of the Ma administration in its first term (2008–2012) was 19.2% of the total, while that of the previous two DPP administrations (2000–2007) was 18.2% (Figure 9.2). The Ma administration has also set aside NT$95 billion (about US$3.01 billion) over a 10-year period to support 17 vulnerable industries affected by ECFA.[4] The Chinese government on the other hand has also promised to minimize ECFA's negative impact on Taiwan's disadvantaged population.[5]

A survey conducted by a group of Taiwanese political scientists after the first four years of the open-door China policy and the re-election of Ma shows interesting results. The general finding is that the DPP has lost

---

[4]President Ma Holds Press Conference to Discuss Signing of ECFA, 1 July 2010. http://english.president.gov.tw/Default.aspx?tabid=491&itemid=21920&rmid=2355, accessed on 18 June 2015.

[5]Guotaiban Wang Yi zhuren jieshou Taiwan meiti zhuanfang (Interview with Wang Yi, Minister of Taiwan Affairs Office of State Council), 31 March 2010, http://www.chinanews.com/tw/news/2010/03-31/2200729.shtml, accessed on 18 June 2015.

advantages in almost all the important fields related to China policy, a reflection that the Ma administration has to a large extent addressed both political and economic concerns. Table 9.2 shows the responses of different groups to a survey question on "how would you rate Ma Ying-jeou and Tsai Ing-wen using 0 to 10 scale, if 0 means candidates are completely incapable of protecting Taiwan's interests, and 10 means that candidates are completely able to protect Taiwan's interests?" Though the nationalists' average rating of Tsai was one point higher than that of Ma, Ma scored higher on overall average rating.

This is an indication that while the nationalists still prefer Tsai's China policy due to its stronger tilt on political nationalism, the overall public was generally satisfied with Taiwan's national security and Ma's ability to protect Taiwan interests. Even the disadvantaged groups had rated Ma on the same footing as Tsai on this issue. The survey also asked respondents to compare the performance of the KMT and the DPP in handling some important national issues, such as cross-strait relations, economic development, social inequality, social welfare and Taiwan's international status, which the DPP said had been negatively impacted directly or indirectly by the KMT's open-door China policy.

Figures 9.3 to 9.6 show that with the exception of social inequality (Figure 9.6), respondents including DPP's core support base believed that the KMT was better than the DPP in handling these issues. Figure 9.7 indicates that while the overall public and the disadvantaged prefer the KMT to improve social welfare, the nationalists prefer the DPP.

These findings generally suggest that the DPP's lambast of the KMT's open-door mainland China policy has failed to achieve its desired effect.

Table 9.2 Average Rating of Tsai's and Ma's Capability of Protecting Taiwan Interests, 2012

	Tsai's Capability of Protecting Taiwan Interests	Ma's Capability of Protecting Taiwan Interests
Average rating by the nationalists	6.6	5.5
Average rating by the disadvantaged	5.9	5.9
Average rating by the overall public	5.8	6.1

Data source: TEDS2012P.

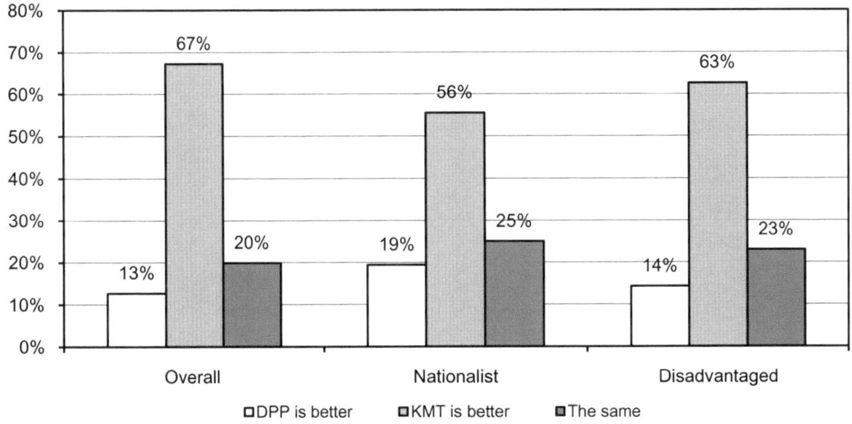

Figure 9.3 Percentage of People in Different Social Groups Believing DPP/KMT Is Better/the Same on Cross-Strait Relations, 2012

Data source: TEDS2012P.

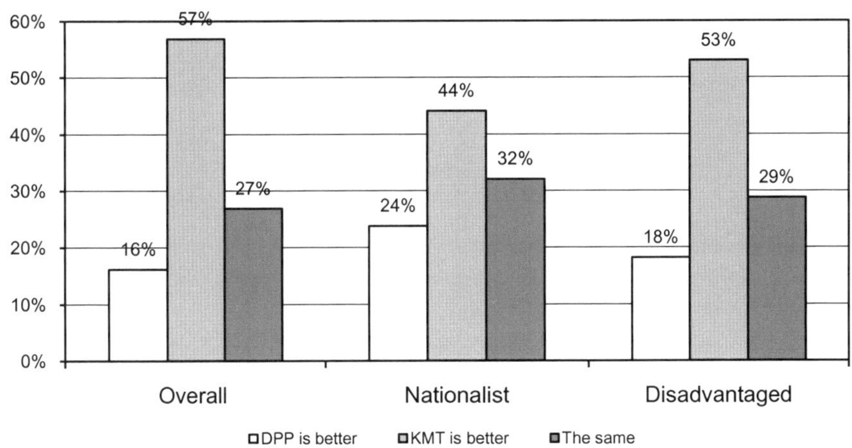

Figure 9.4 Percentage of People in Different Social Groups Believing DPP/KMT Is Better/the Same on Economic Development, 2012

Data source: TEDS2012P.

Even the DPP's core support base, in particular the disadvantaged groups, has shown a swing toward the KMT on important China-related policy fronts. This development could be attributed to the Ma administration's

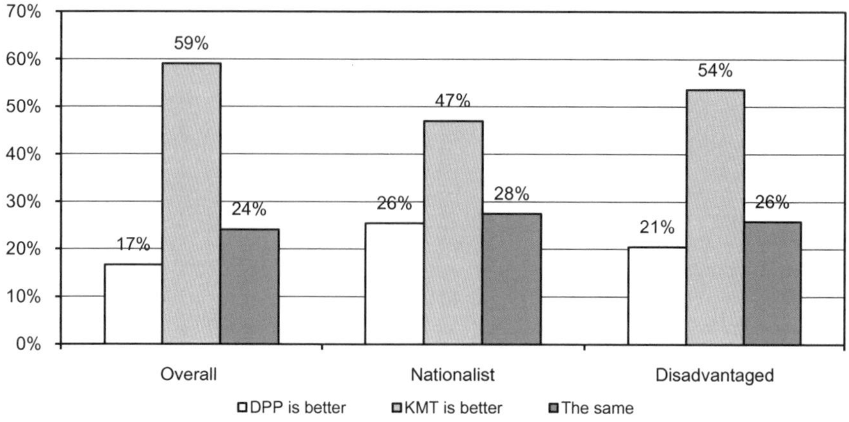

Figure 9.5 Percentage of People in Different Social Groups Believing DPP/KMT Is Better/the Same on Improving Taiwan's International Status, 2012

Data source: TEDS2012P.

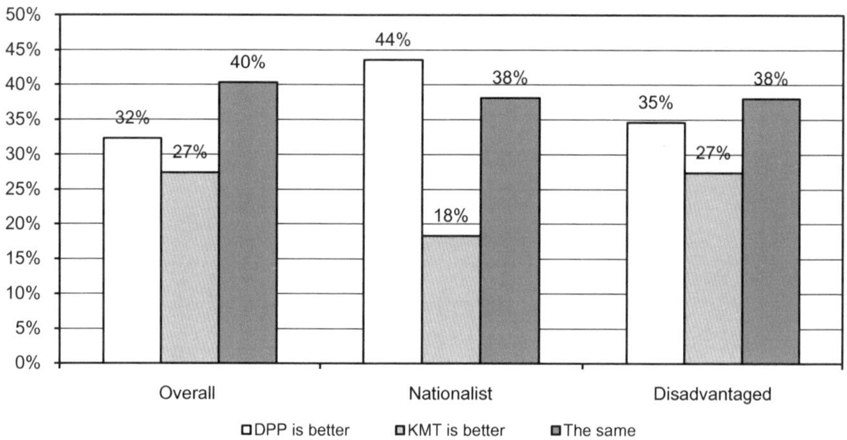

Figure 9.6 Percentage of People in Different Social Groups Believing DPP/KMT Is Better/the Same on Handling Social Inequality, 2012

Data source: TEDS2012P.

dual effort of promoting cross-strait relations and defending Taiwan's national security, while providing assistance to the disadvantaged. This preference swing left the DPP with no choice but to adjust its China policy.

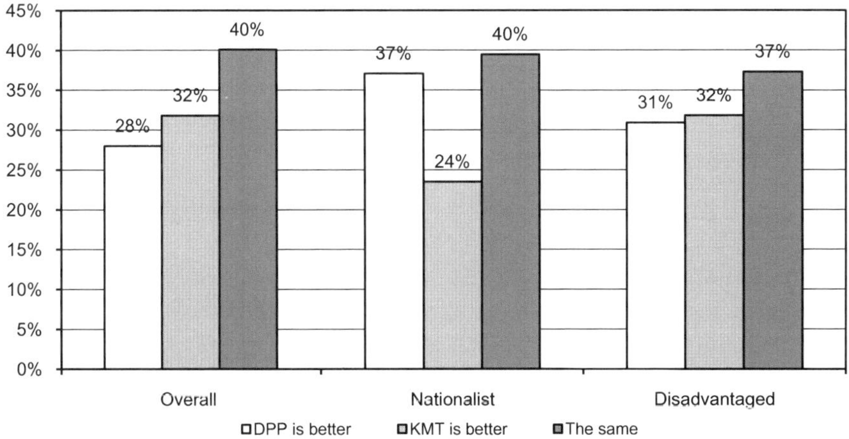

Figure 9.7 Percentage of People in Different Social Groups Believing DPP/KMT Is Better/the Same on Improving Social Welfare, 2012

Data source: TEDS2012P.

The Three DPP Heavyweights and the Last Mile

Since the 2012 presidential election, while popular opinions within and outside the DPP seemed to favor significant changes to its China policy, the change process has been slow. Two main factors have delayed the change process. The first is not a new but stronger "China threat" discourse that has emerged in the DPP and among liberal Taiwanese scholars. The second is factional politics among the three party heavyweights, namely, Su Tseng-chang, Tsai Ing-wen and Frank Hsieh Chang-ting.

The DPP defeat in the 2012 presidential election not only led to heated debate on its China policy, but also ignited serious concern about the Chinese government's influence in the election. Many DPP members and scholars believed that the Chinese government had a hand in mobilizing a large number of Taiwanese business owners and employees in mainland China to return to Taiwan to vote for Ma Ying-jeou during the election. With their return, many more local Taiwanese were believed to have been influenced to vote for Ma. The DPP attributed this "China factor" as among the major contributors to Ma's re-election, while some scholars even called 2012 "the first year of the China factor era."[6] Since then, the China factor, a popular term coined by the DPP and liberal scholars denoting mainland China's new threat to Taiwan, was utilized not only in Taiwan politics, but also in a variety of fields, such as media, pop culture and economy. The DPP argues that all these fields have been negatively influenced by the Chinese government, leading to a deterioration in Taiwan's core institutions, such as democracy, freedom of media, small and medium enterprises.

A more significant and direct factor determining the DPP's China policy is the factional politics among Su, Tsai and Hsieh. For the three heavyweights, the China policy should help the DPP win the presidential election in 2016 and improve their personal political power within the party and in national politics. All three heavyweights have a history of changing their stance on China policy under different political challenges and opportunities. When Su was premier for the Chen Shui-bian administration during 2006–2007, he tried to moderate Chen's radical nationalism policy toward mainland China but failed in the face of objections from the fundamentalists. The fundamentalists called his moderate China policy "Su's revisionist line" and denounced him severely.[7] Nevertheless, after he was elected DPP chairman in 2012, he has deviated from his previous moderate line and leaned toward the fundamentalist stance. Ideologically speaking, Tsai was very close to the fundamentalists as one of the key contributors to Lee Teng-hui's Two-State Theory in 1999.[8] Nevertheless, under her leadership from 2008 to 2012, the DPP abandoned Chen Shui-bian's radical line and became moderate toward mainland China. Her current stance on mainland China is mid-way between the other two heavyweights.

Hsieh was quite open to mainland China when he was the Kaohsiung mayor in the early 2000s. He proposed "Kaohsiung and Xiamen are two

---

[6] http://www.appledaily.com.tw/appledaily/article/forum/20121225/34727076/, accessed on 18 June 2015.

[7] http://www.npf.org.tw/getqr/10861; http://news.xinhuanet.com/tai_gang_ao/2006-07/26/content _4880882.htm, accessed on 14 July 2013.

[8] http://www.kmt.org.tw/english/page.aspx?type=article&mnum=113&anum=8355; http://taiwan. huanqiu.com/opinion/2011-09/2015592.html, accessed on14 July 2013.

cities in the same country according to our constitution."[9] But as the DPP presidential candidate in the 2008 presidential election, he relentlessly attacked Ma's open-door mainland China policy. Since 2012 he has retracted from this stance to become the first in the DPP to interact directly with the Chinese government and its think tanks and to propose the most pragmatic and liberal China policy in the DPP. Hsieh has good reasons to steer the China policy change in the DPP. Since he lost the 2008 presidential election, he has been largely marginalized in the DPP. A change in the China policy would provide him with a good opportunity to regain influence in the party. Nevertheless, his chances of becoming the DPP's 2016 presidential candidate are still slim, even if the DPP could achieve real breakthrough on China policy under his influence. The core concept of his China policy proposal is "one constitution with different interpretations." Hsieh proposes to use Taiwan's and mainland China's constitution as the common ground for jump-starting the official talk between the DPP and the CCP as the constitution is the most legitimate and stable institution for both sides. While his proposal seems to be able to avoid the "one-China principle" on paper, it is actually an implicit acceptance of the "one-China principle," as Taiwan's constitution holds that both Taiwan and mainland China belong to the ROC. For this, Hsieh has been criticized constantly by pro-independence fundamentalists.

For Su, the coming challenge is to keep his Chair position in the 2014 intra-party election before he could be nominated by the party in 2015 for the 2016 presidential election. He needs the support of the fundamentalists for his re-election in 2014, which is more urgent than the 2016 presidential election. He thus could not afford to alienate the fundamentalists with his China policy. Any substantial changes in his China policy stance could only be made after he secures his leadership in mid-2014 and leads the party to perform well in the seven-in-one elections in late 2014. His official stance now is to follow the Resolution on Taiwan's Future in the Party Charter, which is viewed as the moderate line that rejects the "one-China principle."

[9] http://www.chinareviewnews.com/crn-webapp/doc/docDetailCNML.jsp?coluid=7&kindid=0&d ocid=102137530, accessed on 15 July 2013.

Since Tsai lost the 2012 presidential election, she has been focusing on "reconnecting with society"; she commented less frequently and more moderately on China policy. To be nominated for the next presidential election, Tsai could not avoid declaring her stance on China policy at an appropriate time. Tsai has continued to stand by the previous political and economic nationalism concerns about national security and the disadvantaged groups' concern for welfare. Her stance is mid-way between Su and Hsieh, but with a slight tilt toward the latter.

Since 2008, fundamentalist heavyweights such as Yu Shyi-kun have little chance of securing either the party's Chair or the presidential candidate position. However, the large number and strong solidarity of fundamentalists is enough weight for them to constrain the moderate heavyweights from accepting different forms of "one-China principle." The fundamentalist heavyweights want adherence to the Party Charter's Normal Nation Resolution for the DPP to actively pursue Taiwan's *de jure* independence.

In general, there is now a strategic division of labor among Su, Tsai and Hsieh on China policy adjustment. Hsieh's job is to push the moderate line to its limit and propose a policy that may be tolerated by mainland China. If he succeeds, the new China policy may be adopted by Su and Tsai. Tsai is keeping a low profile on China policy and working the ground to understand society's expectations of the DPP's future China policy. Su, on the other hand, is working hard to ensure that the changing China policy will not alienate the fundamentalists and the American government. Therefore, the three heavyweights are trying to find a China policy that would be tolerable to both mainland China and the fundamentalists, and welcomed by Taiwanese society and the American government.

CHAPTER 10: GLOBALIZATION, SOCIAL JUSTICE ISSUES, POLITICAL AND ECONOMIC NATIONALISM IN TAIWAN: AN EXPLANATION OF THE DPP'S LIMITED REVIVAL DURING 2008–2012[1]

Following the Democratic Progressive Party's (DPP) overwhelming defeat by the Kuomintang (KMT) in both the legislative and the presidential elections in Taiwan in early 2008, it was hard to imagine that the DPP could restore its popular support in just two and a half years. The DPP's second administration of 2004–2008 was widely viewed as an unpopular one.[2] Towards the end of that term, the DPP was severely criticized not only by various opposition forces such as the KMT, but also by a large group from within the DPP. Scholars and pundits have already identified the failures of former President Chen Shui-bian 陈水扁 and his administration which led to their defeat in the 2008 elections, including the administration's dissatisfactory economic performance, supposedly

[1] This chapter is a slightly revised version of my paper published in 2013: Globalization, Social Justice Issues, Political and Economic Nationalism in Taiwan: An Explanation of the DPP's Limited Resurgence during 2008–2012, *The China Quarterly*, Vol. 216, pp. 1018–1044.

[2] See, e.g., Chai, 2008; Copper, 2008; Copper, 2009; and Lin, 2009a, p. 421.

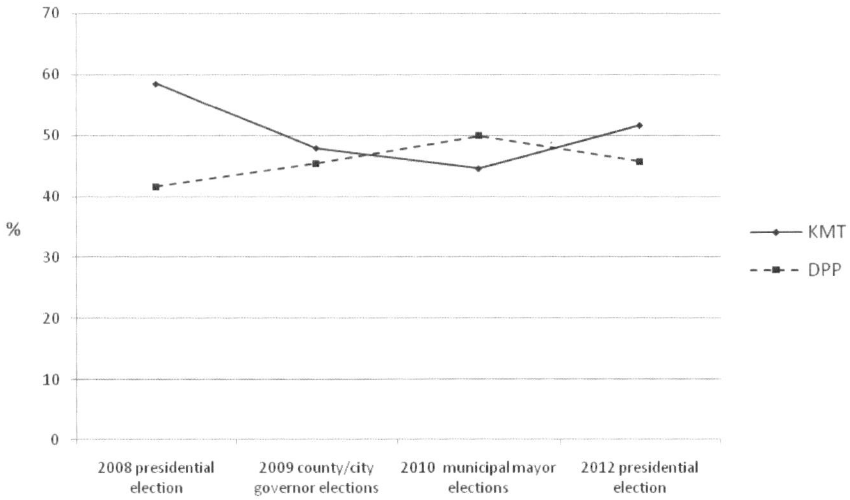

Figure 10.1 KMT's and DPP's Vote Shares in Local and Presidential Elections, 2008–2012

Source: Central Election Commission, ROC (Taiwan), http://www.cec.gov.tw/.

owing to its close-door China policy, the corruption scandals surrounding President Chen and his family members, increased ethnic conflicts and social instability, and the deterioration in Taiwan–US relations caused by Chen's radical and provocative pro-independence policies.[3]

Nevertheless, as Figure 10.1 shows, since its electoral defeat in 2008, the DPP has been steadily gaining popular support in local elections, and did particularly well in the five important metropolitan city elections in November 2010 (although the DPP won one less mayoral seat than the KMT, its total vote count was over 5% more). The city councilor elections, held together with the mayoral elections, also point to an increase in DPP support. The KMT used to dominate city councils, no matter which party won the mayoral seats,[4] but on this occasion the DPP's vote

[3] *Ibid.* Also see Rigger, 2010 and news.ifeng.com. 2008. Chen Shui-bian *zhizheng banian, tiaobuchu Huang Zhongxi guaiquan* (Chen Shui-bian's eight years administration not able to get rid of Huang Zhongxi's historic law), http://news.ifeng.com/special/chenshuibian/, accessed on 23 October 2012.

[4] Copper, 2010, p. 53.

share and seats in all the five councilor elections increased significantly. Its average vote share was only 3.3% less than that of the KMT (35.34% vs. 38.6%), while the total number of its councilor seats was on a par with that of the KMT at 130. Moreover, popular support amassed by the DPP throughout the whole island from the five city mayoral elections and the 2009 county/city governor elections gave the party 48.21% of the votes, more than the KMT's 45.76%.[5] Consequently, after the five city elections, the DPP Chairwoman, Tsai Ing-wen 蔡英文, declared that "the DPP is already able to compete on an equal footing with the ruling party."[6] During the presidential and legislative election in early 2012, the DPP, boosted by its renewed popular support, hit the KMT hard on many social justice issues, making the election race extremely close. In the end, the DPP obtained mixed results from this election: it increased its legislative seats from 27 to 40 in 2008, but lost the presidential election to the KMT by a 6% margin, although its vote share increased 4% from 41.6% in 2008. In summary, the DPP's election record from 2008 to 2012 indicates that although it successfully managed to restore its popular support in local and legislative elections, this political comeback reached its limit in the presidential election.

In trying to understand the DPP's limited resurgence, most explanations emphasize the short-term political and economic factors since 2008 that have either contributed to or constrained the DPP's political recovery. For example, on the DPP side, the new Chairwoman, Tsai Ing-wen, has overseen substantial party reform to rid the DPP of the negative legacies left behind by its former President and Chairman, Chen Shui-bian. Moreover, the performance of DPP local governors has improved significantly since 2008 and ranked much higher than that of the KMT governors in 2010. The party also adopted new and moderate campaign strategies in Taipei 台北市 and Sinbei 新北市 during the five metropolitan city elections. On the KMT side, the Ma Ying-jeou 马英九 administration failed to lift Taiwan's economy by the end of 2009, and the new administration

[5] Chinapost.com.tw. 2010. KMT, DPP neck-and-neck in council elections, 29 November, http://www.chinapost.com.tw/taiwan/national/national-news/2010/11/29/281743/KMT-DPP.htm, accessed on 23 October 2012.

[6] *Ibid.*

was also criticized by the public for its ineffective handling of some important national issues, such as the flood caused by Typhoon Morakot in August 2009.[7] Naturally, increasing popular dissatisfaction with the Ma administration boosted popular support for the DPP and contributed to its improved performance in local elections. On the other hand, many believe that the conservative China policy of 2012 DPP presidential candidate, Tsai Ing-wen, considerably hindered her chances of winning the election.[8]

The aforementioned factors have indeed contributed to or hampered the DPP's political comeback. Nevertheless, this study proposes a broader perspective focusing on the development of, and relations among, globalization, social justice issues and political and economic nationalism in Taiwan to gain a deeper understanding of the DPP's limited revival since 2008. Specifically, this perspective includes the following propositions.

First, as in many other countries, the Taiwanese government has generally been expected by the public to fulfill two major responsibilities: To increase national wealth through expanding the economy, and to allocate national wealth fairly through various policies, such as taxation and social welfare policies. The government's second responsibility is usually framed as addressing social justice issues in Taiwan.

Second, globalization is a double-edged sword: It can contribute to the country's economic development and help the government to fulfill its first responsibility, but on the other hand, it can bring about various environmental and social problems, such as increasing income inequality, which in turn make it more difficult for the government to fulfill its second responsibility.

Third, since the late 1990s, cross-strait economic activities have gradually become the most important form of Taiwan's globalization. Increasing Taiwanese investment in mainland China at the expense of that in Taiwan has contributed to Taiwan's rising income inequality and other social justice issues, and has consequently affected many Taiwanese and increased the salience of various social justice issues in Taiwan's politics.

---

[7] Qi, 2010a, 2010b; Copper, 2010.

[8] Qi, 2012.

Fourth, with an increased social welfare budget, the DPP administration of 2000–2008 was able to control income inequality better and consequently gained relatively more support from the poorer sections of society. Since 2008 and at the national level, the DPP has shifted its policy focus from identity-oriented political nationalism to social justice-oriented economic nationalism. At the local level, it has further decoupled social justice issues from economic nationalism in order to tackle local social justice issues better without the constraints of nationalist ideology. These strategy changes have been instrumental in resurrecting popular support for the DPP, especially in local and legislative elections. However, the DPP's gradual moderation of political nationalism has led to the decline of nationalist sentiment among those Taiwanese not in a position to benefit from globalization and increased cross-strait economic activities, which in turn made them less antagonistic to the KMT's mainland China policy in the presidential election.

Finally, in the 2012 presidential election, the KMT's stability and development card, which placed emphasis on the government's duty to create national wealth fast, eventually beat the DPP's social justice card, which prioritized the government's responsibility for allocating national wealth fairly. The main reason behind the KMT victory (and the DPP's defeat) is that the KMT convinced the majority of Taiwanese that only its mainland China policy could maintain the significantly improved cross-strait relations essential to Taiwan's economic revival. In addition, since 2008, the KMT administration has generally maintained the former DPP administration's social welfare efforts, which helped it to see off the DPP's attacks on social justice issues.

This case study aims to improve understanding of Taiwan's party politics since 2000 by first challenging the popular image of a failed 2000–2008 DPP administration, which was widely believed to be only good at mobilizing "irrational" Taiwanese nationalist sentiment to maintain popular support. Second, it contributes to a deeper knowledge of the characteristics of DPP supporters who, especially the so-called deep-green (*shenlü* 深綠) fundamentalists, have a popular public image of being overly nationalist and less rational for supporting the unpopular DPP administration. However, as this study will show, they support the DPP not only because they share a strong Taiwanese nationalist sentiment with the DPP, but also because the DPP's social welfare policies and economic nationalism rhetoric speak to their rational concerns about their own economic security. Therefore, their support for the DPP is down to both nationalist and rational self-interest reasons.

Third, this article shows that, since 2008, the DPP's priority shift from political nationalism to social justice-oriented economic nationalism has contributed to the DPP's resurgence, especially in local and legislative elections. However, its moderate political nationalism was still believed by many to be detrimental to the improved cross-strait relations. In a sense, Taiwanese people feel comfortable giving local and legislative power to the DPP because the DPP seems more willing and capable to fulfill the government's responsibility of addressing various social justice issues. However, the voters gave the power to the KMT because it seemed more likely to fulfill the government's responsibility of developing Taiwan's economy based on a more flexible political nationalism that promotes cross-strait relations.

Finally, the increasing salience of social justice issues in Taiwan's democratization and recent political development has already received the attention of some scholars. In contrast to their studies, which usually separate social justice issues from Taiwanese nationalism, this study attempts to show the new social justice turn of Taiwanese nationalism. In other words, since 2008, the Taiwanese nationalism championed by the DPP has been embracing a more social justice-based agenda and trying to combine political and economic nationalism in a more balanced way. This may have significant implications for both Taiwan's domestic politics and cross-strait relations.

Following this perspective, the next section discusses the capital flight from Taiwan to mainland China, its contribution to the rising unemployment and income inequality in Taiwan, and the DPP administration's improved social welfare budget. The article goes on to demonstrate how the less well-off segments of Taiwanese society gradually switched their support from the KMT to the DPP from 1996 to 2008. It then further explores the dual characteristics of this group of voters in Taiwan — their stronger nationalist sentiment and concerns about economic security — and shows how they relate these to the DPP's different balance between political and economic nationalism. The article then explains the DPP's limited resurgence since 2008 and ends with a discussion of some of the implications of this study.

Globalization, Social Justice Issues and the DPP's Efforts to Improve Taiwan's Social Welfare System

Most countries have found that globalization cuts both ways. It maximizes global investors' profit by optimizing the utilization of capital, labor, land, technology and many other productive resources in different countries, and as a result, develops those countries' economies. On the other hand, it also brings a variety of social justice issues to both developed and developing countries. One of the most prominent and persistent issues is the increasing wealth disparity in many parts of the world.[9] The causal relations between globalization and wealth disparity are complex, but the basic mechanism is that those who have capital and better skills gain much more income from economic globalization than those who have no such resources. As the two groups' unequal gains accumulate constantly, income inequality in these countries increases. While globalization has become irresistible to most countries, governments are expected by their people to minimize social justice issues related to globalization, such as the better control of income inequality.

Taiwan's main form of globalization has been cross-strait economic activities.[10] The increasing investment flow from Taiwan to mainland China has been one of the most important factors contributing to Taiwan's social justice issues.[11] For Taiwanese investors and the highly skilled labor that can follow the capital, investing in mainland China can result in better profits and well-paid jobs; in contrast, for the less skilled who have no chance to work there because of competition from much cheaper mainland Chinese labor, this investment flight means fewer jobs in Taiwan.[12] In developed economies like Taiwan, unemployment significantly contributes to economic inequality. Figure 10.2 shows the overall development

[9] Dallmayr, 2002; Mills, 2009.

[10] Lin, *et al.*, 2011, pp. 17–18.

[11] *Ibid.*, pp. 17–50.

[12] Chen, 2004.

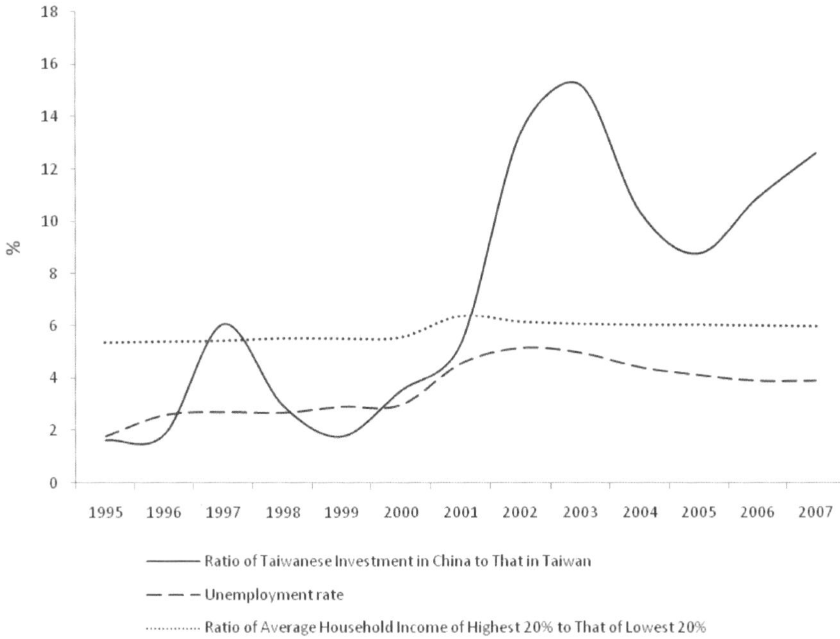

Figure 10.2 Development Trends of Investment, Unemployment and Inequality in Taiwan, 1995–2007

Source: Investment Commission, MOEA, Liang'an maoyi yu touzi yingxiang pinggu baogao (Evaluation Report on Cross-Strait Trade and Investment Impact), June 2007, 17, http://www.moeaic.gov.tw/system_external/ctlr?PRO=PublicationLoad&id=27; June 2008, 63, http://www.moeaic.gov.tw/system_external/ctlr?PRO=PublicationLoad&id=57; Department of Statistics, Ministry of Economic Affairs, Form E-1 Labor Force & Employed, http://2k3dmz2.moea.gov.tw/gnweb/English/Indicator/wFrmEnIndicator.aspx; Directorate General of Budget, Accounting and Statistics, Executive Yuan, ROC. 2010. 99 *nian jiating shouzhi diaocha baogao* (Survey of family income and expenditure), 10, http://win.dgbas.gov.tw/fies/a11.asp?year=99.

trends of three indicators from 1995 to 2007 in Taiwan. Generally, the ratio of investment in mainland China to that in Taiwan has significantly increased over this 12-year period. The correlations between the three indicators, as shown by Table 10.1, are highly positive and significant, suggesting that increasing investment in mainland China at the expense of that in Taiwan may contribute to the rise of unemployment and income inequality in Taiwan.

It is not just those at risk of unemployment — supposedly a small section of the population — who feel the pressure of globalization; a much

Table 10.1 Pearson Correlations between the Three Indicators of Investment, Unemployment and Inequality, 1995–2007

	Unemployment Rate	Ratio of Average Household Income of Highest 20% to that of Lowest 20% (Inequality)
Ratio of Taiwanese investment in China to that in Taiwan	0.842** (n = 13)	0.731** (n = 13)
Unemployment rate	1	0.932** (n = 13)

Note: ** Correlation is significant at the 0.01 level (2-tailed).
Source: As for Figure 10.1.

larger share of the population believed that their social and economic status had declined over the past few decades. Lin's research shows that, in 1992, while about 40% of Taiwanese identified themselves as middle class, that figure had fallen to about 32% in 2007. In contrast, during the same period, the percentage of Taiwanese identifying themselves as lower middle/lower/working class increased from about 50% to about 64%.[13] This clearly indicates an increased sense of economic insecurity in Taiwanese society.

Unemployment, income inequality and economic insecurity as a result of globalization are common to many parts of the world and have profoundly influenced institutional and non-institutional politics such as elections and social movements. There has been a rise in populist, leftist, progressive and social democratic appeals in many countries' elections, as well as a variety of anti-globalization movements across the world over the past few decades, and Taiwan is no exception. Although the politics of Taiwan's democratization and its consolidation during the past three decades have been mainly characterized by political cleavages caused by ethnic and unification/independence issues, some scholars have recently turned their attention to the role of social justice issues. For example, regarding class politics, Yang finds that around the mid-1980s, it was not the middle classes but the rural and urban working classes that showed

[13] Lin, 2009b.

stronger support for the opposition (*dangwai* 党外) movement and the DPP.[14] Hu, Lin and Wong discuss the revival of class politics in Taiwan since the 1990s,[15] and Kevin Wong explores the emergence of class division since 2000 owing to the economic integration of Taiwan and mainland China, and looks at how the DPP strategically politicized the enlarging cleavage to attract support from less skilled labor.[16] In reference to social welfare issues in Taiwan's politics, Aspalter shows that, since the 1980s, increasing electoral competition from the opposition movement and the DPP forced the authoritarian KMT regime to expand its conservative social welfare system, which had until then mostly benefited the mainlanders, to cover much larger segments of the population.[17] Joseph Wong believes that the increasing salience of progressive politics aimed at addressing various social justice issues in Taiwan indicates the deepening of Taiwan's democracy.[18]

In general, the above studies imply that to understand Taiwan's electoral politics better, in addition to the popular ethnic and nationalist issues, social justice issues such as different parties' social policies should also be taken into account. Furthermore, the studies also suggest that the DPP, as a center-left party opposed to the center-right KMT, has been the leading force in addressing Taiwan's various social justice issues. Following this line of thought, the bonds between the DPP and its support base may be better understood from a new angle of social justice. In other words, the main reasons that people support the DPP may not only be due to the DPP's nationalist stance on Taiwan's independence issues, as the popular perspective of Taiwanese political nationalism suggests, but also because of its policies on social justice issues. Therefore, to understand the decline and rise of popular support for the DPP, we should look into the interactive dynamics between the DPP and its social base around both nationalist and social justice issues.

---

14 Yang, 2007.

15 Hu, Lin and Kwok, 2010.

16 Wong, 2010.

17 Aspalter, 2002.

18 Wong, 2003.

In general, social justice issues reflect cleavages and conflicts between privileged, rich and powerful people and the underprivileged, poor and ordinary ones on a variety of issues related to wealth and the allocation of resources. Indeed, while it is acknowledged that the DPP is seen as a pro-independence party, what is less well known is that most Taiwanese people see the DPP as the ordinary people's party, in contrast to the KMT, which is mostly viewed as the rich and powerful people's party. This is clearly shown in Figures 10.3 and 10.4.[19] For example, in 2008 nearly half of all people surveyed believed that the KMT represented the interests of the rich and powerful, whilst 51.1% believed that the DPP represented the ordinary person.

The present study proposes that the Taiwanese nationalism promoted by the DPP has been a combination of political and economic nationalism: political nationalism aims at Taiwan's *de jure* independence from mainland China, while the objective of economic nationalism is to protect the welfare of less affluent or advantaged Taiwanese through a restrained China policy. The Chen Shui-bian administration

[19] Unless otherwise noted, the data used in this study are from the following five datasets: 1. Democracy, Political Parties and Taiwan's Mass Politics: Research on the Electorate in the 1996 Presidential Election (NSC 85-2414-H031-004-Q3), Principal Investigator: Professor Ying-lung You; 2. An Interdisciplinary Study of Voting Behavior in the Presidential Election in 2000 (NSC 89-2414-H-004-021-SSS), Principal Investigator: Professor Yih-yan Chen; 3. Taiwan's Election and Democratization Studies, 2004 (TEDS2004P) (NSC92-2420-H-031-004), Principal Investigator: Professor Shiow-duan Hawang; 4. Taiwan's Election and Democratization Studies, 2005–2008(IV): the Survey of the Presidential Election in 2008 (TEDS2008P) (NSC 96-2420-H-004-017), Principal Investigator: Professor Ching-hsin Yu; and 5. Telephone Interview of the Presidential and Legislative Elections, 2012 (TEDS2012-TP), Principal Investigator: Professor Chi Huang. The coordinator of the multi-year project TEDS is Professor Chi Huang (National Chengchi University). More information is on the TEDS website (http://www.tedsnet.org). The author appreciates the assistance of the institute and individuals aforementioned in providing data. The author alone is responsible for views expressed herein. In all these datasets, if the answer to the survey question is "I don't know," "I don't want to answer," "I have no opinion," or "it's hard to say," the answer is recoded as a missing value. Also, some categorical variables are recoded into fewer categories according to the research purpose.

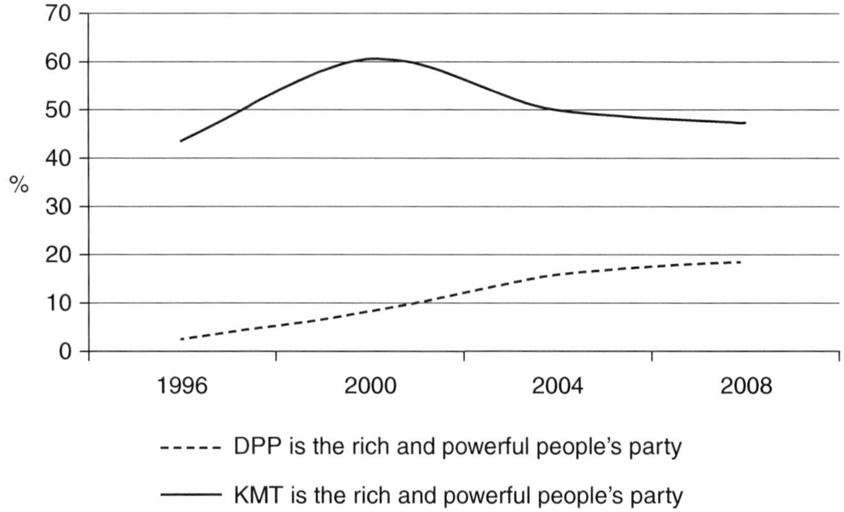

Figure 10.3 Percentage of People Who Believe that KMT/DPP Represents the Interests of the Rich and Powerful

Source: See Footnote 18.

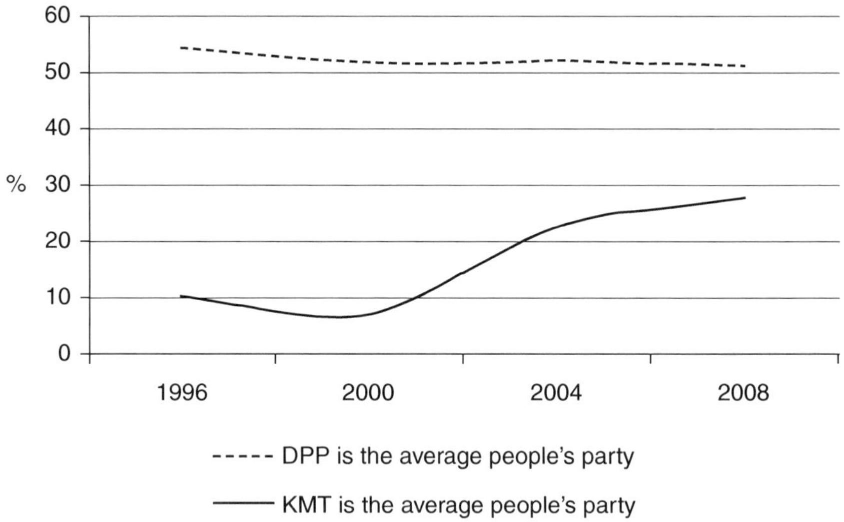

Figure 10.4 Percentage of People Who Believe that KMT/DPP Represents the Interests of the Average People

Source: See Footnote 18.

of 2004–2008 radicalized political nationalism to consolidate its support from the deep-green faction after it was attacked by both the opposition forces and members from within the DPP. This radicalization seemed to serve Chen's personal political purposes well, but caused conflict and instability in society and between Taiwan, mainland China and the US, and finally, alienated moderate supporters from within and outside the party. However, the failure of radical political nationalism does not necessarily mean that the Chen administration also failed in promoting economic nationalism. Its performance on tackling social justice issues may help the DPP to maintain its credibility as a center-left party championing economic Taiwanese nationalism.

The DPP has been a pro-social welfare party with a strong social democratic orientation since its foundation in 1986. Before it took power in 2000, social welfare issues such as pensions had been one of its major appeals in local and national electoral campaigns. Studies have shown that owing to the DPP's strong push for more equal and better social welfare, Taiwan's social welfare system significantly improved in the 1990s.[20] During its eight years in office, although the DPP became less progressive in some social welfare and environmental fields, and was consequently criticized by some civil organizations, it actually significantly increased central government expenditure on social welfare. From the figures presented in Figure 10.5, it can be calculated that while the average percentage of the social welfare budget in the central government's total budget was 12.4% from 1993–1999 under the KMT regime, it was 18.2% during the DPP administration, an increase of 5.8%.

Figure 10.6 shows that, with the help of income and tax transfers provided by taxation and social welfare policies, the constantly rising trend of income inequality was suppressed during the DPP administration. Actual income inequality dropped almost continuously over the last six years of the DPP administration, from 6.39 in 2001 to 5.98 in 2007. In contrast, during the two KMT administrations (1991–1999; 2008–2010), income inequality had an apparently rising trend, increasing from 4.97 to 5.50 during 1991–1999 and from 6.05 to 6.17 during 2008–2011.

[20] Aspalter, 2002; Huang, 2009; Lin, 2005.

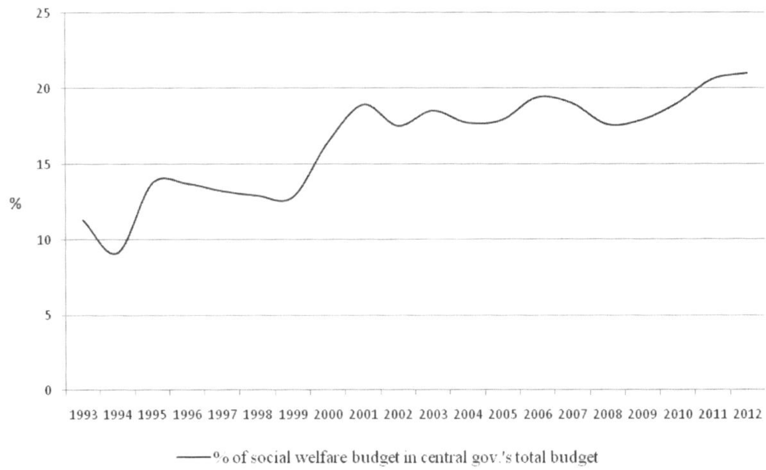

Figure 10.5 Percentage of Social Welfare Budget in Central Government's Total Budget, 1993–2012

Source: Chan, 2012, 32; Executive Yuan. 2012. *Budget Plan of the Central Government* (2012), 32.

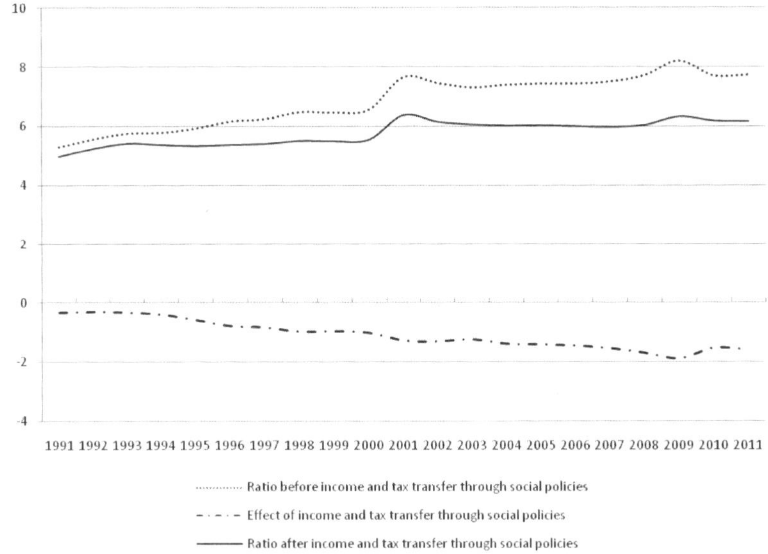

Figure 10.6 Ratio of Average Household Income of Highest 20% to that of Lowest 20% (Measure of Income Inequality): 1991–2011

Source: Directorate General of Budget, Accounting and Statistics, Executive Yuan, ROC. 2011. 100 *nian jiating shouzhi diaocha jieguo zonghe fenxi* (General analysis of family income and expenditure survey results), http://win.dgbas.gov.tw/fies/doc/result/100/a11/Analysis.doc.

DPP's Support Base

The major beneficiaries of the DPP administration's improved social welfare efforts were the financially less well-off. Did the DPP successfully win their hearts? The regression of votes for the DPP in the 2008 presidential election shown in Table 10.2 provides a positive answer.

Table 10.2 Binary Logistic Regression of Individuals' Votes for the DPP, 2008

Independent Variables	Coef. (Odds Ratio)
Ethnicity	
Mainlander	–2.304***(0.100)
Hakka	–0.428†(0.652)
Minnan (ref.)	
Gender	
Male	0.484***(1.622)
Female (ref.)	
Age	–0.012†(0.988)
Education	
Lower (junior high or below)	0.660**(1.934)
Middle (senior high or vocational)	0.205(1.228)
Higher (college or above) (ref.)	
Family's financial situation	
Improved	**–0.819†(0.441)**
About the same	**–0.599***(0.572)**
Deteriorated (ref.)	
Opinion about Taiwan's future relation with mainland China	
Pro-unification	–2.675***(0.069)
Pro-status quo	–1.753**(0.173)
Pro-independence (ref.)	
National identity	
Chinese	–3.395 ***(0.034)
Both Taiwanese & Chinese	–1.193***(0.303)
Taiwanese (ref.)	
Intercept	1.818***(6.162)
–2LL	1208.585***
N	1331

Note: †$p \leq 0.1$, *$p \leq 0.05$, **$p \leq 0.01$, ***$p \leq 0.001$, vote for the KMT is the reference category.
Source: TEDS2008P.

The dependent variable in the regression is binary: A DPP vote vs. KMT vote. The interested independent variable is each respondent's family's economic situation. It is a categorical variable including three possible answers to the question: "Would you say that, over the past year, your own household's financial situation has (1) improved, (2) stayed about the same or (3) deteriorated?"

The regression also includes gender, age, ethnicity, education and two nationalist sentiment indicators as control variables. One of the nationalist sentiment indicators is self-claimed national identity, including Taiwanese, Chinese and both Taiwanese and Chinese. The other indicator is the respondent's opinion on Taiwan's future relationship with mainland China, which also includes three categories: Pro-independence, pro-unification and pro-status quo. The respondents who identified themselves as Taiwanese only or had pro-independence opinions are defined as having Taiwanese nationalist sentiment. The regression shows that people whose financial situations had deteriorated were more likely to vote for the DPP in 2008 presidential election.

Next, it is necessary to know the social characteristics of those whose households had suffered financially. Table 10.3 indicates that, in 2008, people who were less educated (i.e., junior high or below), southern Taiwan residents or farmers were most likely to be worse-off, and most likely to vote for the DPP in their social category defined, respectively, by education, residence region and class/occupation. In addition, among the five age groups, the oldest group (60 and above) had suffered the most financially and showed the second highest level of support for the DPP. Workers were the second most financially worse-off group among the four class groups and showed the second highest level of support for the DPP. Their level of DPP support was much closer to that of farmers than to those of the upper and lower middle classes. Therefore, workers were more like farmers in terms of vote choice. In general, it seems clear that the household finances of the elderly, less educated, southern Taiwan residents, workers and farmers had deteriorated the most, and that these groups were more likely to vote for the DPP.

The most obvious commonality shared by these five social groups is that it is generally assumed that, in a highly globalized economy like Taiwan, they will be in an economically less privileged position. The older generation, the less educated, workers and farmers usually have little opportunity

Table 10.3 Percentage of Worse-Off Families and Votes for the DPP in Each Social Group, 2008

(Unit: % of people in each social group, i.e., row %)

	Family Financial Situation had Deteriorated over Past Year (2007)	**Voted for the DPP in 2008**
Age		
20–29	40	37.8
30–39	39.4	30.9
40–49	51.6	34.6
50–59	52.4	44.4
60 and above	**57**	**40.1**
Education		
College and above	32.2	30.7
Senior high and Vocational	45.1	33
Junior high and Below	**60.3**	**47.2**
Region		
North and Middle	44.6	30.8
South	**53.8**	**51.1**
Occupation/Class		
Upper-middle Class	32.1	33.1
Lower-middle Class	52.2	29.7
Workers	**52.4**	**46.3**
Farmers	**62**	**50.5**
Privileged vs. Less privileged		
Privileged	39.3	25.1
Less privileged	**52.3**	**44.4**

Source: TEDS2008P.

to follow the capital flight to mainland China and reap the benefits of globalization. People in southern Taiwan are also less likely to gain from globalization, as cross-strait economic activities, such as trade and investment, are usually concentrated in northern and central Taiwan. At the same time, they are more likely to be negatively affected by the outward flow of investment. Therefore, we can define people from one or more of those groups as "the less privileged" in Taiwan's globalization. Conversely, those who have none of these characteristics may be termed "the privileged."

It is important to know whether the less privileged have always been more likely than others to support the DPP in presidential elections. Table 10.4 shows a clear trend that after the DPP took power in 2000, the less privileged switched their support from the KMT to the DPP. Specifically, in the 1996 presidential election, people from the less privileged groups were more likely to vote for the KMT, and in 2000,

Table 10.4 Binary Logistic Regressions of Individuals' Votes for the DPP, 1996–2012

Independent Variables	1996 Coef.	2000 Coef.	2004 Coef.	2008 Coef.	2012 Coef.
Ethnicity					
Mainlander	−1.656*	−1.598***	−1.436***	−2.355***	−2.401**
Hakka	−0.128	−0.957***	−0.071	−0.448*	−0.561***
Minnan (ref.)					
Gender					
Male	0.056	0.236	0.101	0.385**	0.431**
Female(ref.)					
Type of social group					
Less privileged	**−0.813*****	**0.193**	**0.535*****	**0.521*****	**0.315***
Privileged (ref.)					
Opinion about Taiwan's future relations with mainland China					
Pro-unification	−2.255***	−1.404***	−1.952***	−2.643***	−2.104***
Pro-status quo	−1.492***	−1.394***	−1.596***	−1.722***	−1.379***
Pro-independence (ref.)					
National identity					
Chinese	−1.677***	−1.854***	−1.925***	−3.548***	−1.659***
Both Taiwanese & Chinese	−1.293***	−0.870***	−1.724***	−1.226***	−1.422***
Taiwanese (ref.)					
Intercept	0.468†	1.493***	2.233***	1.021***	1.117***
−2LL	645.715***	1108.251***	1170.673***	1230.198***	1284.318***
N	972	1025	1222	1341	1291

Note: $^{\dagger}p \leq 0.1$, $^{*}p \leq 0.05$, $^{**}p \leq 0.01$, $^{***}p \leq 0.001$, vote for the KMT is the reference category.
Source: See footnote 18, except for the 2012 model, which uses TEDS2012 (NSC 100-2420-H002-030). TEDS2012's principal investigator is Professor Yun-han Chu.

there was no significant difference between the less privileged and the privileged in their voting decisions; but in 2004, the less privileged became more likely to vote for the DPP, and their significantly stronger support for the DPP continued in 2008 and 2012. Additionally, Table 10.5 shows that, relatively speaking, in 2008 the less privileged segments of Taiwanese society were more likely to choose "social

Table 10.5 Percentage of People in Each Social Group Choosing Social Welfare as the Chen Administration's Best Achievement in His Second Term, 2008

(Unit: % of people in each social group, i.e., row %)

	Social Welfare	**Other Achievements**
Age		
20–29	12.5	87.5
30–39	14.7	85.3
40–49	19.2	80.8
50–59	18.2	81.8
60 and above	**25.0**	**75.0**
Chi-square test	$n = 1592$, $\chi^2 = 17.992$, $df = 4$, $p = 0.001$	
Education		
College and above	9.7	90.3
Senior high and vocational	16.2	83.8
Junior high and below	**25.3**	**74.7**
Chi-square test	$n = 1591$, $\chi^2 = 36.783$, $df = 2$, $p < 0.001$	
Region		
North and Middle	15.3	84.7
South	**21.8**	**78.2**
Chi-square test	$n = 1591$, $\chi^2 = 10.147$, $df = 1$, $p = 0.001$	
Class		
Upper-middle class	12.8	87.2
Lower-middle class	14.1	85.9
Workers	**22.0**	**78.0**
Farmers	**35.1**	**64.9**
Chi-square test	$n = 1213$, $\chi^2 = 34.343$, $df = 3$, $p < 0.001$	
Privileged vs. Less privileged		
Privileged	**11.3**	**88.7**
Less privileged	**21.3**	**78.7**
Chi-square test	$n = 1591$, $\chi^2 = 26.415$, $df = 1$, $p < 0.001$	

Source: TEDS2008P.

welfare" as the DPP administration's best achievement. Therefore, it seems that the DPP administration's performance on social welfare issues had a significantly positive and lasting effect on their support from the less privileged groups.

In general, the findings about the social characteristics of Taiwan's less privileged groups tallies with two previous studies on the characteristics of the DPP's deep-green supporters. Cheng shows that, around the mid-2000s, deep-green supporters were likely to be older, less educated and of the working class.[21] Wang, Cheng and Chen similarly found that, in 2007, deep-green support was strongest amongst older people, people with less education and those from rural areas, especially southern Taiwan.[22]

Concerns of the Less Privileged Taiwanese and the DPP's Political and Economic Nationalism

To understand better the underlying motivations of the less privileged Taiwanese's support for the DPP, it is necessary to look further at their shared characteristics. As shown by Figure 10.7, Taiwanese nationalist sentiment has always been stronger among the less privileged groups than the privileged.[23] Specifically, in 1996 the proportion of the less privileged with Taiwanese nationalist sentiment is 12.4% higher than that of the privileged. This gap increased to 17.1% in 2008. Many studies have shown that those with Taiwanese nationalist sentiments are more likely to support the DPP, so it seems reasonable to suspect that the less privileged Taiwanese's stronger support for the DPP is entirely down to their stronger Taiwanese nationalist sentiment. However, the regressions in Table 10.4 demonstrate that, even after controlling for Taiwanese nationalist sentiment, the less privileged Taiwanese were still significantly more likely to vote for the DPP in 2004, 2008 and 2012. In other words, having Taiwanese nationalist sentiment and being less privileged both have independent and positive effects on people's support for the DPP.

---

[21] Cheng, 2007.

[22] Wang, Cheng and Chen, 2009.

[23] As in the previous section, those who are pro-independence or identify themselves as Taiwanese-only are defined as people having Taiwanese nationalist sentiment.

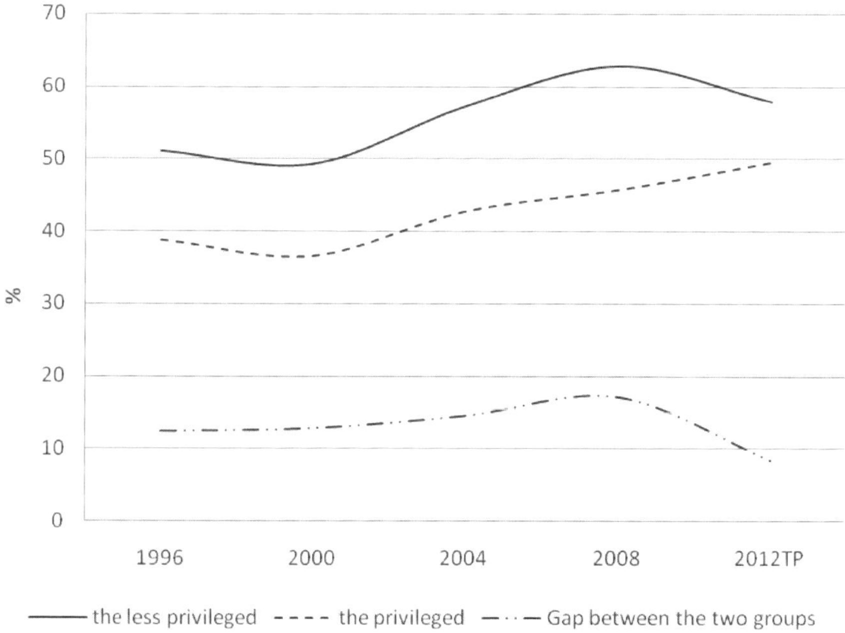

Figure 10.7 Level/Percent of Nationalist Sentiment among the Less Privileged and the Privileged, 1996–2012

Source: See Footnote 18.

This leads to a further question: In addition to stronger Taiwanese nationalist sentiment, what other reasons lead voters from a less privileged background to support the DPP? The previous section indicates that it may be owing to the DPP administration's better performance on social welfare issues which benefited this section of Taiwanese society. Another major characteristic of the less privileged provides a clue. Table 10.6 shows that, in 2008, those from less privileged groups were more likely to believe that both Taiwan and themselves would become worse off under the open-door China policy; they are also less likely to believe that both Taiwan and themselves would become better off under that policy.[24]

[24]The only exception is the age group of 60 and above. Among the five age groups, this group has the second lowest percentage of people believing that they would become better off under the open-door policy. The age group of 50–59 has the lowest percentage, which is only slightly lower than the 60 and above group.

Table 10.6 Percentage of People in each Social Group Possibly Approving or Disapproving the Open-Door China Policy, 2008

(Unit: % of people in each social group, i.e., row %)

	Will Taiwan Be Better Off, Worse Off, Or The Same Under The Open-Door China Policy?			Will You Be Better Off, Worse Off, Or The Same Under The Open-Door China Policy?		
	Better off	**Worse off**	**The same**	**Better off**	**Worse off**	**The same**
Age						
20–29	53.2	21.2	25.5	15.2	15.8	69
30–39	49.9	26.4	23.7	15.9	18.6	65.4
40–49	45.1	31.2	23.7	17.5	22.7	59.8
50–59	42	40.5	17.5	10.4	24.6	65
60 and above	**35.4**	**41.4**	**23.2**	**12**	**30.7**	**57.9**
Chi-square test	$n = 1579, \chi^2 = 46.326, df = 8$, p<.001			$n = 1635, \chi^2 = 29.743, df = 8, p < 0.001$		
Education						
College and above	62	20.1	17.9	20.5	11.9	67.7
Senior high and vocational	49.3	28.3	22.4	15.9	19.7	64.4
Junior high and below	**29.4**	**42.5**	**28.1**	**8.7**	**31.1**	**60.2**
Chi-square test	$n = 1576, \chi^2 = 97.934, df = 4, p < 0.001$			$n = 1634, \chi^2 = 63.684, df = 4, p < 0.001$		
Region						
North and middle	50.9	26.1	23	16.9	18.1	65
South	**35.7**	**41.2**	**23.2**	**9.1**	**30.4**	**60.5**
Chi-square test	$n = 1579, \chi^2 = 41.775, df = 2$, p<.001			$n = 1637, \chi^2 = 40.080, df = 2, p < 0.001$		

Class					
Upper-middle class	53.9	27.7	18.3	17.7	17.5	64.8
Lower-middle class	53.8	22.4	23.8	18.8	15.9	65.3
Workers	**34.8**	**36.9**	**28.3**	**9.7**	**27.6**	**62.7**
Farmers	**23.5**	**50**	**26.5**	**8.0**	**37.5**	**54.5**
Chi-square test	$n = 1209, \chi^2 = 65.895, df = 6, p<0.001$			$n = 1243, \chi^2 = 45.705, df = 6, p < 0.001$		
Privileged vs. Less privileged						
Privileged	**59**	**20.6**	**20.4**	**20**	**13.8**	**66.2**
Less privileged	**38.1**	**37.2**	**24.7**	**11.2**	**26.7**	**66.2**
Chi-square test	$n = 1579, \chi^2 = 72.277, df = 2, p<0.001$			$n = 1636, \chi^2 = 51.350, df = 2, p < 0.001$		

Source: TEDS2008P.

The stronger nationalist sentiment found among the less privileged Taiwanese and their concerns about the open-door China policy were echoed in the DPP's nationalist rhetoric.[25] In general, since 2000, this nationalist rhetoric has comprised of political nationalism aimed at protecting Taiwan's current *de facto* independence and pursuing its future *de jure* independence, and economic nationalism aimed at protecting the less privileged groups' welfare with a conservative China policy. For both nationalisms, mainland China is viewed as the largest threat by the DPP. Therefore, the DPP has argued that Taiwan needs a conservative and restrained China policy in both political and economic fields and that the KMT's open-door China policy will jeopardize both Taiwan's *de facto* independence and the welfare of less privileged Taiwanese.

What distinguishes the nationalist rhetoric of Chen Shui-bian in his second administrative term of 2004–2008 from that of Tsai Ing-wen during 2008–2012 is the change in focus from political to economic nationalism. To divert public attention away from the scandals surrounding his family and administration and to maintain the deep-green's support, Chen radicalized political Taiwanese nationalism by enshrining the goal of Taiwan's independence and the act of loving Taiwan. The message that this brought to the public was that nothing was more important than pursuing Taiwan's independence and loving Taiwan, and that no one upheld this more than Chen and his administration. It also justified Chen's closed-door policy towards mainland China: although it might be detrimental to Taiwan's economy, it was a necessary step in order to protect Taiwan's independence. In summary, the whole argument of this radical political nationalism was that Taiwan's independence was the highest national priority and pursuing this goal was the most sincere manifestation of loving Taiwan; Chen and his administration's policies were the best way to achieve Taiwan's future independence and therefore they loved Taiwan most; anyone who challenged their policies was opposed to Taiwan's independence and therefore was a "China conspirator" who did not love Taiwan.

---

[25] Some scholars have pointed out this economic concern of Taiwanese nationalism upheld by the marginalized groups in the process of economic integration between Taiwan and mainland China. See Chen, 2004.

In contrast, after the DPP lost power in 2008, party moderates, including Tsai Ing-wen, gradually took over the party and reined in Chen's radical political nationalism, which had become a major liability for the party. The DPP moderates seem to be both idealists and pragmatists. They are committed to a vision of political Taiwanese nationalism, which is Taiwan's *de jure* independence, but have a clear understanding of the tremendous difficulties of pursuing this goal. They oppose the use of radical ways to address these difficulties, and particularly dislike the political manipulation of independence issues for personal gain in politics. In terms of cross-strait relations, they share the radicals' worries about mainland China's efforts to incorporate Taiwan through economic means, but do not think that completely isolating Taiwan from mainland China is a rational choice. Instead, they suggest gradual, careful and transparent exchanges between the two sides of the Taiwan Strait.

Although Tsai and other moderates abandoned radical political nationalism, they still have concerns about mainland China's threat to Taiwan's national security and future independence. On the other hand, in order to protect the less privileged Taiwanese who are threatened by increased cross-strait investment, they have prioritized economic nationalism. These dual concerns have become apparent in the DPP's opposition to the Economic Cooperation Framework Agreement (ECFA) since 2008. In terms of national security, the DPP has argued that the ECFA will lead to Taiwan's economic integration with mainland China and then its eventual political integration, as anticipated by the Chinese government. In her debate with President Ma Ying-jeou on ECFA issues, Tsai stated that the DPP's preferred option would be for Taiwan to open to "the world," especially developed economies such as the US, before approaching mainland China. This is in contrast to the KMT's ECFA scheme of opening to mainland China first, and then going to "the world" through mainland China.[26]

Another major concern raised by the DPP in its argument against the ECFA is its potential negative impact on Taiwan's social equality. The DPP believes that the ECFA will only benefit a few large enterprises and

---

[26] docs.google.com. 2010. Transcript of Ma Ying-jeou and Tsai Ing-wen's debate on ECFA, https://docs.google.com/View?id=dgv9n52c_6164pdj9ct, accessed on 23 October 2012.

the more privileged section of society; Taiwan's small and middle enterprises (SME), the middle and lower classes, and those living in middle and southern Taiwan will gain little or even lose out in terms of wages and business opportunities. It believes that the gap in incomes will significantly widen in Taiwan as a result and cites Hong Kong as an example to support their argument: income inequality increased in Hong Kong after it signed the Closer Economic Partnership Arrangement (CEPA) with mainland China.[27]

DPP's Limited Resurgence, 2008–2012

To understand the DPP's comeback in local and legislative elections and its limitations in the presidential election, it is necessary to evaluate the Ma Ying-jeou administration's general performance since 2008. In the 2008 presidential election, Ma Ying-jeou's unprecedented landslide victory was driven by popular dissatisfaction with then-president Chen Shui-bian and his administration in four areas: The corrupt practices of Chen, his family members and his close government officials; the disappointing economic performance supposedly caused by his closed-door China policy; increasing ethnic conflicts as a result of his radical pro-independence and ethnically divisive policies; and the deterioration in Taiwan's international relations, especially with the US, caused by Chen's provocative pro-independence policies. The Taiwanese people expect the Ma administration to perform better in these areas, and in general, Ma's report card does not disappoint: Ma and his administration have no serious corruption scandals; Taiwan's economy has survived the 2008 world financial crisis and the ECFA with mainland China is expected to boost Taiwan's economic revival quickly; ethnic tension in Taiwan has declined visibly; and Taiwan's relations with the US have improved.

However, a closer look at the Ma administration's key economic and social performance indicators in Table 10.7 reveals that its performance was actually worse than that of the Chen 2004–2007 administration in some important fields. In terms of GDP growth, Table 10.7 shows that the Chen administration maintained a fairly stable growth rate. In contrast, the

[27] *Ibid.*

Table 10.7 Comparison of Key Economic and Social Performance Indicators under the Ma and Chen Administrations

Year	GDP Growth Rate (%)	Unemployment Rate (%)	Monthly Real Wage Index of Non-Agriculture Workers (2004 = 1)	Income Inequality
Chen administration				
2004	6.19	4.44	1.00	6.03
2005	4.70	4.13	0.99	6.04
2006	5.44	3.91	0.99	6.01
2007	5.98	3.91	0.99	5.98
2004–2007 Average	5.58	4.10	0.99	6.02
Ma administration				
2008	0.73	4.14	0.96	6.05
2009	–1.81	5.85	0.92	6.34
2010	10.72	5.21	0.96	6.19
2011	4.03	4.39	0.97	6.17
2008–2011 Average	3.42	4.90	0.95	6.19

Source: Copy and recalculation of the data from Directorate General of Budget, Accounting and Statistics and Council of Labor Affairs, Executive Yuan, ROC.

world financial crisis of 2008 impacted Taiwan negatively, registering extremely slow and negative GDP growth in the first two years of the Ma administration. It was only in 2010 that the Taiwanese economy bounced back with a two-decade high of 10.72%. However, the rebound was short-lived; in 2011, Taiwan's economic growth dipped to 4.04%. Overall, Taiwan's economy experienced its worst economic setbacks during Ma's first term in office. With an average annual growth rate of 3.42%, Ma's economic performance was worse than Chen's (5.58%).

In terms of issues related to social justice such as unemployment levels, income inequality and the real wage index, the Ma administration also performed worse than the Chen administration. The average unemployment rate and income inequality were both higher under Ma than the average numbers during the Chen administration. On average, the real wage during the Ma administration declined by 5% from the 2004 level, while it only declined by 1% during the Chen administration. Unemployment and real wage decline impact the masses more tangibly than any positive impact of GDP growth, and so the DPP criticized the economic recovery under the Ma administration for being a "recovery unfelt by people."[28]

With the earlier comparison, it is not difficult to understand why the DPP campaigned on social justice issues in both the local and national elections after 2008, and as a result, gained increasing support. In the national presidential election, because nationalist issues such as cross-strait relations were a major concern for the majority of voters, the DPP linked social justice issues to nationalism and presented the public with a policy of strong economic nationalism. As we have discussed previously, the DPP's argument that Ma's open-door mainland China policy would not only jeopardize Taiwan's *de facto* independence, but would also have a negative impact on various social justice issues provided the reasoning behind the DPP's promotion of social justice-oriented economic nationalism against mainland China. However, in local and legislative elections, the DPP usually decoupled social justice issues from economic nationalism to a large extent because nationalism played a much less important role in local elections. For example, during the five municipal elections in November 2010, the DPP more or less ceased their attacks on the ECFA and concentrated instead on highlighting the KMT local governors' incompetence in addressing various social justice issues.

The DPP's general strategy is to use a different focus at the local level from the national level. At the national level, the DPP has moderated its political nationalism and prioritized the social justice-oriented economic nationalism to maintain the support of the less privileged Taiwanese and attract swing voters. The regression of the Taiwanese's vote choice in the 2012 presidential election in Table 10.4 indicates that the DPP successfully maintained this group's support in the election. At the local level, it not only diminished political nationalism, but also decoupled social justice issues from economic nationalism. This decoupling has reduced the

[28]dpppolicy.blogspot.sg. 2011. *Ma zhengfu "wugan fusu" tiuxang* (Ma administration's recovery picture not felt by the people), 5 July, http://dpppolicy.blogspot.sg/2011/07/blog-post.html, accessed on 23 October 2012.

constraints of nationalist ideology in local elections, and has consequently improved the DPP's flexibility in framing local social justice issues and proposing policy solutions to local voters. In general, this strategy worked well for the DPP, especially at the local level; the puzzle is why the DPP still lost to the KMT in the presidential election.

In the 2012 presidential election, owing to huge public concern with cross-strait relations, the result rested largely on the KMT and the DPP's China policies. As previously discussed, Ma Ying-jeou's economic and social performance did not particularly outshine Chen Shui-bian's. However, using a flexible political nationalism along with the principles of "no unification, no independence and no use of force" and the "1992 consensus," his efforts to improve cross-strait relations have been substantial, visible and, most importantly, successful. The signing of the ECFA is considered by the Ma administration to be one of the most important contributory factors in Taiwan's economic revival.

To counter the "1992 consensus," Tsai Ing-wen proposed the "Taiwan consensus" as the cornerstone of her China policy. She described the "Taiwan consensus" as the democratic way to achieve a consensus in Taiwan, which would provide a more legitimate basis for the future administration's China policy. However, the outcome of the "Taiwan consensus" would not be known until this democratic process, in the form of a referendum, was held. The "Taiwan consensus" appeared to be a way for Tsai to escape from her disadvantaged position on cross-strait issues. In reality, however, it did not address the public's concern about whether her China policy could further improve or even maintain current cross-strait relations. To allay the fears of swing voters about her China policy, Tsai gradually shifted her position on the ECFA from complete rejection to acceptance. She also promised that the current amicable cross-strait relations would be maintained under her future administration. This promise lost ground when the Chinese government insisted that good cross-strait relations would only be possible if Tsai accepted the "one-China policy" implied in the "1992 consensus." Although Tsai and the DPP have toned down their radical political nationalism since 2008, it is still impossible for them to accept either the "1992 consensus" or "one-China policy." Throughout the election campaign, Tsai enjoyed much less public trust and support than Ma on cross-strait issues. Tables 10.8–10.10 show the results of a survey

Table 10.8 Are You Satisifed or Dissatisfied with President Ma's Performance in Managing Cross-Strait Relations in the Past Three Years?

(Unit: % of people in each social group, i.e., row %)

	Satisfied	Dissatisfied
Privileged	66.8	33.2
Less privileged	58.5	41.5
Chi-square test	$n = 3908$, $\chi^2 = 28.333$, $df = 1$, $p < 0.001$	
Overall	62.2	37.8

Source: TEDS2012-TP.

Table 10.9 Has Taiwan's Overall Economy Improved, Declined or Remained the Same because of ECFA?

(Unit: % of people in each social group, i.e., row %)

	Improved	Declined	The Same
Privileged	34.9	17.1	48
Less privileged	31.5	25.7	42.8
Chi-square Test	$n = 4177$, $\chi^2 = 44.552$, $df = 2$, $p < 0.001$		
Overall	33	21.9	45.1

Source: TEDS2012-TP.

Table 10.10 Should We Continue to Use "1992 Consensus" to Negotiate with Mainland China?

(Unit: % of people in each social group, i.e., row %)

	Continue	Discontinue
Privileged	69	31
Less privileged	58.4	41.6
Chi-square test	$n = 3183$, $\chi^2 = 38.933$a, $df = 1$, $p < 0.001$	
Overall	63.4	36.6

Source: TEDS2012-TP.

conducted shortly before the presidential election on Ma's performance and policy of managing the cross-strait relations. Two findings are telling. The less privileged were still less likely than the privileged to be satisfied with Ma's performance on managing cross-strait relations, to believe that

Taiwan's overall economy had improved because of the ECFA, and to support the continuation of the "1992 consensus." This may further explain the less privileged groups' relatively weak support for the KMT (and relatively strong support for the DPP). However, on the other hand, even within the less privileged groups, more people were happy with Ma's performance and policy on cross-strait relations than were unhappy. This may imply that the support generally received by the less privileged Taiwanese groups might have been impacted by the latter's high approval of Ma's cross-strait performance and policy in the presidential election. The last rows in Tables 10.8–10.10 also indicate that, shortly before the election, more people overall approved of Ma's mainland China policy and the continuation of the "1992 consensus" than disapproved.

Several other factors might have impacted the less privileged Taiwanese groups' overall support for the DPP in the presidential election. First, Figure 10.7 indicates that shortly before the election, the less privileged Taiwanese's nationalist sentiment had declined by 5% from its 2008 level. This could be owing to a combination of the DPP's moderated political nationalism and the significantly improved cross-strait relations under the Ma administration's liberal mainland China policy. Second, Figure 10.5 shows that since 2008, the Ma administration has generally maintained the social welfare improvements instigated by the Chen administration, with an average percentage of the social welfare budget in the total budget during the Ma administration of 2008–2011 being 0.6% higher than that during the Chen administration of 2004–2007. Finally, the Chinese government, in response to worries about further alienating the less privileged groups in Taiwan, has promised to minimize the ECFA's negative impact on them[29] and Ma's administration has also decided to compensate some of those who could lose out under the agreement.[30] This might lessen the appeal of the DPP's economic nationalism to the less privileged.

---

[29] Chinanews.com.cn. 2010. *Guotaiban Wang Yi zhuren jieshou Taiwan meiti zhuanfang* (Interview with Wang Yi, Minister of Taiwan Affairs Office of State Council), 31 March, http://www.chinanews.com.cn/tw/news/2010/03-31/2200729.shtml, accessed on 23 October 2012.

[30] president.gov.tw. 2010. President Ma holds press conference to discuss signing of ECFA, 1 July, http://english.president.gov.tw/Default.aspx?tabid=491&itemid=21920&rmid=2355, accessed on 23 October 2012.

Conclusion and Implications

This article argues that to get a clearer understanding of Taiwan's party politics since 2000, and particularly the DPP's limited resurgence since 2008, we should pay more attention to the links between globalization, social justice issues, and political and economic nationalism in Taiwan. To put it simply, globalization has negatively impacted large groups of less privileged people and widened the income gap in Taiwan, which in turn has made the less privileged more receptive to social justice-oriented economic nationalism. Therefore, a nationalist and center-left party with a better record for improving social welfare and controlling income inequality, and which promotes a social justice-oriented economic nationalism, may obtain support from the less privileged groups in society. This is the case for the reversal of the DPP's fortunes since it lost power in 2008.

The DPP has learned from its 2008 electoral catastrophe that radicalizing political nationalism brought more problems than it solved for both Taiwan and the DPP. Therefore, at the national level the DPP has moderated its political nationalism and shifted its policy focus to economic nationalism. Political nationalism mobilizes loyalty by appealing to ideological and symbolic factors, such as national identity and ethnic cleavage, and economic nationalism attracts support by promising both to address social justice issues and protect the ordinary people's welfare. Therefore, the DPP's new balance between political and economic nationalism has impacted Taiwan's national politics positively. The significance of highly ideological, emotional and divisive nationalist issues has declined and a variety of social justice issues closely related to ordinary people's livelihoods has become more salient in Taiwan's national politics. At the local level, the DPP has further downplayed political nationalism and decoupled local issues from economic nationalism. This has also led to positive changes as it has allowed for the de-nationalism of local politics, which in turn has made policy debates more concrete and meaningful.

Although the DPP was able to revive its popular support with a better balance of political and economic nationalism, this comeback hit a wall in the 2012 presidential election. The Ma administration did not outperform the Chen administration in many aspects, but it's achievements in creating better cross-strait relations became its best vote-winning platform. In contrast, the DPP's moderate political nationalism was still not flexible enough to propose a more liberal and pragmatic China policy and thus negatively impacted its popular support in this election.

According to the present study's findings, if the KMT and the mainland Chinese governments wish to win over the less privileged Taiwanese groups, they will have to pacify their nationalist sentiment and provide them with economic benefits. If only one of these concerns is addressed, the remaining other concern may be enough to maintain the less privileged Taiwanese's support for the DPP. In other words, they will need to provide the less privileged with both "romance" and "bread."[31] This also generally supports Wang, Chen and Keng's finding that both symbolic and self-interest considerations significantly affect Taiwanese people's policy positions.[32]

The history of Taiwanese politics over the past several decades suggests that it is too early to conclude that a typical two party-dominated system, with the center-right KMT and the center-left DPP, has been institutionalized in Taiwan. In response to the DPP campaigning on social justice issues, the KMT has also enhanced its policy efforts to help those losing out under the ECFA. The DPP's increasing emphasis on social justice issues may be primarily for winning elections; nevertheless, since Chen Shui-bian overly played highly ideological, emotional and divisive nationalist issues and consequently exposed the dark side of radical political nationalism to society, it seems impossible for the DPP to rely only on traditional ethnic and identity issues to maintain broad popular support. Social justice-oriented economic nationalism is a new battlefield created by the DPP since 2008 and has helped to restore its popular support. Therefore, it is likely that the DPP will continue with a balanced combination of political and economic nationalism that emphasizes both national security and the ordinary people's welfare in its promotion of Taiwanese nationalism and struggle for local and national power.

[31] The terms romance and bread are from Wu, 2005.

[32] Wang, Chen and Keng, 2010.

REFERENCES

Aspalter, C. 2002. *Democratization and Welfare State Development in Taiwan*. Burlington, VT: Ashgate.

Brown, M.J. 2004. *Is Taiwan Chinese? The Impact of Culture, Power, and Migration on Changing Identities*. Berkeley: University of California Press.

Brustein, W. 1988. The Political Geography of Belgian Fascism: The Case of Rexism. *American Sociological Review* 53(1), 69–80.

Brustein, W. 1991. "The Red Menace" and the Rise of Italian Fascism. *American Sociological Review* 56(5), 652–664.

Chai, W. 2008. Taiwan's 2008 Elections and Their Impact on U.S.–China–Taiwan Relations. *Asian Affairs: An American Review* 35(2), 83–92.

Chan, H.-S. 2012. Yijiazi yilai Taiwan shehui fuli zhengce de yanbian (Sixty Years' Evolution of Social Welfare Policy in Taiwan). Paper presented at the conference *Shehui fuli moshi — cong chuancheng dao chuangxin yantaohui* (*Conference on Social Welfare Models: From Traditions to Innovations*), Beijing, 15–19, April 2012.

Chen, J. 1998. *Hai wai Tai du yun dong shi* (*A History of the Overseas Taiwan Independence Movement*). Taipei: Qianwei Publishing.

Chen, J. 2006. *Taiwan du li yun dong shi* (*History of the Taiwan Independence Movement*). Taipei: Yushan Publishing.

Chen, L. 2000. Taiwan Xuanmin Zhengdang Rentong de Chixu yu Bianqian (Change and Continuity of Taiwanese Voters' Party Identification). *Xuanju Yanjiu* (*Elections Study*) 7(2), 109–133.

Chen, M.-C. 2004. Sinicization and Its Discontents: Cross-Strait Economic Integration and Taiwan's 2004 Presidential Election. *Issues and Studies* 40(3/4), 334–341.

Chen, Y. 1994. *Shi Ming Taiwan shi lun di xu gou* (*Shi Ming's Fabrication of Taiwan History*). Taipei: Renjian Publishing.

Cheng, S.-F. 2007. Shenlü xuanmin zhi tansuo (A Preliminary Study of Deep-green Voters). *Wen Ti Yu Yan Jiu (Issues and Studies)* 46(1), 33–61.

Chu, Y.-H and J.-W. Lin. 2001. Political Development in the 20th-century Taiwan: State-building, Regime Transformation and the Construction of National Identity. *The China Quarterly* 165,102–129.

Copper, J.F. 2008. Taiwan's Failed President. *Asian Affairs: An American Review* 34(4), 179–192.

Copper, J.F. 2009. The Devolution of Taiwan's Democracy during the Chen Shui-bian Era. *Journal of Contemporary China* 18(60), 463–478.

Copper, J.F. 2010. *Taiwan's 2010 Metropolitan City Elections: An Assessment of Taiwan's Politics and a Predictor of Future Elections*. Baltimore, MD: University of Maryland School of Law.

Dallmayr, F.R. 2002. Globalization and Inequality: A Plea for Global Justice. *International Studies Review* 4(2), 137–156.

Glenn, J.K. 2003. Parties out of Movements: Party Emergence in Postcommunist Eastern Europe. In J.A. Goldstone (ed.), *States, Parties, and Social Movements*. Cambridge, UK; New York: Cambridge University Press, 147–169.

Gold, T. 1986. *State and Society in the Taiwan Miracle*. Armonk, New York, and London:M.E. Sharpe

Goldstone, J.A. 2003. *States, Parties, and Social Movements*. Cambridge, UK; New York: Cambridge University Press.

Gould, R.V. 1991. Multiple Networks and Mobilization in the Paris Commune, 1871. *American Sociological Review* 56(6), 716–729.

Gould, R.V. 1995. *Insurgent Identities: Class, Community, and Protest in Paris from 1848 to the Commune*. Chicago: University of Chicago Press.

Hechter, M. 1999. *Internal Colonialism: The Celtic Fringe in British National Development*. New Brunswick, N.J.: Transaction Publishers.

Hechter, M. 2000. *Containing Nationalism*. Oxford; New York: Oxford University Press.

Hsieh, J.F.-S and E.M.S. Niou. 2005. Measuring Taiwanese Public Opinion on Taiwanese Independence. *The China Quarterly* 181, 158–168.

Hu, A., T.-H.Lin and R.S.K. Wong. 2010. Jieji zhengzhi de fuxing? Taiwan de minzhu zhuanxing yu jieji toupiao, 1992–2004 (Revival of Class Politics? Democratic Transition and Class Voting in Taiwan, 1992–2004). Paper presented at *2010 Taiwanese Sociological Association Conference*, Taipei, 4–5 December 2010.

Huang, S.-L. 2009. *Taiwan shehui fuli fazhan zhi zhengzhi jingji fenxi (Political Economic Analysis of Taiwan Social Welfare Development)*. Master's thesis, National Dong Hwa University.

Jacobs, J.B. 2005. "Taiwanization" in Taiwan's Politics. In J. Makeham and A.-C. Hsiau (eds.), *Cultural, Ethnic, and Political Nationalism in Contemporary Taiwan*: *Bentuhua*. NY: Palgrave Macmillan, 17–54.

Li, Q. 2003. Preface: Taiwan Culture's Engineer. In W. Zhuang (ed.), *Taiwan wen hua lun: zhu ti xing zhi jian gou* (*Theories of Taiwan Culture*: *Construction of Taiwan subjectivity*). Taipei: Yushan Publishing.

Lin, J. 1993. *Tai du yan jiu lun ji* (*A Collection of Studies on the Taiwan Independence Movement*). Xindian City: Taipei: Haixia Xueshu Publishing.

Lin, C.-S. 2006. *Gong Tong Ti: Shi Jie Tu Xiang Xia de Taiwan* (*Community: Taiwan in the Global Context*). Xindian City: Zuoan Wenhra Publishing.

Lin, C.-S. 2009. *Lishi juchang: tongku zhizheng banian* (*History as Theatre: Eight Years of a Painful Regime*). Taipei: INK.

Lin, T.-H., 2009. Taiwan de hougongyehua: jieji jiegou de zhuanxing yu shehui bupingdeng, 1992–2007 (Taiwan after Industrialization: Changing Class Structure and Income Inequality, 1992–2007). *Taiwan shehuixuekan* (*The Taiwanese Journal of Sociology*) 43, 93–158.

Lin, T.-H., etc. Hong Jingshu, Li Jianhong, Wang Zhaoqing and Zhang Fengyi. 2011. *Beng shidai — caituanhua, pinqionghua yu shaozinühua de weiji* (*A Collapsed Generation: The Business Consortiums, Impoverization, and Birth Rate Decline Crisis*). Taipei: Taiwan Labor Front.

Lin, W.-I. 2005. 1990 niandai yilai Taiwan shehui fuli fazhan de huigu (Overview of Taiwan's Social Welfare Development since the 1990s). *Shequ fazhan jikan* (*Community Development Quarterly*) 109, 12–35.

Marx, K. 1964. *The Class Struggles in France* (*1848–1850*). New York: International Publishers.

McAdam, D. 1999. *Political Process and the Development of Black Insurgency, 1930–1970*. Chicago: University of Chicago Press.

McAdam, D. and R. Paulsen. 1993. Specifying the Relationship between Social Ties and Activism. *The American Journal of Sociology* 99, 640–667.

McAdam, D. and S. Tarrow. 2009. Ballots and Barricades: On the Reciprocal Relationship between Elections and Social Movements. *Perspectives on Politics* 8(2), 529–542.

Mills, M. 2009. Globalization and Inequality. *European Sociological Review* 25(1), 1–8.

Nan, F. 1980. *Di guo zhu yi yu Taiwan du li yun dong* (*Imperialism and the Taiwan Independence Movement*). Taipei: Siji Publishing.

Nan, F. 2008. Taiwan Chu Zai Yu Ku Wu Lei de Chuo Qi Qing Jing Zhong (Taiwan Is Sobbing). In G. Chen (ed.), *Ku Qi de Taiwan: Kan Min Jin Dang Zhi Zheng Ba Nian(Sobbing Taiwan: Exploring the DPP's Eight Years Regime)*. Zhonghe City: INK Publishing.

Olzak, S. 2004. Ethnic and Nationalist Social Movements. In S.A. Soule, D.A. Snow, H. Kriesi (eds.), *The Blackwell Companion to Social Movements*. Oxford, UK: Blackwell Publishers.

Qi, D. 2010a. *Two Years in Opposition: Taiwan's Democratic Progressive Party Moves from Defeat to Revival? EAI Background Brief No. 567*. Singapore: East Asian Institute, National University of Singapore.

Qi, D. 2010b. *Taiwan's 2010 Municipal Elections. EAI Background Brief No. 584*. Singapore: East Asian Institute, National University of Singapore.

Qi, D. 2012. *Taiwan's 2012 Presidential and Legislative Elections. EAI Background Brief No. 691*. Singapore: East Asian Institute, National University of Singapore.

Rigger, S. 2010. The Democratic Progressive Party: from Opposition to Power, and Back Again. In Wei-Chin Lee (ed.), *Taiwan's Politics in the 21st Century: Changes and Challenges*. Singapore: World Scientific Publishing, 41–67.

Roy, D. 2003. *Taiwan: A Political History*. Ithaca: Cornell University Press.

Sheng, X. 2002. Tongdu Yite yu Taiwan Xuanmin de Toupiao Xingwei (Independence Issue and Taiwanese Voting Behavior: An Analysis of 1990s). *Xuanju Yanjiu* (*Elections Study*) 9(1), 41–80.

Shi, M. 2001. *Taiwan min zu zhu yi yu Taiwan du li ge ming* (*Nationalism in Taiwan and the Revolution of Taiwan Independence*). Taipei: Qianwei Publishing.

Shi, Z. 2007. *Democracy* (*Made in Taiwan*): *The "Success" State as a Political Theory*. Lanham, MD: Lexington Books.

Skocpol, T. 1979. *States and Social Revolutions: A Comparative Analysis of France, Russia, and China*. Cambridge, New York: Cambridge University Press.

Snow, D.A., Jr. L.A. Zurcher and S. Ekland-Olson. 1980. Social Networks and Social Movements: A Microstructural Approach to Differential Recruitment. *American Sociological Review* 45, 787–801.

Song, C. (Munakata, T.). 1996. *Taiwan du li yun dong si ji* (*A Private Narrative of the Taiwan Independence Movement*). Taipei: Qianwei Publishing.

Tarrow, S.G. 1998. *Power in Movement: Social Movements and Contentious Politics*. Cambridge: New York: Cambridge University Press.

Tilly, C. 1978. *From Mobilization to Revolution*. MA: Addison-Wesley Pub. Co.

Tilly, C. 2003. Afterword: Agendas for Students of Social Movements. In J.A. Goldstone (eds.) *States, Parties, and Social Movements*. Cambridge, UK; New York: Cambridge University Press.

Traugott, M. 1980. Determinants of Political Orientation: Class and Organization in the Paris Insurrection of 1848. *American Journal of Sociology* 86, 32–49.

Tucker, R.C. 1961. Towards a Comparative Politics of Movement-regimes. *The American Political Science Review* 55, 281.

Wang, F. 1998. Zuqun Yishi, Minzu Zhuyi yu Zhengdang Zhichi: 1990 Niandai de Zuqun Zhengzhi (Ethnic Consciousness, Nationalism and Political Party Support: Taiwan's Ethnic Politics in 1990s). *Taiwan Shehuixue Yanjiu* (*Taiwanese Sociological Research*). 1, 129–210.

Wang, F. 2005. Why Bother about School Textbooks: An Analysis of the Origin of the Disputes over *Renshi Taiwan* Textbooks in 1997. In J. Makeham and A.-C. Hsiau (eds.), *Cultural, Ethnic, and Political Nationalism in Contemporary Taiwan*: *Bentuhua*. NY: Palgrave Macmillan.

Wang, Y. (O, Ikutoku). 1993. *Taiwan: Ku men di li shi* (*Taiwan*: *A Depressed History*). Taipei: Zili Wanbao Publishing.

Wang, Y. (O, Ikutoku) (ed.) and R. Wu. 2002. *Wang Yude zi zhuan: Chu shi zhi er er ba hou tuo chu Taiwan* (*A Biography of Yude Wang: From the Birth to Fleeing Taiwan*). Taipei: Qianwei Publishing.

Wang, T.Y., L.-H. Chen and S. Keng. 2010. Symbolic Politics, Self-interests and Threat Perceptions: An Analysis of Taiwan Citizens' Views on Cross-Strait Economic Exchanges. In Wei-Chin Lee (ed.), *Taiwan's Politics in the 21st Century*: *Changes and Challenges*. Singapore, London: World Scientific, 159–184.

Wang, T.Y., S.-F. Cheng and L.-H. Chen. 2009. Deep-green Supporters and Political Tolerance in Taiwan: An Analysis of Kennedy's Hypothesis. *Issues and Studies* 45(1), 1–30.

Wong, J. 2003. Deepening Democracy in Taiwan. *Pacific Affairs* 76(2), 235–256.

Wong, K.T. 2010. The Emergence of Class Cleavage in Taiwan in the Twenty-first Century: The Impact of Cross-Strait Economic Integration. *Issues & Studies* 46(2), 127–172.

Wu, N.-T. 2005. Mianbo yu aiqing: Chutan Taiwan minzong minzu rentong de biandong (Romance and Bread: A Preliminary Study of Identity Change in Taiwan). *Taiwan Journal of Political Science* 9(2), 5–39.

Xiao, X. 1999. *Xin Taiwan ren di xin: guo jia ren tong di xin tu xiang* (*Minds of New Taiwanese: The New Images of National Identities*). Taipei: Yuedan Publishing.

Xu, H. 2002. Taiwan Zhengdang Bantu de Chonghua: Minjindang, Guomindang yu Qinmindang de 'Minji' de Bijiao (The Realignment of Political Parties in Taiwan: A Comparison of the DPP, the KMT and the PFP's Support Base). *Dongwu Zhengzhi Xuebao* (*Dongwu Political Science Journal*). 14, 83–134.

Yang, D. 2007. Classing Ethnicity: Class, Ethnicity and the Mass Politics of Taiwan's Democratic Transition. *World Politics* 59, 503–538.

Zhang, C. 2002. *"Tai du"ni liu* (*Eddy of the Taiwan Independence Movement*). Fuzhou City: Fujian People Publishing.

Zhang, F. and W. Qiu. 2005. *Lü se nian dai*: *Taiwan min zhu yun dong 25 years* (*Green Years*: *25 Years of Taiwan Democracy Movement*). Taipei: Lüse Lüxing Culture and Education Foundation.

Zhang, Y., H. Hu, and Q. Zeng. 2000. *Taiwan du li yun dong di xian sheng*: *Taiwan gong he guo* (*A Pioneer in the Taiwan Independence Movement*: *The Republic of Taiwan*). Taipei: Wu Sanlian Taiwan Historical Materials Foundation.

INDEX

1947, 43, 44, 115
1979, 16, 36
1986, 4, 7, 30, 37, 39, 225
2000, 3–5, 8, 15, 20, 21, 25, 26, 31–34, 36, 38, 39, 41, 42, 46, 49–53, 55–59, 68–70, 72, 74–76, 86, 90, 111–114, 117, 118, 128–130, 133, 147, 150, 159, 167, 193, 202, 217, 225, 230, 236, 244
2000–2004, xiv, xix, 7, 73, 91, 103
2000–2008, v, vi, xiii, xix, 1, 5, 7, 13, 14, 29, 30, 36, 47, 48, 58, 67, 68, 70, 73, 111, 148, 154, 157, 193, 202, 203, 217
2000–2012, v
2004, xix, xx ,3–5, 7, 8, 14, 15, 26, 33, 37, 38, 42, 43, 51, 53, 55, 56, 58, 68, 69, 77, 79–81, 83, 84, 93, 94, 96, 100, 102–107, 112, 116, 117, 122, 123, 128–130, 147, 159, 186, 187, 190, 202, 203, 230–232, 238, 239, 240, 243
2004–2008, xiv, 71, 83, 91, 128, 141, 160, 213, 225, 236
2008, vi, vii, xv, xvii, xix–xxi, 3–5, 7, 15, 25–27, 30, 36, 43, 55–57, 60, 62, 64–66, 68, 69, 82, 84, 90, 92–94, 98, 100–108, 122, 123, 125, 127–131, 133, 136–140, 149, 150, 154, 157, 158, 160, 162, 164–167, 171, 172, 174–176, 181, 183, 185–189, 196, 203, 204, 210, 211, 213–220, 223, 225, 227–230, 232, 234, 237–239, 243–245
2008–2010, xviii, 175, 188, 225
2008–2012, xv, xvi, xviii ,155, 204, 205, 236, 238
2010, vi, xv, xx, 158, 163, 165, 167, 171, 173–175, 178, 184, 186–189, 198, 214, 220, 239, 240, 191
2012, vi, vii, xv, xvi, xviii–xx, 158, 163, 167, 168, 171, 172, 179, 181–183, 185, 187, 189, 191, 196, 199, 200–204, 206–210, 212, 215–217, 226, 230–233, 240, 241, 244

anti-independence, 4, 10, 11, 36, 43, 46, 60, 63, 69, 117, 132
authoritarian, v, 4, 6, 10, 18, 31, 32, 35, 36, 38, 45, 114, 143, 222

black sheep, vii, xiv, 113–115, 120, 134
Brown, 31, 32, 38, 39
Brustein, 24

CCP (Chinese Communist Party), 32, 37, 43, 44, 75, 113, 114, 199, 200, 211
Chen Chih-chung, 181
Chen Shui-bian, 8, 52, 74, 185
Chiang Ching-kuo, 36, 44
Chiang Kai-shek, 36, 44
China conspirator, 236
China factor, 209, 210
China policy, vi, vii, 172, 182, 184, 185, 192, 198, 199, 201–206, 208–212, 214, 216, 217, 223, 233, 236, 238, 240, 241, 243, 245
Chinese government, 3, 5, 6, 15, 38, 45, 47, 74, 77–81, 83, 86, 89, 90, 113, 114, 147, 149, 153, 166, 167, 185, 189, 192, 193, 205, 209–211, 237, 243
class, xi, 23, 24, 100–102, 126, 127, 130, 131, 133, 135, 139, 140, 142, 154, 177, 182, 184, 187, 193, 221, 222, 228, 231, 232, 235
Concession, xiv, 74
1992 consensus, 184, 192, 195, 198, 200, 241, 243
Confrontation, xiv, 17, 74, 82
congress, 19, 77, 80, 81, 158, 177
corruption, 6, 7, 26, 42, 71–73, 83, 85, 87, 90–93, 104, 105, 107, 108, 112, 115, 121, 134, 140–142, 147, 148–150, 157, 158, 161, 162, 176, 181, 184, 185, 189, 194, 214, 238
cross-strait relation, 4, 78, 132, 133, 136, 137, 139, 158, 160, 184, 185, 187–195, 198–200, 206–208, 218, 237, 241–243, 245

Dangwai, 33
de-China, 119, 120
deep-green, 48, 225, 232, 236
de facto independence, 51, 52, 200, 201, 205, 236, 240
de jure independence, 50, 51, 52, 80, 89, 113, 114, 160, 166, 200, 201, 212, 223, 236
democratic consolidation, 166, 173
democratization, 35, 36, 38, 39, 119, 218
dichotomous characteristics of state and movement, 16
dichotomy in social science, 16
dilemma, vi, 8, 13, 75–79, 85, 111, 121, 142, 145, 161
disadvantaged, 21, 123, 124, 127, 135, 167, 168, 184, 192, 194, 202–208, 212, 241
divergent popular support, 67
double-edged sword, xv, 73, 107, 108, 112, 121, 136, 139–141, 147, 196, 216
DPP, v–vii, xiii, xiv–xviii, xix–xxi, 3–22, 25–27, 29, 30, 33, 35–49, 52–57, 59, 61–81, 83–88, 90–95, 100–105, 107–109, 111–113, 116–118, 120–123, 128, 131, 132, 134–141, 143, 146–151, 153, 154, 157–169, 171, 173–183, 187–191, 193–211, 213–218, 222–225, 227–233, 236, 237, 240, 241, 243–245
DPP ID, xvii, xix, xx, 49, 50, 54–60, 63–66, 69, 70, 72, 92, 95, 96, 98, 100–102, 106
dummy member, 163

ECFA, xxi, 158, 164, 166, 168, 169, 173, 179, 182, 184, 185, 187–189, 192, 205, 237, 238, 241–243

economic nationalism, vii, 123, 124, 204, 205, 212, 216–218, 223, 225, 236, 237, 240, 243–245
electoral politics, v, vi, 19, 33, 144, 146, 202, 222

Faction, 168
28 February 1947, 32, 34, 43, 114
fondness of Chen, 92, 93, 95, 103–105, 107, 109
four noes and one without, 41, 52, 75, 90
four wants and one without, 89
Friends of Little Ing, 179

globalization, vii, 158, 216, 217, 219, 220, 221, 229, 244
government-oriented strategy, 8, 14, 16, 77, 79, 105, 147
government role, 16, 54, 55, 57, 59, 63, 69, 70, 71, 82, 145, 147

Hakka, 25, 38, 62, 64, 65, 66, 227, 230
Hau Lung-pin, 178, 180
Hoklo, 25, 38, 62, 64, 65, 66, 118
Hong Kong, xi, 32, 74, 167, 238
Hsieh Chang-ting, 90, 209
Huang Chao-shun, 178, 180
Hu Chi-keung, 178, 180

imperial-subjectization, 31
independence, vii, xv, xvii, 8, 10, 13, 15, 19–22, 29, 30, 32–34, 38, 41, 43, 45, 46, 49, 50–54, 58, 60–67, 74–76, 78–80, 86, 87, 89, 90, 94, 97, 99, 106, 111, 115–118, 122, 132–134, 158, 160, 162, 178, 189, 190, 200, 201, 204, 221, 222, 227, 228, 230, 236–238, 241
inequality, 166, 167, 184, 192, 197, 205, 206, 216–219, 221, 225, 238, 239, 244
institutional politics, 18–21, 153
investment, 47, 48, 75, 85, 86, 205, 216, 219–221, 229, 237

James Soong, 46, 52, 183, 193, 195
Japan, 4, 30, 31–35, 190

Kaohsiung, 36, 85, 164, 168, 169, 171, 174, 175, 178, 180, 181, 210
Kaohsiung Incident, 36
Kejia (Hakka), 25, 38, 62, 64–66, 94–96, 98, 106, 138, 227, 230
KMT, xviii, xx, 4, 10, 11, 18–21, 25, 31–39, 41–46, 49, 52, 60, 62, 68, 69, 74–78, 80, 81, 83–85, 94, 95, 113, 114, 116, 118, 119, 130, 137, 138, 140, 157–159, 162, 164–167, 169, 172–184, 188–190, 193–197, 199, 200, 202–204, 206–209, 213–215, 217, 218, 222–225, 228, 230, 240, 241, 243, 245

Lee Teng-hui, 36, 38, 45, 46, 53
less privileged, 228–233, 236, 237, 240, 242–245
Lien Chan, 114, 174
Lin Cho-shui, 116, 132

mainland China, vii, xi, 3–6, 11, 13, 25, 30–34, 39, 41, 43–45, 47–51, 62, 71, 74, 75, 77–81, 83, 85–87, 89, 93, 94, 113–115, 118, 119, 123, 124, 132, 135, 136, 153, 158, 160, 166, 172, 176, 182, 184, 185, 188, 190, 192, 194, 197, 199, 200–203, 205,

206, 209–212, 216–220, 222, 223, 225, 227–229, 236–238, 240, 243
McAdam, vii, 7, 16, 17, 21, 24, 25, 143, 144, 146, 151, 152, 249, 250
mainland China policy, 173, 176, 182, 183, 192, 196, 197, 243
Mandarin, 118, 119
martial law, 18, 32, 33, 37, 38
Marx, 23, 24
Ma Ying-jeou, 36, 158, 159, 183, 186, 189, 196, 199, 206, 209, 215, 237, 238
Minnan (Hoklo), 25, 38, 62, 64–66, 94–96, 98, 106, 118–120, 122, 138, 227, 230
mobilization, 17, 20, 25, 134, 136, 177, 179, 184
mode of production, 23, 24
movement government, 141
movement government framework, v, vi, 8, 9, 11, 12, 15, 22, 23, 26, 27, 29, 48, 54–56, 59, 69, 71–73, 76, 79, 82, 83, 91–93, 103–105, 108, 111, 136, 139, 143, 146–149, 151
movement leader, v, vi, 7, 8, 11, 13, 14, 78, 111, 143, 145
movement-oriented strategy, vi, 8, 9, 14, 15, 79, 84, 105, 112, 147
movement regime, 9, 10
movement role, 8, 54, 57, 59, 69–71, 77, 79, 82, 140, 147, 148
movement strategy, xv, 72, 73, 91–93, 95, 102–105, 107–109, 112, 117, 123, 136, 139–142, 147, 148, 149–151, 154

national identity, 49, 60, 61, 63, 93, 95, 228, 244
nationalism, xi, 4, 7, 15, 42, 90, 112, 113, 134, 154, 210, 217, 236, 240, 245
nationalistic sentiment, 5, 15, 72, 73, 81–84, 90, 92, 93, 95, 100–105, 107, 108, 112, 127, 128, 130, 136, 147, 154, 161
New Tide Faction, 160, 168
non-institutional politics, 17, 153, 221
Normal Nation Resolution, 45, 90, 200
NP (New Party), 46, 60, 62, 80, 94, 95

one-China, 86, 199, 200, 211, 212
one-China policy, 44, 74, 78, 87, 241
one country on each side, 78
open-door policy, 123, 124, 135, 137–139

pan-blue, 45–48, 55, 56, 60, 69, 174, 194
pan-blue exclusion clause, 163
pan-green, 45–48, 60, 68, 174
party politics, 29, 198, 217, 244
peace agreement, 185, 190, 194, 196
PFP (People First Party), 46, 52, 60, 62, 80, 94, 95, 183, 193
political nationalism, vii, 204, 206, 217, 218, 222, 223, 225, 236, 237, 240, 241, 243–245
politicization, 117, 118, 120, 134
presidential election, vi, vii, 3, 4, 6–8, 15, 19, 26, 39, 41–43, 46, 48, 52, 56, 69, 70, 74, 79–82, 89, 90, 91, 117, 122, 136, 137, 147, 154, 158, 163, 167, 168, 171, 172, 174, 176, 182, 185, 186, 188, 193, 196–199, 201–203, 209–212, 215, 217, 227, 228, 230, 238, 240–244

privileged, 42, 114, 135, 166, 223, 229–231, 235, 238, 242
pro-China, 42, 116, 119, 120, 134, 173, 182, 194, 196, 200
pro-democracy, 4, 5, 18, 19, 33, 35, 36, 37, 88, 114, 134
pro-independence, 3, 4, 5, 6, 14, 15, 18–22, 29, 33, 34, 36, 37, 39, 42–47, 49–54, 56–58, 60, 61, 68–70, 72, 73, 76–78, 88–90, 95, 100, 102, 103, 105, 107, 117–119, 121, 128–130, 134, 154, 160, 165, 172, 179, 181, 183, 185, 200, 202, 211, 214, 223, 228, 238
pro-unification, 36, 46, 49, 61, 66, 67, 93, 183, 190, 202, 228
Provisional Government of Taiwan Republic, 34

radicalization, xiv, 73, 82–84, 108, 148, 149, 150, 157, 225
radical strategy, 43, 72, 83, 84, 85, 87, 88, 90, 112, 113, 115, 116, 118–123, 127, 128, 130, 132, 134–137, 139, 141, 142, 150, 154
referendum, 3, 4, 6, 34, 52, 75, 78, 80–83, 88, 89, 158, 164, 192, 194, 241
role conflict, 13

SARS, 79, 80
Sean Lien, 174
Second Republic Constitution, 89
Shih Ming-teh, 88
Sinbei, 171, 174, 175, 178, 179, 181, 191, 215
social justice, vii, 184, 187, 191, 193, 195–198, 215–219, 221–223, 225, 239–241, 244, 245
social movement, xi, 10, 17–19, 21, 36, 88, 117, 134, 152
social network, 23, 24
social structure, 24, 25
social support, vi, 4–6, 8, 9, 15, 16, 26, 29, 30, 50, 54, 59, 71–73, 82, 107, 108, 145
social welfare budget, 196, 203, 205, 217, 225, 243
southern Taiwan, 100–103, 109, 122, 123, 135, 139, 154, 165, 180, 181, 192, 193, 198, 202, 228, 229, 232, 238
status quo, 6, 17, 49, 61, 62, 64–67, 74, 75, 87, 93, 94, 97, 99, 106, 190, 193, 202, 227, 228, 230
Su Jia-chyuan, 178–180
support base, vi, 3, 6, 7–9, 11, 12, 14, 15, 20, 22–27, 29, 33, 37, 43, 48, 49, 54–61, 63, 68–70, 82, 111, 122, 141, 142, 144, 145, 147, 148, 154, 158, 164, 180, 202, 203, 206, 207, 222
Su Tseng-chang, 178, 180, 198, 201, 209
symbiotic relation, 153

Taipei, 32, 88, 159, 171, 172, 174, 175, 178–181, 195, 215
Taiwan consensus, 184, 192, 241
Taiwanese identity, xi, 29, 50, 53–55, 57–59, 61, 67–70, 72, 73, 76, 95, 100, 103, 105, 107
Taiwanese nationalism, 68–70, 72, 76, 81, 85, 113, 130, 189, 190, 196, 197, 202, 218, 223, 225, 236, 237
Taiwanese-only identity, 49, 56
three middles, 193

TIM (Taiwan Independence Movement), v–vii, xiii, xiv, 4, 6–8, 10–12, 18–20, 22, 25–27, 29–39, 42, 43, 50–54, 59, 63, 67–72, 75, 76, 78, 84, 86, 88, 90, 105, 107–109, 112, 116, 120, 121, 132, 142, 146, 153, 154
Traugott, 25
Tsai Ing-wen, xv, 154, 157, 161, 174, 178, 179, 182, 183, 197, 199, 201, 206, 209, 215, 216, 236, 237, 241
TSU (Taiwan Solidarity Union), 45–47, 60, 62, 94

UN, 3, 43–45, 47, 88–90
unemployment, 47, 86, 123, 164, 173, 177, 182, 184, 186, 187, 192, 196, 205, 218, 219, 220, 239
US, viii, xi, 4–6, 11, 32, 33, 35, 41, 43, 44, 74, 78–80, 83, 87, 166, 185, 190, 191, 195, 196, 214, 225, 237, 238

WUFI (World United Formosans for Independence), 35, 37
Wu Rwei-ren, 134

Yang Chiu-hsing, 169, 175, 180
Yu Shyi-kun, 200, 212